Identity and Discrimination

Identity and Discrimination

Timothy Williamson

Reissued and Updated Edition

WILEY-BLACKWELL

A John Wiley & Sons, Ltd., Publication

This revised edition first published 2013
© 2013 Timothy Williamson
Edition history: Basil Blackwell Ltd. (1e 1990)

Blackwell Publishing was acquired by John Wiley & Sons in February 2007. Blackwell's publishing program has been merged with Wiley's global Scientific, Technical, and Medical business to form Wiley-Blackwell.

Registered Office
John Wiley & Sons Ltd, The Atrium, Southern Gate, Chichester, West Sussex, PO19 8SQ, UK

Editorial Offices
350 Main Street, Malden, MA 02148-5020, USA
9600 Garsington Road, Oxford, OX4 2DQ, UK
The Atrium, Southern Gate, Chichester, West Sussex, PO19 8SQ, UK

For details of our global editorial offices, for customer services, and for information about how to apply for permission to reuse the copyright material in this book please see our website at www.wiley.com/wiley-blackwell.

The right of Timothy Williamson to be identified as the author of this work has been asserted in accordance with the UK Copyright, Designs and Patents Act 1988.

Library of Congress Cataloging-in-Publication Data

Williamson, Timothy.
  Identity and discrimination / Timothy Williamson.
    p. cm.
  Originally published: Oxford, UK ; Cambridge, Mass. : B. Blackwell, 1990.
  Includes bibliographical references (p.) and index.
  ISBN 978-1-118-43259-4 (pbk. : alk. paper)   1. Identity (Philosophical concept)
2. Discrimination.   I. Title.
  BD236.W55 2013
  126–dc23

                                                          2012036605

A catalogue record for this book is available from the British Library.

Cover design by Richard Boxall Design Associates.

Typeset in 10.5/13pt Sabon by Aptara Inc., New Delhi, India

Printed in Malaysia by Ho Printing (M) Sdn Bhd

1   2013

To my mother; for my father

Contents

Preface to the Revised Edition   *ix*
Preface to the First Edition   *xiii*

Introduction   1

1 Concepts of Indiscriminability   4
   1.1 Indiscriminability and Cognition   5
   1.2 Formal Features of Indiscriminability   10
   1.3 The Intentionality of Indiscriminability   14
   1.4 Direct and Indirect Discrimination   20
   1.5 Further Reflections   21

2 Logics of Indiscriminability   24
   2.1 Logical Apparatus   24
   2.2 The Non-Transitivity of Indiscriminability   34

3 Paradoxes of Indiscriminability   43

4 Concepts of Phenomenal Character   48
   4.1 Presentations of Characters   50
   4.2 Presentation-Sensitivity   54
   4.3 The Identity of Characters   62

5 Logics of Phenomenal Character   65
   5.1 Maximal *M*-Relations   65
   5.2 Ignorance and Indeterminacy   73
   5.3 Matching the Same Experiences   82

6   Paradoxes of Phenomenal Character   88
  6.1   The Paradox of Observational Predicates   89
  6.2   The Paradox of Phenomenal Predicates   93
  6.3   The Failure of Observationality   99
  6.4   Sorites Arguments and Necessary Ignorance   103

7   Generalizations   109
  7.1   Maximal M-Relations as Minimal Revisions   109
  7.2   Examples   114
  7.3   Necessary Conditions for Personal Identity   116
  7.4   Sufficient Conditions   121
  7.5   Close Relations   123

8   Modal and Temporal Paradoxes   126
  8.1   A Modal Paradox   126
  8.2   Two Temporal Paradoxes   135
  8.3   Comparisons   142

9   Criteria of Identity   144
  9.1   Forms   144
  9.2   Functions   148

Appendix   Maximal M-Relations and the Axiom of Choice   154

Notes (to the First Edition)   158
Additional Notes (to the Revised Edition)   165
References (to the First Edition)   171
Additional References (to the Revised Edition)   176
Index   179

Preface to the Revised Edition

Identity and Discrimination was first published in 1990. It appeared in Basil Blackwell's Philosophical Theory monograph series, edited by John McDowell, Philip Pettit and Crispin Wright. Like most volumes in that series, it was taken out of print in 1993 as a result of a change in publishing policy. Since then I have been hearing complaints that it is hard to obtain. Although I have subsequently changed my view on some of the topics with which it deals, not least on vagueness, as a whole it still strikes me as useful enough to be worth republishing.

The main text has been left unaltered, even though it contains some things that I would no longer say and many things that I would now say differently. On most of those points, I have had my more recent say elsewhere.

In the case of vagueness, my views were evolving as I wrote *Identity and Discrimination*. Having started as an orthodox supervaluationist, shortly before I finished the book I came on the idea of margins for error, and its potential use in defence of an independently attractive epistemic interpretation of vagueness. It appears on pp. 104–7. However, I was not yet sure of my ground, and tentatively opted for a hybrid view, epistemicist about some cases, supervaluationist about others. Subsequent reflection and experience convinced me that a uniformly epistemicist view can be robustly defended, and has systematic advantages over a mixed alternative, since much of the cost of backsliding from classical logic and bivalent semantics is incurred if it happens even once. I defended an uncompromisingly uniform epistemicism in *Vagueness*. Although some details of the account there need refinement, I see no good reason to compromise on the logic and semantics.

Another respect in which the approach of *Identity and Discrimination* is tentative concerns the treatment of phenomenal character, the topic of chapters 4–6. It is often supposed to be a central feature of consciousness, defined by appeals to 'what it is like'. I did not (and do not) find appeals to 'what it is like' of much explanatory or even descriptive value. Although talk of what it is like may once have served as a useful corrective to behaviourism, it has become a piece of lazy-mind jargon that obstructs serious understanding of how we experience the world. Constraining phenomenal character in terms of indiscriminability promises to impose some much-needed discipline on the discussion. However, I also worried about the hint of verificationism in attempts to capture the supposed psychological reality of phenomenal character in such terms. I therefore adopted an experimental attitude, developing a formal strategy for handling the specific structural problem in which I was interested for such accounts of phenomenal character while warning that the strategy was no panacea (p. 112). I later came to the conclusion that one leading conception of the phenomenal is an artefact of uncritical epistemology (*Knowledge and its Limits* p. 173). In any case, indiscriminability is a real feature of cognitive life, whose structure needs investigating.

Chapters 1–3 develop an account of discrimination as recognition of distinctness, which enables the logic of indiscriminability to be explained as resulting from the interaction of the logic of epistemic possibility with the logic of identity. The realization that indiscriminability should be understood in terms of knowledge was an early step towards the knowledge-first epistemology of *Knowledge and its Limits*. The epistemic conception of indiscriminability has subsequently been put to work by various authors in recent discussion of disjunctivist theories of perception, which have some similarities with, but also some differences from, knowledge-first epistemology (*Knowledge and its Limits* pp. 44–8).

In 'Additional Notes (to the Revised Edition)', I have given a few references to subsequent writings by others where it seemed particularly useful to do so. Naturally, I have made no attempt to provide bibliographies of recent work on large relevant themes such as vagueness, phenomenal consciousness and essentialism. Nor have I indicated the places where I am no longer happy with what I said in 1990; this preface should be sufficient indication. I have added comments on a few points of interest, including some material from my note 'Fregean

Directions' (*Analysis* 1991) in a new note to chapter 9. These additions are kept separate from the original text of the book, which remains as it was printed in 1990, except for straightforward minor corrections on pp. 9, 35, 45, 57, 65, 66, 72, 77, 84, 107, and 115.

A note on the origins of the book may amuse a few readers. Early in 1974, as a first year undergraduate reading Mathematics and Philosophy at Balliol College Oxford, I became fascinated by Frege's idea of identifying obscure entities (such as directions) with equivalence classes of less obscure entities (such as lines) under a comparatively clear equivalence relation (such as parallelism), and especially by Russell's attempts to extend the method of logical constructions to the world of our experience. I was moved less by the supposed metaphysical or epistemological benefits of the method than by its intellectual elegance. But what particularly intrigued me was an obstacle it faced in some cases: the non-transitivity of the natural candidate for the relevant equivalence relation. Suppose, for example, that we wish to define the perceptible determinates of a given determinable, such as weight. A salient proposal is to equate the identity of the perceptible determinate qualities with indiscriminability in the given respect. But they are not equivalent, because identity is always transitive while indiscriminability in a respect is notoriously not: two differences each too small to be discriminated may add up to a difference large enough to be discriminated.

It occurred to me that by applying Zorn's Lemma, an equivalent of the Axiom of Choice, one can prove that some partition of the objects to be assigned perceptible qualities lumps together only ones mutually indiscriminable (in the relevant respect), and is maximal in the sense that any coarsening of it lumps together some discriminable objects. Such a maximal partition defines an equivalence relation, with the formal features of a criterion of identity for the relevant perceptible qualities, and in a sense comes maximally close to the natural but incoherent original idea. It struck me as a promising fallback position. However, I also realized that, by an easy extension of the argument, the solution is not unique: whenever indiscriminability is non-transitive, more than one partition is maximal. I experimented with criteria for choosing amongst solutions, although I knew on grounds of symmetry that no formal criterion will always select a unique one: just consider the simplest possible case, a reflexive, symmetric, non-transitive relation of indiscriminability on a domain of three objects. I

generalized the applications of the technique, for example to a characterization of meanings in natural language, where the non-transitive
relation on linguistic expressions is approximate synonymy, and to
the non-Cantorian infinite numbers toyed with in section 7.2. By the
summer of 1974 I had most of the material in sections 5.1, 5.3, 7.1
and 7.4 of the present book.

Despite my increasing scepticism about the philosophical presup-
positions of a Russellian programme of logical construction, I contin-
ued to work intermittently on the ideas, and proved that the lemma
about maximal equivalence relations on which the technique depends
is itself equivalent to the Axiom of Choice (see pp. 156–7). I wrote up
the material in 1975 and submitted it to *The Journal of Philosophy*.
After a long wait, I received what I now know to have been a 'revise
and resubmit' letter, asking (reasonably enough) for the philosophical
significance of the material to be clarified. At the time, ignorant of the
conventions of philosophy journals, I read the letter as a patronising
rejection and put the paper away in disgust. I abandoned the topic
for almost a decade. My doctoral dissertation at Oxford was on 'The
Concept of Approximation to the Truth', as a topic in the philosophy
of science, without reference to vagueness: of two precise but false
theories, one may in some sense be closer to the truth than the other
is. Its only contribution to *Identity and Discrimination* was that it
became the starting point for an article on the logic of comparative
similarity, used in passing in section 7.5. Perhaps it was no coincidence
that the two projects shared the theme of approximation. Years later,
I rewrote the paper on identity completely, avoiding commitment to
metaphysical and epistemological assumptions that I could no longer
accept. It finally appeared in *The Journal of Philosophy* for 1986 as
'Criteria of Identity and the Axiom of Choice'. The rest of *Identity
and Discrimination* was written without further delay (see the Preface
to the first edition). I hope that, through this revised edition, it will
encourage others to go further in exploring the fine structure, both
logical and epistemological, of the interaction between identity and
discrimination.

Preface to the First Edition

This book is not longer than it is. The reader may feel that no apology is needed, but should recall the price of comparative brevity: neglect of alternative views, compromises in formal rigour. In particular, I have assumed without argument that the last thing to give up is a principle of classical logic; even its opponents should agree that no case against it is complete without an understanding of what can be done within its limits; this book aims to contribute to that understanding. Logicians will note that quotation marks have been omitted where ambiguity does not threaten.

Material from my 'Criteria of Identity and the Axiom of Choice', *The Journal of Philosophy* 83 (1986), pp. 380–94, appears, completely rewritten, in chapters 5 and 7 and the appendix; I thank the editors of *The Journal of Philosophy* for permission to print it here. I have been greatly helped by responses to oral presentations of ideas in this book. Early versions of chapter 8 were given as talks at Brandeis University and Williams College in 1987 (I thank Peter Lipton in particular). Chapter 9 stems from a paper read to a conference on Identity at Dubrovnik in 1987; David Charles replied. Much of chapters 1 and 6 evolved in a class I gave at Oxford University in Michaelmas 1988. It developed further when I made parts of chapters 1, 2 and 4 the basis of two talks at the University of California at Los Angeles in 1989. I should also like to thank Graeme Forbes, Eli Hirsch, Michael Morris, Stig Alstrup Rasmussen, Nathan Salmon and Crispin Wright for written comments on various parts of the material. Robin Gandy, Dan Isaacson, Bill Newton-Smith and Andrew Pigdon may have forgotten older debts. A first draft was completed at Trinity College, Dublin, and efficiently typed by Anne Burke. Later drafts have been written at University College, Oxford, of which I am not the first Fellow to have written a book about identity; I take the work of my colleague David Wiggins to justify certain assumptions which I have tacitly made. The contrasting influences of the work of Michael Dummett and Saul Kripke are active in many parts of the book. Most important of all, my wife Elisabetta gave me encouragement when it was most needed.

Introduction

Intelligent life requires the ability to discriminate, but not with unlimited precision. A way of discriminating is usually ineffective below a certain threshold. When two things differ by just more than the threshold they can be discriminated, but an intermediate thing may differ from both by less than the threshold, and therefore be discriminable from neither. Discriminability is a rough guide to distinctness; discriminable things are always distinct, distinct things are often but not always discriminable. By the same token, indiscriminability is a rough guide to identity: in longer words, an approximate criterion. If indiscriminability is a shadow of identity, the shape of the latter is distorted but recognizable in the shape of the former. The logic of identity generates a logic of approximate criteria of identity, in some ways similar and in some different (identity is reflexive, symmetric and transitive; indiscriminability is reflexive, symmetric and non-transitive). It is the theme of this book. In particular, techniques are developed for working approximate criteria of identity into exact ones.

Chapter 1 analyses discrimination between things as activation of the knowledge that they are distinct, and indiscriminability as the impossibility of activating such knowledge. The analysis permits an explanation of the reflexivity, symmetry and non-transitivity of indiscriminability in terms of the reflexivity, symmetry and transitivity of identity. However, that is to treat indiscriminability as a relation, and there is a sense in which it is not one, because it is as intentional as any other cognitive phenomenon: things may be discriminable when presented in one way and not when presented in another. The intentional and non-intentional senses are compared. Chapter 2 is more technical; it uses an epistemic interpretation of modal logic to formalize the two senses, and to make precise connections between their formal properties and more general claims about the logic of knowledge. Chapter 3 uses

Identity and Discrimination: Reissued and Updated Edition. Timothy Williamson.
© 2013 Timothy Williamson. Published 2013 by Blackwell Publishing Ltd.

this apparatus to formulate conditions in which an observational predicate applies to both or neither of two indiscriminable things, thereby giving rise to a sorites (slippery slope) paradox.

Can indiscriminability ever be an *exact* criterion of identity? The phenomenal character of an experience is supposed to be wholly given to its subject; if such characters exist, they are subjective qualities in the sense that they form a kind for which identity and indiscriminability coincide. According to a well-known argument there are no subjective qualities, for a non-transitive relation of indiscriminability cannot coincide with the transitive relation of identity. Chapter 4 defends phenomenal characters against that argument, by showing it to run foul of the intentionality of indiscriminability already discussed. Discrimination between phenomenal characters depends on which experiences present them. A positive condition is derived on the relation in which two experiences stand when they have the same phenomenal character. Chapter 5 shows that the condition is satisfied, but by more than one relation. The question is raised whether the concept of sameness in phenomenal character is indeterminate between those relations, or refers to just one of them even if we must be ignorant of which. The account of phenomenal character is contrasted with the view that experiences are the same in phenomenal character just in case they match the same experiences. Chapter 6 uses the plurality of candidate relations of sameness in phenomenal character to explore and defeat sorites paradoxes like those of chapter 3 as threats to phenomenal character. Generalizations to other sorites paradoxes are discussed; as before, they can be understood in terms of either indeterminacy or ignorance.

A necessary and sufficient criterion of identity is an equivalence relation: it is reflexive, symmetric and transitive. The treatment of phenomenal character can be seen as a matter of finding equivalence relations which best approximate a given necessary criterion that is insufficient because non-transitive; various equally good approximations are candidate necessary and sufficient criteria. Chapter 7 generalizes the technique to other cases, including the identity of species and persons, and makes the appropriate concept of approximation precise. A comparison is made with the problem of finding equivalence relations which best approximate a given sufficient condition that is unnecessary because non-transitive. Chapter 8 applies the same technique to sorites paradoxes about the identity of artifacts as their constituent materials vary from possible world to possible world or from time to time. In the light of the foregoing, chapter 9 begins to clarify the confused notion of a criterion of identity. A criterion of identity for things of some kind may be a relation that is not a species of identity and relates things of some other kind, as having the same phenomenal character is not a species of identity and relates experiences, not their phenomenal characters. It is suggested that a criterion of identity is a metaphysical principle apt to explain certain epistemic phenomena.

1

Concepts of Indiscriminability

This chapter is a study in the epistemology of identity. Of course, what is true of knowledge in general is true of knowledge of identity in particular, and for most purposes it would be both inefficient and prejudicial to focus on the latter rather than the former. Nevertheless, the relation of identity exhibits a unique formal character, which is reflected as in a distorting mirror by the formal character of knowledge of identity. The interaction of general features of knowledge with general features of identity needs special attention. The phenomenon of indiscriminability provides one way into this area, the way to be followed here. Since the indiscriminability of objects is less a route to knowledge that they are identical than a block to knowledge that they are distinct (or so it will be argued), it might be less misleading to say that this chapter deals with knowledge of non-identity.

Indiscriminability, unlike identity, is non-transitive. It is not always the case that when a is indiscriminable from b and b is indiscriminable from c then a is indiscriminable from c, for otherwise there could not be series in which the differences between successive members are both too small to be discriminated and yet add up to a discriminable difference between the first member and the last. The non-transitivity of indiscriminability is often treated as a specific and rather mysterious feature of sensory experience, from which startling philosophical conclusions may be drawn. The underlying aim of this chapter is to understand it as a general cognitive phenomenon.

Section 1 develops a cognitive model of discrimination.[1] Section 2 uses the model to explain some formal features of indiscriminability, such as its failure to be transitive, Section 3 uses it to expound a sense in which discrimination is intentional. In section 4 this intentionality is observed to threaten an attempt to define a

Identity and Discrimination: Reissued and Updated Edition. Timothy Williamson.
© 2013 Timothy Williamson. Published 2013 by Blackwell Publishing Ltd.

transitive notion of indiscriminability in terms of a non-transitive notion. Section 5 ties up loose ends.

1.1   Indiscriminability and Cognition

What is indiscriminability? Surface form indicates that things are indiscriminable if and only if it is not possible to discriminate between them. One may therefore expect an account of indiscriminability to comprise accounts of discrimination and, perhaps less importantly, of the relevant kind of possibility.

What is it to discriminate? The verb has an active meaning, in a more than purely grammatical sense. To discriminate is to do something. That is not, of course, to say that discrimination is a bodily (rather than mental) act, still less that it is whatever falls under a certain behavioural (rather than intentional) description. Discrimination has at the very least a cognitive component. For the processes involved in discrimination can also lead to ignorance or error. If I fail to discriminate between the lengths of two lines, one slightly longer than the other, there is something I have failed to find out. If, misled by perspective, I judge one line to be longer than another, and they turn out to be of equal length, my would-be discrimination was incorrect. Failures of discrimination are cognitive failures, so discrimination is a cognitive act.

Naturally, it is open to anyone to use the word 'discrimination' in a non-cognitive sense, perhaps defined in terms of differential responses to stimuli, where 'stimulus' and 'response' are somehow themselves understood non-cognitively. One might even say that a window can discriminate between a ball and a feather, if one breaks it and the other does not. However, that just looks like a metaphorical extension of the concept; we pretend that the window is a knowing subject. In literal terms, the window is at most the instrument of *our* discrimination. Derived senses of the word will not be pursued here.

What kind of cognitive act is discrimination? If discriminating could be assimilated to judging, then false or incorrect discriminations should be possible, as well as true or correct ones. They seem not to be. If I judge this vintage to be fuller-bodied than that, and they turn out to be the same vintage, poured from the same bottle, I have not falsely or incorrectly discriminated the vintage from itself; I have not discriminated at all. I may have seemed to discriminate the vintage in this glass from the vintage in that, but I have not actually done so. In general, a good way of refuting someone's claim to be able to discriminate between this and that is to show that this is that. The cognitive failures associated with discrimination occur in its absence.

Discrimination thus seems closer to knowledge than to belief; false discrimination, like false knowledge and unlike false belief, is a contradiction in terms. Indeed, there is good reason to push this likeness to the point of identity, for if we can characterize discrimination as knowledge, we shall be in a position to explain both why discrimination cannot be in error and why the alternatives to it are ignorance and error.

It would not be quite right simply to assimilate discriminating to knowing, for the former is a process and the latter – like believing – a state. One might use 'recognition' and 'judgement' to express the processes analogous to knowledge and belief, respectively, since judgement but not recognition can be false. Just as knowledge entails belief (on most views), so recognition entails judgement. The hypothesis would then be that discrimination is a kind of recognition, not merely of judgement.

Discrimination involves states as well as processes. The state of being able to discriminate stands to the process of discrimination as the state of being able to recognize stands to the process of recognition. A more specific comparison might be with memory. There is the process of remembering that tomorrow is my birthday, active recall, and there is the state of being able to remember that tomorrow is my birthday. The process is a kind of activation of the state, an exercise of the ability which it is the state of having. However, if I am able to remember that tomorrow is my birthday, I already know that tomorrow is my birthday – I am not merely able to know it; in contrast, I may be able to discriminate between two things, even though I have not yet encountered them and have as yet no relevant knowledge, simply because my present cognitive capacities would permit me to discriminate if I did encounter them. The knowledge activated in discrimination need not pre-exist the process. Thus the closest we can reasonably come to assimilating discrimination to knowledge is the hypothesis that it is the activation of knowledge, where this activation may be described either as acquisition or employment, depending on whether the subject calls on knowledge already possessed.

What knowledge is activated in discrimination? What is its content? The identity of a and b rules out discrimination between them. It would be natural to explain this in terms of the content of the knowledge activated in discrimination, by the incompatibility of this content with the identity of a and b. The simplest hypothesis meeting these requirements is this: to discriminate between a and b is to activate the knowledge that a and b are distinct. One cannot discriminate between a and a because there can be no knowledge that a and a are distinct to be activated; knowledge entails truth. The idea of discriminating as activating knowledge of distinctness is explored in this and subsequent chapters; it will emerge as adequate to a wide variety of cognitive phenomena.

Not every kind of knowledge is relevant to every kind of discrimination. When we speak of discriminating between wines, we do not usually mean reading the labels on the bottles, although in special circumstances we might speak of this as a quick but not always reliable means of discrimination unavailable to the illiterate. In this respect the sense of the word 'discrimination' is context-relative; different kinds of knowledge are meant in different contexts. The word 'knowledge', in contrast, will not be used in this context-relative way; it will be read as stably covering all relevant kinds. Thus although discrimination between a and b entails knowledge that a and b are distinct, not all knowledge that a and b are distinct entails discrimination between a and b in the sense appropriate to a given context, since the knowledge may not issue from the right source.

There is no good reason to restrict the kinds of knowledge which constitute kinds of discrimination. The relevant sources may be sensory modalities, statistical techniques, the use of litmus paper or parish records. Any source which yields knowledge of the properties or relations of a and b may indicate that a has a property which b lacks, or stands in a relation to something to which b does not, thus revealing the distinctness of a and b by Leibniz's Law; identity entails sharing of properties and relations. Any source of knowledge of properties or relations can therefore correspond to a kind of discrimination.

There is also no good reason to restrict the kinds of object which can be discriminated. For, by the same reasoning, for any object *a* of whose properties or relations one can have non-trivial knowledge, there will be an object *b* such that one can know that *a* and *b* are distinct, and in that sense discriminate between them. One can discriminate between paints, or between painted surfaces or walls, or between their colours, or between one's experiences of those colours, for knowledge of distinctness is possible in all these cases. The subjects who discriminate will also be as various as the subjects who know, or at least who know facts of distinctness: people, animals, perhaps machines, and groups of these.

Given this account of discrimination, it is easy to define indiscriminability: *a* is indiscriminable from *b* for a subject at a time if and only if at that time the subject is not able to discriminate between *a* and *b*, that is, if and only if at that time the subject is not able to activate (acquire or employ) the relevant kind of knowledge that *a* and *b* are distinct.

This account is no doubt something of an idealization; as an attempt to state necessary and sufficient conditions for the correct use of the word 'discrimination' in ordinary English it would presumably go the way of most attempts to state necessary and sufficient conditions. Instead it displays a paradigm of discrimination, like pure water. What satisfy the account are clear cases of discrimination; what do not satisfy it but come near to doing so are less clear cases, which it may nevertheless be useful to think of in the same terms. A baby or animal may discriminate sugar from salt, even if it seems excessive to describe them as having the propositional knowledge that sugar is not salt. One might even say that it discriminates between London and Paris (its attitude to passers-by varies) while being reluctant to admit that it thinks of either city. In increasingly attenuated senses, flowers discriminate between day and night, litmus paper between acid and alkali, the window between the feather and the ball. The use of the word is not wholly inept, for such conceptualized sensitivity to difference bears some similarity to the cognitive paradigm. Knowledge is missing, but information may be received. This chapter and the next two, however, deal with more strictly knowledgeable forms of discrimination. They are more amenable to a certain kind of understanding, and the phenomena it discerns should have their analogues in the less articulate cases.

Knowledge is intentional. If, at a party, the sandal-wearer

is the vegetarian and the tea-drinker is the George Orwell expert, I can know that the sandal-wearer and the tea-drinker are distinct without knowing that the vegetarian and the George Orwell expert are distinct. The example requires the definite descriptions to take narrower scope than the knowledge operator (the *de dicto* reading), of course; it fails if they take wider scope (the *de re* reading). If I know, of the sandal-wearer and the tea-drinker, that they are distinct, I thereby know, of the vegetarian and the George Orwell expert, that they are distinct. Which reading applies to discrimination? If I discriminate between the sandal-wearer and the tea-drinker, do I thereby discriminate between the vegetarian and the George Orwell expert? It looks as though both readings are possible, a point which would tell in favour of a cognitive model of discrimination.

A reading of 'discriminate' is *non-intentional* just in case it logically validates the following inference schema:

$$a \text{ is discriminated from } b$$
$$a = c$$
$$b = d$$

Ergo, c is discriminated from d.

The schematic letters 'a', 'b', 'c' and 'd' are replaceable by any singular terms. If the schema is not validated, the reading is *intentional*.

One's ability to discriminate between a and b will in general be sensitive to the ways in which they are presented to one; even one's ability to discriminate between colours depends upon the light in which one sees them. However, sense can always be made of the non-intentional reading in terms of the intentional one, if only by the stipulation that a and b are discriminated non-intentionally if and only if there are modes of presentation under which they are discriminated intentionally. Only on the non-intentional reading can discrimination, and therefore indiscriminability, be a relation between the objects to be discriminated, by Leibniz's Law. It will simplify matters in the short run to adopt this reading. In the long run, however, this neglect of modes of presentation distorts our view of the phenomena to be understood, or so it is argued below, and their role will later be given explicit acknowledgement.

1.2   Formal Features of Indiscriminability

Indiscriminability is generally agreed to be a reflexive, symmetric and non-transitive relation. One cannot discriminate between a and itself, nor can one discriminate between a and b without thereby discriminating between b and a; however, one can sometimes discriminate between a and c when one can discriminate between neither a and b nor b and c. An advantage of the present cognitive account is that it enables these formal features to be explained on general grounds, as follows.

(1)   Reflexivity. It is not possible that a is distinct from a, since identity is necessarily reflexive; it is therefore not possible to know that a is distinct from a, since knowledge entails truth; so it is not possible to activate the knowledge that a is distinct from a, and so no subject is able to do so; a is therefore indiscriminable from a. The reflexivity of identity thus indirectly explains the reflexivity of indiscriminability.

(2)   Symmetry. Suppose that b and a are discriminable: someone is able to activate the knowledge that b is distinct from a. Might they nevertheless be unable to activate the knowledge that a is distinct from b? It seems not; indeed, it seems that the knowledge that b is distinct from a would *constitute* knowledge that a is distinct from b. Imagine trying to work out which of these pieces of knowledge a subject had by trying to discover whether the representation of a was to the right or the left of the representation of b in the relevant sentence token of the subject's language of thought. A subject who assented to the sentence 'Cicero is not Catiline' but refused assent to the sentence 'Catiline is not Cicero' seems to be too confused to count as knowing that Cicero is not Catiline, perhaps even to count as believing that, unless the words are not being understood in the relevant way. Whether or not the pieces of knowledge are identical, conditions on knowledge and understanding seem to make the ability to activate one equivalent to the ability to activate the 'other', without any commitment to the false general thesis that knowledge is closed under logical consequence (crucially, knowledge of the relevant propositions has

not been said to require knowledge of more complex propositions). Moreover, the argument exploited no change in the parameters of discrimination – subject, time, source of knowledge, and so on. If b is discriminable from a in a certain sense, a is discriminable from b in the same sense; contrapositively, if a is indiscriminable from b then b is indiscriminable from a. Thus the symmetry of identity indirectly explains the symmetry of indiscriminability.

(3) Non-transitivity. At least part of what needs to be explained on the present view is the failure of the transitivity of identity to entail the transitivity of indiscriminability. On the other hand, one cannot hope to show that *no* relation of indiscriminability is transitive, for some sources will give complete knowledge of identity and distinctness for some limited domains; in these cases discriminability will be equivalent to distinctness, and therefore indiscriminability to identity, so that it will be transitive. What one can do is to give specific examples of non-transitive indiscriminability relations, and use them to show where attempted arguments from the transitivity of identity to the transitivity of indiscriminability break down. The simplest example is as follows. Let a, b and c be three distinct objects, and let the relevant source of knowledge about them be merely the testimony that a is distinct from c. Thus a and c are discriminable, since a subject with access to the appropriate source can know that they are distinct. However, nothing whatsoever can be learned from that source about b. It leaves open the possibility that b is a; it also leaves open the possibility that b is c. Thus a is indiscriminable from b and b from c, since one cannot know in the appropriate way that they are distinct. So the relation of indiscriminability in question is non-transitive. The underlying logical point is that although the distinctness of a from c entails that either a is distinct from b or b is distinct from c (to contrapose the transitivity of identity), one can know that such a disjunction is true without being able to work out which disjunct is. A way of verifying a disjunction need not be a way of verifying one or other disjunct. It is worth noting that this point could still hold even if knowledge were closed under logical consequence.

For all that has been said so far, the indiscriminability relations of most philosophical interest – such as those associated with direct observation, in some appropriate sense of the term – might still be transitive. However, we know independently that they are not. Given a series of red paints, each very slightly darker than the one before, I may be able to discriminate between the first red and the last without being able to discriminate between any red and its immediate successor (all by the naked eye).

The point deserves further reflection, for it has been challenged on the basis of an information-processing model of perceptual discrimination (see Hardin 1988 for further details). Suppose that a system is to determine whether or not signals are distinct (in type), but that its inputs consist of signals mixed with a certain amount of random interference (noise). The system would be excessively prone to error if it judged signals to be distinct whenever the corresponding inputs were, for qualitatively identical signals will often lead to qualitatively distinct inputs because of variation in the randomly added noise. If its judgements are to be reliable, it should judge that the signals are distinct only when the difference between the inputs is large enough for the probability that it is entirely due to variation in the random noise to be acceptably small. However, if two signals are qualitatively distinct, by however little, the addition of noise in the long run tends to yield an average difference between inputs greater than in the case of qualitatively identical signals, and the probability that this difference results from qualitatively identical signals can be reduced below any desired threshold by sufficiently prolonged exposure to the signals (with probability 1). Our perceptual systems may well work in this way. Thus, it might be suggested, objects presented to this system are indiscriminable in a given context if and only if they cause qualitatively identical signals in that context: but qualitative identity is a transitive relation, so indiscriminability is. Of course, if the system's exposure to the signal is limited to a fixed time – five minutes, say – then indiscriminability will be non-transitive, since for any such time there will be almost but not quite qualitatively identical signals which cannot be discriminated with the required degree of reliability within the given time; transitivity will fail for a series of such signals. The reliability constraint certainly seems to be required by the idea that discrimination is the activation of *knowledge* that the signals come from numerically distinct objects. However, any such time limit would be arbitrary, and give a distorted picture of the underlying phenomena. Or so the argument goes.

An obvious objection to the argument is that it fails to do

justice to the role of consciousness in constituting the kind of discrimination at issue. No doubt a transitive relation of indiscriminability has been described, but that relation is not the one in which we are most interested, at least not when we are investigating perceptual appearances. We are concerned with the way things seem to a pre-reflective observer, and thus the relevant kinds of discrimination are non-inferential. In reply to the claim that all perceptual discrimination involves statistical inferences of the sort just discussed, it is reasonable to stipulate that we are concerned with the way things seem to an observer who has not consciously reflected on them, so that 'non-inferential' may be glossed as 'not involving conscious inference'. Thus the argument for the transitivity of the relevant kind of indiscriminability goes through only if the system can make all the required inferences unconsciously; it is not enough for a professional psychometrician with a calculator to make them. There could indeed be such creatures: presented with any two differently coloured surfaces, however similar, they might experience a sense of slowly gathering conviction that the colours were distinct; it would simply be a matter of looking long and hard enough. We, however, are not such creatures. The longer and harder we look at two surfaces whose colours are distinct but sufficiently similar, the more confused we become; there is a limit to the length of runs of statistical data which we can unconsciously integrate in that way. This fact has an effect on the nature of our experience. It also imposes a non-arbitrary time limit on non-inferential discrimination of the relevant kind, and thus renders the corresponding relation of indiscriminability non-transitive.

The point has nothing to do with the supposed subjectivity of colour, as a secondary quality. Exactly parallel arguments would apply to naked-eye discrimination in respect of length, a primary quality and therefore supposedly objective.

If no distinction were drawn between inferential and non-inferential discrimination, a simpler argument would threaten to make indiscriminability transitive (compare Jackson and Pinkerton 1973, Jackson 1977 pp. 112–15, Sanford 1981 pp. 380–2). Suppose that I can discriminate between a and c, but not between b and c. Thus I can get into the position of having discriminated between a and c without having discriminated between b and c; what is then to stop me from recognizing that to be my position, and thence inferring that *a* is not *b* by Leibniz's Law? I should then have inferential knowledge, based on the relevant source, that *a* and *b* are distinct, thereby having discriminated between *a* and *b*. Thus if *a* but not *b* is discriminable from *c* then *a* is discriminable from *b*; by contraposition, if *a* is indiscriminable from *b* and *b* from *c* then *a* is indiscriminable from *c*. This argument evidently fails for non-inferential forms of discrimination. It has other flaws too, such as the absence from it of any reason to suppose that we can know what discriminations we have made, or not made, and that we can get this knowledge in an appropriate way, but these difficulties may be less pressing in the case of perceptual discrimination; they will be discussed later. What the argument does seem to show is that any relation of indiscriminability can be used to define a transitive relation of indiscriminability, where *a* and *b* are indiscriminable in the new sense just in case they are indiscriminable in the old sense from exactly the same things. Although this conclusion is correct as stated, one must treat it with caution once account is taken of the ways in which the objects of discrimination are presented, and it is to this topic that we now return.

1.3   The Intentionality of Indiscriminability

The standard notions of reflexivity, symmetry, transitivity and non-transitivity are defined for, and only for, binary relations. Thus in describing indiscriminability as non-transitive, one presupposes that it is a binary relation. It follows that any breakdown in the transitivity of indiscriminability will involve at least three objects of attempted discrimination. For suppose that *a* is indiscriminable from *b*, and *b* from *c*, but that *a* is not indiscriminable from *c*; since indiscriminability is reflexive, *a* and *c* are certainly distinct. If *a* and *b* were identical, they would stand in the same relations; since *b* but not *a* stands in the relation of indiscriminability to *c*, they are distinct. By a similar argument, *b* and *c* are distinct. Thus three objects of attempted discrimination are involved even in the simplest case of non-transitivity. The argument invokes Leibniz's Law for relations, but it is surely correct to do so.

Nevertheless, the transitivity of indiscriminability appears to fail in some cases involving only two objects of attempted discrimination. The first example to be given may strike some as a cheat, but it usefully highlights the relevant schema, and will be followed by examples of a more familiar kind.

Goldbach's Conjecture famously says that every even number greater than two is the sum of a pair of prime numbers. It has been neither proved nor refuted; such a proof or refutation may or may not be forthcoming in the future. Even so, the Conjecture will be assumed to be either true or false. Since we do not presently know that the Conjecture is not true, '0=0' is presently indiscriminable in truth value from it, for us. Since we do not presently know that the Conjecture is not false, it is presently indiscriminable in truth value from '0=1', for us. But we can certainly discriminate '0=0' from '0=1' in truth value now. The example does of course involve three distinct sentences, and the three distinct structured propositions they express – 0=0, Goldbach's Conjecture and 0=1 – but these are not the objects of the relevant attempts to discriminate. We can tell all three sentences apart, and all three structured propositions, without the least difficulty; there is no failure *there* of transitivity, and equally, nothing which enables mathematicians to answer the question in which they are interested. Rather, the objects of the relevant attempts to discriminate are the truth values, of which by hypothesis there are exactly two, of these sentences or propositions. One could restate the example in the following terms: the truth value of '0=0' is indiscriminable from the truth value of Goldbach's Conjecture; the truth value of Goldbach's Conjecture is indiscriminable from the truth value of '0=1'; the truth value of '0=0' is not indiscriminable from the truth value of '0=1'. On this way of speaking, the functor '— is indiscriminable from . . .' contains two opaque contexts, in which co-referring singular terms are not intersubstitutable *salva veritate*. Suppose, for instance, that the Conjecture is true; then the two definite descriptions 'the truth value of "0=0"' and 'the truth value of Goldbach's Conjecture' have the same referent, the True (which may arbitrarily be identified with a certain set, for example), but the insertion of the former in the gap in '— is indiscriminable from the truth value of "0=1"' yields a falsehood, whereas the insertion of the latter yields a truth. On this intentional reading, truth values are not discriminable or indiscriminable absolutely, but only relative to their presentations. It does not matter for present purposes whether these are thought of as linguistic expressions, the Fregean thoughts or Russellian propositions expressed, or any of several other possibilities. What does matter is that the objects of attempted discrimination are the objects presented, not the presentations of them, and that while there are three of the latter, there are only two of the former.

The mathematical example confirms the point implicit in the foregoing analysis, that the failure of the transitivity of indiscriminability is not a specifically perceptual phenomenon (it would also be easy to give mathematical examples involving three objects rather than two). However, it does strikingly occur in perception; some perceptual examples involving only two objects are therefore in order.

I turn on the radio and hear three songs in succession, having missed the announcement of the singers. I can hear that the singer of the first song is not the singer of the third, but I can hear neither that the singer of the first song is not the singer of the second nor that the singer of the second is not the singer of the third. Thus, in my circumstances and given my capacities, the singer of the first song is indiscriminable from the singer of the second, and the singer of the second from the singer of the third, but the singer of the first is not indiscriminable from the singer of the third. It is perfectly compatible with all this that the singer of the second should turn out to be the same person as either the singer of the first or the singer of the third. If she does, there are only two objects of discrimination – two singers. In this context one may think of the singings of the songs as the presentations of the singers. There are indeed three of these, but they are not the objects of the relevant attempts to discriminate; my ability to discriminate any one of the singings from the other two is not in question. My difficulty is in telling the difference between the singers they present.

Both examples involve three presentations and two objects presented. The object presented by x is indiscriminable from the object presented by y, which is in turn indiscriminable from the object presented by z, although the object presented by x is discriminable from the object presented by z. All this is consistent with x and y presenting the same object; it is equally consistent with y and z doing so. Since the object presented by x is discriminable from the object presented by z, they are certainly distinct, so at least two objects are needed. The description also requires x, y and z to be distinct presentations. If x were z, the object presented by x would be the object presented by z, which has just been seen not to be the case. If x were y, the discriminability of the object presented by x from the object presented by z would contradict the indiscriminability of the object presented by y from the object presented by z; co-referring variables over presentations are intersubstitutable *salva veritate* in a context like this even though co-referring definite descriptions of the objects they present are not (all relative to an assignment of values to variables). Thus the presentations x and y are distinct; by a similar argument, y and z are distinct.

If there are three presentations and only two presented objects, one object is presented twice. Examples of this kind could thus not be found for kinds of object and presentation, if any, for which each object admits of at most one presentation. Such objects have indeed been sought by philosophers in search of foundations for knowledge. Russellian sense data seem to provide an example. They could of course be referred to by means of many different descriptions – 'the dark red spot at the top left of my visual field at midnight', 'the most irritating sense datum I have had all month', and so on – but each is supposed to have only one period of immediate presentation; a sense datum is the object of acquaintance only once. This period is not momentary, according to Russell; it may last a few minutes (Russell 1918, p. 203). Now what is to stop me from noticing that my present red sense datum occupies more of my visual field than did my red sense datum of two seconds ago, and is therefore presumably distinct from it, without being sure exactly when the change took place? In the circumstances, my red sense datum of two seconds ago is indiscriminable from my red sense datum of one second ago, and my red sense datum of one second ago is indiscriminable from my present red sense datum, although my red sense datum of two seconds ago is discriminable from my present red sense datum. For all that I can tell, the change took place entirely within the last second, in which case my red sense datum of two seconds ago and my red sense datum of one second ago are presumably identical; alternatively, the change may have taken place entirely within the penultimate second, in which case my red sense datum of one second ago and my present red sense datum are presumably identical. Perhaps I have clearer memories of how things were two seconds ago than of how they were one second ago, and thus find the former easier to compare than the latter with how things are now. In this case the passage of time differentiates what are in effect distinct presentations of the same sense datum. The point seems generalizable, given that any object of our awareness is so for more than a single moment of time. If sense data admit distinct presentations, so *a fortiori* do less exotic creatures of subjectivity. The same colour looks different in different lights; pains return.

In the last example, the passage of time gave rise to a difference of presentations. Even if the same sense datum was presented in qualitatively just the same way throughout the period from two seconds ago to one second ago, the facts about discriminability required the presentation of the sense datum two seconds ago to be distinct from the presentation of it one second ago. The point evidently does not turn on the special nature of sense data; it would also arise for a film projected on a screen. It is indeed the reason for speaking of presentations rather than modes of presentation, tokens rather than types, since the former but not the latter have changed (on the most natural readings of 'mode of presentation'). Questions obviously exist about the way in which presentations are to be individuated. It follows from the case that there is no positive length of time δt such that whenever an object is presented in qualitatively just the same way from time t to time $t+\delta t$ then the presentations of it at all times between t and $t+\delta t$ are numerically identical (otherwise the presentation two seconds ago would be the presentation one second ago, by transitivity). Can any presentation exist for more than a single moment? *If* this cannot happen when no qualitative change occurs, *a fortiori* it can hardly happen when such change does occur. Suppose that the presentation at time t is always distinct from the presentation at any later time $t+\delta t$; would it follow that there is always room for doubt as to whether the object presented at t is the same as the object presented at $t+\delta t$? These problems are alleviated but not solved by the reflection that the presentations in the earlier examples could be identified with relatively uncontroversial items, sentences in one case, performances of songs in the other, although neither would be upset by finer distinctions. It may be that presentations x and y are identical if and only if it is necessary that anyone who thinks of an object under x thinks of it under y and *vice versa*, but the implications of this principle are unclear in the absence of a developed theory of content. Fortunately, presentations can for present purposes be treated merely as indices, sequences of relevant factors including in at least some cases times; the arguments which follow are not too sensitive to the detailed filling in of this idea.

Some final remarks are in order about the logical form of statements involving intentional and non-intentional uses of 'discriminate' and cognate words. In English sentences of the form 'a is discriminable from b', where 'a' and 'b' are singular terms, the subject is 'a'. This creates grammatical pressure to read the sentence as ascribing a property to the individual a. One takes 'discriminable' non-intentionally, at least with respect to the first argument-place, and therefore with respect to the second too in uniform cases. By contrast, the singular term 'a' in the analysing sentence 'It is possible to activate the knowledge that a is not b' is not the subject, and occurs embedded within several operators. Something like 'a is such that it is possible to activate the knowledge that it is not b' better matches the grammar of the original, on the non-intentional reading; the formal equivalent would use a predicate-forming lambda-operator. However, explicit constructions of this kind will not be used. The non-intentional reading will generally be in play when and only when the singular terms are individual variables. In this special case it is plausible that 'It is possible to activate the knowledge that a is not b' and 'a is such that it is possible to activate the knowledge that it is not b' are logically equivalent. Another assumption is of course involved: that individual variables can occur meaningfully within the scope of propositional attitude operators. Surely this assumption is correct; we can make sense of the half-English sentence 'For some a, John believes that a contains water and Mary knows that a contains gin' (Church 1982 gives a contrasting view). On these assumptions, and using 'a' and 'b' as variables, the formula 'It is possible to activate the knowledge that a is not b' in effect expresses a relation between a and b.

As for intentional discriminability, it is naturally expressed in English by a sentence whose subject stands for the presentation rather than the object of discrimination. The intentional reading is clearer in 'This line is discriminable from that in length' than in

'The length of this line is discriminable from the length of that', although it can be heard in both. Substitution is legitimate for co-referring terms for presentations but not for the objects presented, as in the formula 'It is possible to activate the knowledge that the object presented by x is not the object presented by y'. These points also apply to the interpretation of the formal system in the next chapter.

1.4   Direct and Indirect Discrimination

The intentionality of discrimination bears on attempts to define a notion of indirect discrimination for which indiscriminability would be transitive in terms of a notion of direct discrimination for which indiscriminability is non-transitive. The idea, already mentioned, is that the direct discriminability of this but not that from a third thing is itself an indirect means of discriminating between this and that.[2] This is indiscriminable by indirect means from that just in case this and that are indiscriminable by direct means from exactly the same things, a transitive matter even if direct discrimination is not. What happens if the relevant notion of indiscriminability by direct means is an intentional one?[3]

Given an intentional kind of indiscriminability, indiscriminability$_i$, we can say that the object presented by x is indiscriminable$_{i*}$ from the object presented by y just in case for every presentation z, the object presented by x is indiscriminable$_i$ from the object presented by z if and only if the object presented by y is indiscriminable$_i$ from the object presented by z. If indiscriminability$_i$ could be treated simply as a relation between the objects presented, so could indiscriminability$_{i*}$, and the latter would automatically be an equivalence relation; that is, it would be reflexive, symmetric and transitive. Some problems with this construction have already been mentioned, but the intentionality of indiscriminability$_i$ creates a more urgent one. For the discriminability$_{i*}$ of the object presented by x from the object presented by y does not entail the distinctness of those objects. Suppose that the object presented by x, but not the object presented by y, is discriminable$_i$ from the object presented by z; given the intentionality of discriminability$_i$, it is consistent also to assume that the objects presented by x and y are the same. The object presented by x is discriminable$_{i*}$ from the object presented by y, by definition; yet the subject has been given no kind of access to knowledge that the object presented by x is not the object presented by y, for the subject has been given no kind of access to a situation in which this would be true (even when the definite descriptions are given narrow scope, as they should be). If one reasons 'I have discriminated$_i$ the object presented by x from the object presented by z, but I have not discriminated$_i$ the object presented by y from the object presented by z; therefore by Leibniz's Law the object presented by x is not the object presented by y', one has simply committed a fallacy of illicit substitution of co-referring definite descriptions in an opaque context (given the same assumption as before about scope); one's premises are true and one's conclusion is false. Thus discriminability$_{i*}$ is not the possibility of any kind of discrimination, and indiscriminability$_{i*}$ is not a kind of indiscriminability.

One can of course legitimize the definition of indiscriminability$_{i*}$ by reverting to a non-intentional reading of indiscriminability$_i$. One would then say that a is indiscriminable$_{i*}$ from b just in case for every object c, a is indiscriminable$_i$ from c if and only if b is indiscriminable$_i$ from c, where the variables 'a', 'b' and 'c' range over presentable objects (unlike 'x', 'y' and 'z', which range over presentations). The discriminability$_{i*}$ of a and b would then entail their distinctness. Expressions such as 'the object presented by x' could be substituted for variables such as 'a', provided that the description was given wide scope. However, this move is less than fully illuminating in the absence of an account of the relations between the intentional and non-intentional uses. The sensitivity to presentation seems too germane to the phenomena in which we are interested simply to be ignored in this way.

1.5 Further Reflections

Three further aspects of the importance of presentation may be mentioned.

(1) We can know two things to be distinct simply because they are in different places, even if we can discern no qualitative difference between them. If Tweedledum and Tweedledee are presented to me simultaneously, I know without being told that the twin on my right is not the twin on my left. If they are

presented to me consecutively, I do not know without being told that the twin now in the room is not the twin who left the room five minutes ago. There is little to be proud of in my kind of ability to discriminate between the twins. To specify the kind of discriminability in which we are more likely to be interested, we must advert to the presentations to stipulate that they should be consecutive.

(2) Consider a man who cannot discriminate between elms and beeches. That is not to say that for him every elm is indiscriminable from every beech, nor even that every elm is indiscriminable from some beech (not necessarily the same one in every case) and *vice versa*; some elm may look quite different from every beech, even to him. The point is rather that if you take him to a grove of elms and beeches, he cannot usually sort the trees into two classes, one containing all and only the elms and the other all and only the beeches (he is not required to know which class to associate with the word 'elm' and which with the word 'beech'). In particular, if you present him with an elm and a beech, he cannot usually tell that the former is a different kind of tree from the latter. At the same time he may know theoretically that the genera *Ulmus* (elm) and *Fagus* (beech) are distinct; he may even know of examples of each, labelled as such in the Botanical Gardens. The objects of discrimination are in effect kinds of tree, genera, but as presented by individual trees instantiating them rather than by definitions. Similarly, consider a man who cannot discriminate between liars and truth-tellers. That is not to say that for him every liar is indiscriminable from every truth-teller, nor even that every liar is indiscriminable from some truth-teller (not necessarily the same one in every case) and *vice versa*; some liar may sound quite different from every truth-teller, even to him. The point is rather that if you present him with a liar and a truth-teller, he cannot usually tell that they fall on different sides of the liar/truth-teller divide. At the same time he may perfectly understand what the divide is; he may even know paradigms of each. Thus the objects of discrimination are in effect the qualities of being a liar and of being a truth-teller, but as presented by individual people instantiating them rather than by definitions. More generally, the ability to discriminate between As and Bs can be characterized as the ability to discriminate between the qualities of A-hood and B-hood (or between the kinds, classes or whatever), but only on the

stipulation that these qualities (or kinds, classes or whatever) are presented by their instances (or members) rather than by descriptions. One cannot carry out this subsumption of the ability to discriminate between As and Bs under the preceding account without reference to modes of presentation.

(3)   It is not implied that a subject can activate the knowledge that the object presented by x is distinct from the object presented by y only by thinking *about* the presentations x and y themselves. The subject will normally think only about the objects presented; the requirement is to think about them *under* x and y respectively. Nevertheless, at least one aspect of the subject's knowledge can be articulated perspicuously by the proposition that the object presented by x is not the object presented by y, which is *de re* with respect to presentations rather than objects; it is left open whether the subject has *de re* knowledge concerning the objects, that they are distinct.

The informal analysis in this chapter has only begun to reveal the structure implicit in the non-transitivity of indiscriminability. The next chapter continues the process by developing a formal system. Informal readers may prefer to go straight to chapter 4.

2

Logics of Indiscriminability

Issues about discrimination were seen in the previous chapter to reflect several broader cognitive phenomena: more and less intentional descriptions of knowledge; inferential and non-inferential knowledge; knowledge and ignorance about knowledge. All three contrasts have been successfully investigated elsewhere within the framework of quantified epistemic logic; it provides some useful apparatus for pushing the present inquiry forward (section 2.1). In particular, the aim will be to formulate epistemic conditions for the non-transitivity of indiscriminability (section 2.2). It will emerge as an overdetermined phenomenon; several different kinds of cognitive failure are individually sufficient for it to occur.

2.1 Logical Apparatus

We shall use a formal language with two sorts of variables: type 1 variables $x, y, z, \ldots$ to range over a class of presentations, and type 2 variables $a, b, c, \ldots$ to range over the corresponding class of objects presented. There is just one function symbol, o; it is unary and takes only type 1 variables in its argument place; it is to be read as expressing the function which maps each presentation to the object it presents. It will be assumed that each presentation presents one and only one object, so that o is everywhere well-defined. The general importance of the possibility of empty and ambiguous presentations needs no emphasis, but in the present context it would introduce irrelevant complications.

A type 2 term is either a type 2 variable or of the form ov, where v is a type 1 variable. The only atomic formulae consist of the identity sign $=$ flanked on each side by type 2 terms. The language contains standard truth-functors: $\sim$ (negation), & (conjunction),

Identity and Discrimination: Reissued and Updated Edition. Timothy Williamson.
© 2013 Timothy Williamson. Published 2013 by Blackwell Publishing Ltd.

∨ (disjunction), → (material conditional), ↔ (material biconditional). As discussed below, we shall not need any quantifiers.

The idea is to use the apparatus of modal logic by reading $\Box A$ not as 'It is necessary that A' but as 'The subject is able to activate knowledge that A' (where this knowledge is understood to be appropriate to the kind of discrimination in question).[1] As usual, $\Diamond A$ is defined as $\sim\Box\sim A$; it means that the subject is not able to activate knowledge that it is not the case that A. The operators will be written $\boxed{\text{K}}$ and $\diamondsuit\!\!\!\text{K}$ as a reminder of their epistemic readings. Since the expression 'the object presented by x is discriminable from the object presented by y' has been explicated as 'the subject is able to activate knowledge that the object presented by x is distinct from the object presented by y', it may be symbolized as $\boxed{\text{K}} \sim ox = oy$. Correspondingly, the expression 'the object presented by x is indiscriminable from the object presented by y' may be symbolized as $\sim \boxed{\text{K}} \sim ox = oy$, that is, as $\diamondsuit\!\!\!\text{K}\, ox = oy$ (where the descriptions are to be read as taking small scope).

Why should $\boxed{\text{K}}$ be thought of as a kind of epistemic *necessity*, and $\diamondsuit\!\!\!\text{K}$ as a kind of epistemic *possibility*? Why should the subject's ability to do something be regarded as a case of necessity, as the symbolism insinuates – is it not rather a case of possibility? One answer is by extrapolation: provability is well thought of as a kind of epistemic necessity, and its being provable that A is equivalent to a special case of a hyper-rational subject's being able to activate knowledge that A. Just as the metaphysical possibility of a proof that A corresponds to the epistemic necessity that A, and the metaphysical impossibility of a proof to the epistemic possibility of its negation, so the subject's ability to activate knowledge also corresponds to an epistemic necessity, and the subject's inability to an epistemic possibility. There is no paradox, because the kinds of modality which correspond in this inverted way are different – one epistemic, one metaphysical or ontological. To say that something is epistemically possible is not to say that it could really have been the case. A fuller answer will be available once the logic of $\boxed{\text{K}}$ and $\diamondsuit\!\!\!\text{K}$ has been discussed, since the principles to be postulated as governing them are precisely those in some standard systems of modal logic.

The relevant kind of epistemic necessity should not be thought to involve *certainty*. The use of epistemic modalities is intended as a development of the earlier account of discriminability, not an alternative to it; they should therefore be understood in terms of knowledge rather than certainty. This kind of epistemic necessity does not require the elimination of all conceivable room for doubt, any more than knowledge does. For example, I can know two wines to be distinct by tasting them, and so render their distinctness epistemically necessary, even though a sceptic could raise doubts – perhaps they are the same wine and only my palate has changed. Given that my palate has in fact remained more or less the same, that there is no reason to think otherwise, and so on, the possibility of such doubts undermines neither the knowledge nor the epistemic necessity.

Although the system under construction could be made into a quantified modal logic by the addition of universal and existential quantifiers, in practice we shall find ourselves able to express whatever present purposes require using only quantifier-free open formulae, and it will greatly simplify matters if we do so. That is not to say that we can finesse all the delicate questions about the interaction of quantifiers with modal operators; rather, some of them will be begged. For example, once the universal quantifier was added the use of open formulae and standard quantifier rules could lead to the derivability of the converse Barcan schema $\boxed{K} \forall x A(x) \vdash \forall x \boxed{K} A(x)$, and in some circumstances of the Barcan schema $\forall x \boxed{K} A(x) \vdash \boxed{K} \forall x A(x)$ itself (Kripke 1963 p. 68). Neither schema is obviously valid on the present interpretation of $\boxed{K}$, even for a perfectly rational subject. The converse Barcan schema may fail because, although the subject knows that everything is A, there is some member of the domain of which the subject does not know; *a fortiori*, the subject does not know of it that it is A, and thus does not know of each member of the domain that it is A. The Barcan schema may fail because, although the subject knows of each member of the domain that it is A, the subject does not know that the inventory of the domain is complete, and cannot rule out the possibility that a non-A member has been omitted. Thus the Barcan schema and its converse require the domain to be *surveyable*. In what follows, this simplifying assumption will be made about both the domain of presentations and the domain of objects presented. It is fairly harmless, since the main focus will be on what can *not* be derived; if something cannot be derived in the presence of this assumption, it certainly cannot be derived in its absence. In a more elaborate development the assumption could be avoided by devices such as those in Kripke 1963 (at p. 69).

Individual open formulae will not be understood as though preceded by universal quantifiers; rather, the scope of the implicit universal quantifiers will be the whole sequent. For example, the sequent $a = b \vdash b = a$ expresses the symmetry of identity; it corresponds to $\forall a \forall b \, (a = b \to b = a)$ rather than to $\forall a \forall b \, a = b \to \forall a \forall b \, b = a$. Thus from $A(a) \vdash B(a)$ we can infer $A(b) \vdash B(b)$, but we do not generally have $A(a) \vdash A(b)$ (where A is quantifier-free).

If we think of indiscriminability non-intentionally, as equivalent to a relation between the objects of discrimination, then the following sequents, valid or invalid, express its reflexivity, symmetry and transitivity:

(2.1) $\vdash \Diamond_{\!K}\, a = a$

(2.2) $\Diamond_{\!K}\, a = b \vdash \Diamond_{\!K}\, b = a$

(2.3)* $\Diamond_{\!K}\, a = b, \Diamond_{\!K}\, b = c \vdash \Diamond_{\!K}\, a = c$

The asterisk flags a rejected thesis. If we think of indiscriminability intentionally, as presentation-sensitive, then (2.1–3) give way to:

(2.1o) $\vdash \Diamond_{\!K}\, ox = ox$

(2.2o) $\Diamond_{\!K}\, ox = oy \vdash \Diamond_{\!K}\, oy = ox$

(2.3o)* $\Diamond_{\!K}\, ox = oy, \Diamond_{\!K}\, oy = oz \vdash \Diamond_{\!K}\, ox = oz$

Strictly speaking, (2.1o–3o) express the reflexivity, symmetry and transitivity of a certain relation between presentations, rather than presented objects, which is not itself that of indiscriminability. However, it will sometimes be convenient to speak loosely of (2.3o) as maintaining the transitivity of intentional indiscriminability. The object of the exercise is to investigate the circumstances in which these sequents are derivable.

The underlying propositional logic will be classical; the principles of standard natural deduction systems will be assumed. The logic for identity is also standard: its reflexivity is given by the sequent $\vdash a = a$, and Leibniz's Law is represented by the schema

(LL), $a = b$, $A \vdash B$, where A and B differ only in that B contains b in some places where A contains a (A and B may contain modal operators, since the co-referring terms being substituted are variables).[2]

To make up for the absence of quantifier rules there is a rule of substitution: if # is an operation of substitution and the sequent $A_1, \ldots,$ $A_n \vdash B$ is derivable, then so is the sequent $\#A_1, \ldots, \#A_n \vdash \#B$. Technically, # is an operation of substitution just in case it is a function from the terms and formulae of the language to its terms and formulae such that: if v is a type 1 variable, $\#v$ is so too and $\#ov$ is $o\#v$; if v is a type 2 variable, $\#v$ is a type 2 term; if t and t' are type 2 terms then $\#(t = t')$ is $\#t = \#t'$; $\#{\sim}A$ is ${\sim}\#A$, $\#(A \,\&\, B)$ is $\#A \,\&\, \#B$, and so on. This rule allows us to derive $\vdash b = b$ and $\vdash ox = ox$ from $\vdash a = a$, for example. However, it requires one qualification: no term of the form ov should be substituted for a type 2 variable within the scope of a modal operator. We should otherwise be able to move from the sequent $a = b$, $\boxed{\text{K}}\, a = a \vdash \boxed{\text{K}}\, a = b$ to the sequent $ox = oy$, $\boxed{\text{K}}\, ox = ox \vdash \boxed{\text{K}}\, ox = oy$; but whereas the former is an acceptable instance of (LL), the latter says in effect that if two presentations pick out the same object then it is epistemically necessary that they do (the premise $\boxed{\text{K}}\, ox = ox$ dropping out as redundant for present purposes), which is wholly implausible on the intended narrow-scope reading of the descriptions.

Just as we have the sequent $\vdash a = a$, and thence $\vdash ox = ox$, for the reflexivity of identity, so it is an easy exercise using the rules above to derive the sequents $a = b \vdash b = a$ and $a = b$, $b = c \vdash a = c$, and thence $ox = oy \vdash oy = ox$ and $ox = oy$, $oy = oz \vdash ox = oz$, for its symmetry and transitivity. The crux will be the relation of these sequents to (2.1–3) and (2.1o–3o), which depends on the principles governing epistemic possibility.

In order to derive the reflexivity of indiscriminability, (2.1), from the correct sequent $\vdash a = a$ and (2.1o) from the correct sequent $\vdash ox = ox$, it would be enough to have the rule that if $\vdash A$ is a correct sequent then so is $\vdash \diamondsuit A$.[3] In other and rougher words, this rule says that the subject is unable to activate knowledge of the falsity of a logical truth. Similarly, in order to derive the symmetry of indiscriminability, (2.2), from the correct sequent $a = b \vdash b = a$ and (2.2o) from the correct sequent $ox = oy \vdash oy = ox$, it would be enough to have the rule that if $A \vdash B$ is a correct sequent then so is $\diamondsuit A \vdash \diamondsuit B$. Since this is equivalent to the rule that if ${\sim}B \vdash {\sim}A$ is a

correct sequent then so is $\boxed{\text{K}} \sim B \vdash \boxed{\text{K}} \sim A$, it can be roughly para-
phrased as saying that logical consequences of a piece of activatable
knowledge are themselves activatable knowledge (which does not
mean that it is knowledge the subject already possesses). These
rules are very weak. Even taken together, they do not require
either that truth entails epistemic possibility or that the epistemic
possibility of a disjunction entails that at least one of its disjuncts
is epistemically possible, both of which seem to be reasonable
principles.[4] The derivation of $\diamondsuit\!\!\!\!\!\;\text{\tiny K}\, A \vdash \diamondsuit\!\!\!\!\!\;\text{\tiny K}\, B$ from $A \vdash B$ might still
be doubted where non-inferential knowledge was in question, but the
particular instances of the rule used to derive (2.2) and (2.2o) were
already seen in section 1.2 of the previous chapter to be particularly
unproblematic. However, the most interesting issues concern the
non-derivability of the transitivity of indiscriminability. The way
to study them is to look at the strongest reasonable systems in
which (2.3) and (2.3o) are not derivable, and the principles whose
addition to these systems would lead to their derivability, in order
to see what logical issues the non-transitivity of indiscriminability
reflects.

The first assumption to be made is that the relevant kind of epistemic necessity is transmitted by logical consequence. It corresponds
to a familiar rule from modal logic:

(RK) If $A_1, \ldots, A_n \vdash B$

then $\boxed{\text{K}}\, A_1, \ldots, \boxed{\text{K}}\, A_n \vdash \boxed{\text{K}}\, B$

It is permissible for the set of premises to be the null set (n = 0), so
that the rule of Necessitation is a special case. (RK) says that if the
subject is able to activate each of several items of knowledge of the
appropriate sort, then the subject is able to activate knowledge of
the appropriate sort of anything entailed by these items. So not only
must the subject be able to draw the required inferences, the activation
of the knowledge that A_1 must not interfere with the activation of the
knowledge that A_2 (one thinks of uncertainty principles in quantum
mechanics), otherwise the subject could not activate all the premises
of the premises together; $\boxed{\text{K}}A_1, \ldots, \boxed{\text{K}}A_n$ guarantee only that any one
of the premises can be activated. In addition, the resulting inferential
knowledge must be of the appropriate sort.

A subtler assumption is also involved in (RK). It is normally allowed that a subject can have several items of *de re* knowledge about a single object without being in a position to know that they are knowledge of the same object. Someone might have met a little girl at school and a famous film star without realizing them to be the same person. He knows of the little girl that if she is now rich then she has failed in her ambition to be a train-driver; he also knows of the film star that she is now rich. Let *a* be the person who is now a famous film star and was once a little girl; our man knows that if *a* is now rich then *a* has failed in *a*'s ambition to be a train-driver, and he knows that *a* is now rich. Nevertheless, he is in no position to apply *modus ponens* to conclude that *a* has failed in *a*'s ambition to be a train-driver, whether he thinks of *a* as the little girl or as the film star. If he did draw that conclusion while not realizing the identity it would be an irrational inference and would not lead to knowledge; there is certainly no failure of rationality in not drawing the conclusion. Thus (RK) does not merely require subjects to be good logicians; it also requires them to be in a position to know when the same object is being presented again – not in all cases, but in those which result in *de re* knowledge. The point of these assumptions is not that they are always met but that, as will be seen, indiscriminability may be non-transitive even when they are. In other words, the non-transitivity of indiscriminability depends neither on uncertainty or opacity effects in the acquisition and employment of knowledge nor on the subject's inferential failings; it can occur even when all the activatable knowledge of the relevant kind has been activated, and this knowledge includes all its logical consequences.

The next assumption to be made is that the relevant kind of epistemic necessity entails truth. It corresponds to a familiar schema in modal logic:

(T) $\boxed{\text{K}}\, A \vdash A$

That is, if the subject is able to activate the knowledge that A then it is the case that A. An example of what this schema rules out is the following situation: the presentations x and y actually present the same object, but the subject has the (unexercised) ability to activate the knowledge that they present different objects by knowingly bringing about a situation in which they do, because the subject can control which object a particular presentation presents. Such a situation may or may not be possible, but examples can certainly be found when a wider range of substitutions for A is allowed. Even when I am sitting, I have the ability to activate the knowledge that I am standing; for I have the ability to stand, and when I exercise it I know that I do. Again, the point of the assumption is to show that the non-transitivity of indiscriminability does not depend on the knower's control over the objects of knowledge.

The rule (RK) yields the modal system K. It is already sufficient for the derivation of the rule that if $A \vdash B$ is a correct sequent then so is $\diamondsuit A \vdash \diamondsuit B$, and thus of (2.2) and (2.2o), the symmetry of indiscriminability. The addition of (T) to K yields the modal system KT, also known as M and T. Even in the absence of (RK), (T) is sufficient for the derivation of the rule that if $\vdash A$ then $\vdash \diamondsuit A$, and thus of (2.1) and (2.1o), the reflexivity of indiscriminability ((T) is equivalent to the schema $A \vdash \diamondsuit A$).

So far we lack principles about the iteration of modal operators.[5] We shall assume that if something is epistemically necessary, then it is epistemically necessary that it is epistemically necessary. This corresponds to the schema:

(S4) $\boxed{K} A \vdash \boxed{K} \boxed{K} A$

That is, if the subject is able to activate the knowledge that A then the subject is able to activate the knowledge that the subject is able to activate the knowledge that A. Subjects can recognize their own cognitive achievements. Moreover, the knowledge they gain in doing so can be of the appropriate kind. Again, the point of these assumptions is not that they are always met but that, as will be seen, indiscriminability may be non-transitive even when they are. In other words, the non-transitivity of indiscriminability does not depend on subjects' inability to recognize their own cognitive achievements in the appropriate way. The addition of (S4) to KT yields the modal system KT4, better known as S4.

(S4) is to be compared with the assumption that if something is epistemically possible, then it is epistemically necessary that it is epistemically possible. It corresponds to the schema:

(S5) $\diamondsuit A \vdash \boxed{K} \diamondsuit A$

That is, if the subject is unable to activate the knowledge that it is not the case that A, then the subject is able to activate the knowledge that the subject is unable to activate the knowledge that it is not the case that A. Subjects can recognize their own cognitive failings. Moreover, the knowledge they gain in doing so can be of the appropriate kind. The addition of (S5) to either KT or KT4 yields the modal system KT5, better known as S5, for (S4) is a consequence of (S5) in KT.

(S5) is notoriously a far more dubious principle than (S4) on epistemic interpretations of modal logic. Not only self-love makes it harder to acknowledge one's cognitive failures than one's cognitive successes. It is convenient to take (S5) in the equivalent form $\sim \boxed{K} A \vdash \boxed{K} \sim \boxed{K} A$. Suppose that John has never eaten frogs, but is mistakenly convinced that he remembers doing so; then John is in no position to know that he once ate frogs, but he is also in no position to know that he is no position to know that he once ate frogs. This example turns on John's error, but (S5) is more dubious than (S4) even when error is not in question. There are various interpretations of $\boxed{K}$ as a kind of provability for which 'It is provable that A' entails 'It is provable that it is provable that A', although 'It is unprovable that A' does not entail 'It is provable that it is unprovable that A', since a proof of provability need only point out a single proof, whereas a proof of unprovability requires some sort of survey of all possible proofs. Nevertheless, it would still be worth assuming (S5) if it could be shown that, even in its presence, the transitivity of indiscriminability cannot be derived, for then non-transitivity would turn out not to depend on the failure of (S5). In what follows we shall work with both KT4 and KT5.

Something needs to be said about the semantics of these systems. The intended interpretation of the symbols has already been given by the informal remarks above. However, it will be convenient also to have a formal model theory for the systems, so that certain sequents can be proved to be underivable on the grounds that they fail in some model. This model theory will be of the usual possible worlds sort. It should be thought of as merely an algebraic device of use to independence proofs; the possible worlds are not claimed to be essential to an understanding of the symbols, still less to exist 'out there' as worlds in some metaphysically robust sense (which would be particularly inappropriate for an epistemic reading of the modal operators).

The elements of such a possible worlds model may briefly be rehearsed, in application to the language being considered.[6] There is a set of items called worlds, and a relation of what is called accessibility on them. There is a domain of presentations and a domain of presentable objects; since the Barcan formula and its converse are not in question, these will be held constant from world to world. To interpret o, there is a function f which maps each ordered pair of a world and an element of the domain of presentations to an element of the domain of objects (the same presentation may present different objects in different epistemically possible worlds). To interpret $=$, there is for each world w an equivalence relation E_w on the domain of objects, which may or may not be identity (another reason for not treating the worlds as more than an algebraic device); it is required that if a world w+ is accessible from a world w, and E_w holds between two objects, then so does E_{w+}. By an assignment is meant a (world-independent) mapping of type 1 variables into the domain of presentations and of type 2 variables into the domain of objects. Relative to an assignment and a world w, the denotation of a variable is what the assignment maps it to; if the assignment maps the type 1 variable v to i, then the denotation of the type 2 term ov is f(w, i). If t and t' are type 2 terms, an assignment satisfies the formula $t = t'$ at a world w just in case the relation E_w holds between the denotations, relative to that assignment and w, of t and t'. An assignment satisfies the formula $\sim A$ at a world w just in case it does not satisfy A at w; it satisfies A & B at w just in case it satisfies A at w and B at w, and so on for the other truth functors; it satisfies $\diamondsuit A$ at w just in case it satisfies A at some world w′ accessible from w; it satisfies $\boxed{K} A$ at w just in case it satisfies A at every world w′ accessible from w. A sequent is valid at a world just in case every assignment which satisfies each premise of the sequent also satisfies its conclusion; it is valid in a model just in case it is valid at every world in that model. It is a routine task to show for such models that: every derivable sequent of K is valid in every model; every derivable sequent of KT is valid in every model whose accessibility relation is reflexive; every derivable sequent of KT4 is valid in every model whose accessibility relation is reflexive and transitive; every derivable sequent of KT5 is valid in every model whose accessibility relation is reflexive, symmetric and transitive. The only special point to check is that E_w acts as a relation of indiscernibility at every world which has the ancestral of the accessibility relation to w.

2.2   The Non-Transitivity of Indiscriminability

The sequents (2.3) and (2.3o) symbolize the transitivity of indiscriminability. Why are they not derivable? In particular, why are they not derivable from the transitivity of identity – (2.3) from the correct sequent $a = b,\ b = c \vdash a = c$, and (2.3o) from the correct sequent $ox = oy,\ oy = oz \vdash ox = oz$?

(2.3) and (2.3o) would be derivable from the transitivity of identity if we had a rule which allowed us to move from $A,\ B \vdash C$ to $\Diamond\!\!\!\Diamond A,\ \Diamond\!\!\!\Diamond B \vdash \Diamond\!\!\!\Diamond C$; it would be the equivalent of (RK) for $\Diamond\!\!\!\Diamond$ in place of $\boxed{\text{K}}$. However, this rule is invalid, for it assumes that all possibilities are compossible. For example, it would allow us to move from the correct schema $A, \sim\!A \vdash A\ \&\ \sim\!A$ to the schema $\Diamond\!\!\!\Diamond A,\ \Diamond\!\!\!\Diamond \sim\!A \vdash \Diamond\!\!\!\Diamond (A\ \&\ \sim\!A)$, which is not only intuitively incorrect but leads, in KT or any stronger logic, to the collapse of all modal distinctions, by yielding the schema $\Diamond\!\!\!\Diamond A \vdash A$. It is true, as has already been noted, that such a rule does hold in the special case where only one premise is involved, so that we can move from $A\ \&\ B \vdash C$ to $\Diamond\!\!\!\Diamond (A\ \&\ B) \vdash \Diamond\!\!\!\Diamond C$, but this does not help, since $\Diamond\!\!\!\Diamond A\ \&\ \Diamond\!\!\!\Diamond B \vdash \Diamond\!\!\!\Diamond (A\ \&\ B)$ is not derivable. In particular, we can derive $\Diamond\!\!\!\Diamond (a = b\ \&\ b = c) \vdash \Diamond\!\!\!\Diamond a = c$ and $\Diamond\!\!\!\Diamond (ox = oy\ \&\ oy = oz) \vdash \Diamond\!\!\!\Diamond ox = oz$, but these do not amount to (2.3) and (2.3o). Thus the non-transitivity of indiscriminability can be seen as reflecting the fact that two states of affairs can be epistemically possible without their conjunction being so, in the sense that its transitivity is derivable from the denial of the fact.

However, the failure of one attempt to derive a sequent does not show that it is underivable. For indeed, (2.3) *is* derivable in KT5. This can be shown as follows. Even in K we have 'The Necessity of Identity':

(2.4) $a = b \vdash \boxed{\text{K}}\, a = b$

For $a = b$, $\boxed{\text{K}}\, a = a \vdash \boxed{\text{K}}\, a = b$ is an instance of (LL), and the application of (RK) to $\vdash a = a$ yields $\vdash \boxed{\text{K}}\, a = a$. From (2.4) we can reach $\Diamond\!\!\!\!\Diamond\, a = b \vdash \Diamond\!\!\!\!\Diamond \boxed{\text{K}}\, a = b$ via (RK), and $\Diamond\!\!\!\!\Diamond \boxed{\text{K}}\, a = b \vdash a = b$ is an instance of the schema $\Diamond\!\!\!\!\Diamond \boxed{\text{K}} A \vdash A$, which is derivable in KT5. This gives the principle that the epistemic possibility of identity entails identity:

(2.5) $\Diamond\!\!\!\!\Diamond a = b \vdash a = b$

(2.5) is equivalent to 'The Necessity of Distinctness', the sequent $\sim a = b \vdash \boxed{\text{K}} \sim a = b$. Given (T), $\Diamond\!\!\!\!\Diamond\, a = b$ is then equivalent to $a = b$. But then (2.3) does follow from $a = b$, $b = c \vdash a = c$, for indiscriminability collapses into identity, and the transitivity of the latter guarantees the transitivity of the former.

In KT5, we cannot distinguish between non-intentional indiscriminability and identity. At least two responses to this fact are possible. We can retreat from KT5 to a weaker system such as KT4, or we can treat indiscriminability as intentional within KT5. The latter of these possibilities will be investigated first.

For the presentation-dependent notion of indiscriminability, (2.3o) states the relevant form of transitivity. (2.3o) cannot be inferred by substitution from (2.3), since that would involve illicitly replacing variables by definite descriptions within the scope of a modal operator. Indeed, KT5 does not even yield the equivalent of the necessity of identity for definite descriptions:

(2.4o)* $ox = oy \vdash \boxed{\text{K}}\, ox = oy$

(2.4o) is intuitively incorrect because x and y can be distinct presentations of the same object, and knowledge that they present the same object (as in $\boxed{\text{K}}\, ox = oy$) cannot be reduced to knowledge of a trivial identity (as in $\boxed{\text{K}}\, ox = ox$). In contrast, (2.4) characterizes the knowledge solely in terms of the objects it is about; relative to an assignment of the same object to the variables 'a' and 'b', knowledge that a is a is knowledge that a is b.[7]

What is needed is a proof that (2.3o) is not derivable in KT5. In fact, something stronger will be proved: that the *only* constraints imposed by KT5 on $\Diamond\!\!\!\!\Diamond\, ox = oy$ as a relation between x and y are reflexivity and symmetry ((2.1o) and (2.2o)). The proof will use the possible worlds model theory sketched in the previous section.

Let R be any reflexive symmetric relation on a set X; we ignore the trivial case in which X is empty. The idea is to produce a possible worlds model of KT5 in which R is the extension of the formula $\Diamond\, ox = oy$, thus showing that KT5 imposes no further constraints. The worlds will simply be those unordered pairs $\{i, j\}$ of members of X between which R holds. Every world is accessible from every world; since this is an equivalence relation, the schemata (T) and (S5) are satisfied. The domain of presentations is X itself; the domain of objects is the union of X and $\{q\}$, where q is not in X. Each equivalence relation E_w on the latter domain, interpreting $=$, is simply identity. The function f, interpreting o, is defined as follows: if $\{i, j\}$ is a world, then $f(\{i, j\}, i)$ and $f(\{i, j\}, j)$ are q, and $f(\{i, j\}, k)$ is k whenever k is neither i nor j. All constraints on a KT5 model have been satisfied, so all derivable sequents of KT5 are valid in this model. Let i and j be any members of X, and consider any assignment which maps the variables x and y to i and j respectively. If R holds between i and j then $\{i, j\}$ is a world, and both ox and oy denote q relative to that assignment and that world; that assignment therefore satisfies the formula $ox = oy$ at that world; since that world is accessible from every world, that assignment satisfies $\Diamond\, ox = oy$ at every world. On the other hand, if R does not hold between i and j then i and j are distinct (since R is reflexive), so that ox and oy can have the same denotation only at a world $\{i, j\}$; but there is no such world, since R does not hold between them; the assignment therefore satisfies $ox = oy$ at no world; so it satisfies $\Diamond\, ox = oy$ at no world. Thus the extension of $\Diamond\, ox = oy$ is precisely R. The non-derivability of (2.3o) is an immediate corollary of this point. For we can choose R to be non-transitive, so that it holds between i and j and between j and k but not between i and k. Consider an assignment which maps x to i, y to j and z to k. It will satisfy $\Diamond\, ox = oy$ and $\Diamond\, ox = oz$ at all worlds and $\Diamond\, ox = oz$ at none; (2.3o) will therefore be valid at no world, and so invalid in the model. Since every derivable sequent of KT5 is valid in the model, (2.3o) is not a derivable sequent of KT5.

The non-transitivity of intentional indiscriminability is thus a robust phenomenon in epistemic modal logic. For KT5 is one of the strongest modal systems of philosophical interest; on the current reading, it presents facts about cognition as themselves entirely open to cognition. Such a claim is in general far too strong; the point is that even it does not yield (2.3o). Since (2.3o) is not derivable in KT5, it is not derivable in any subsystem of KT5 either. If all the principles which are plausible on the current reading can be derived in KT5, they do not entail (2.3o).

The failure of intentional indiscriminability to be transitive in KT5 can be traced to the subject's inability to tell which object some of the presentations present. For when the subject does have access to such identifying knowledge, intentional indiscriminability collapses into the non-intentional variety, whose transitivity has been seen to be derivable in KT5. Let the object of the presentation x be a; then the subject can tell which object is presented by x just in case the subject has the ability to activate the information that the object presented by x is a, a supposition expressed by the formula $\boxed{K}\,ox = a$. If the subject can tell which objects are presented by x and y, then the object presented by x is intentionally indiscriminable from the object presented by y if and only if they are non-intentionally indiscriminable. The point can be expressed in a pair of sequents:

(2.6a) $\boxed{K}\,ox = a,\ \boxed{K}\,oy = b,\ \langle\!\langle K\rangle\!\rangle\,ox = oy \vdash \langle\!\langle K\rangle\!\rangle\,a = b$

(2.6b) $\boxed{K}\,ox = a,\ \boxed{K}\,oy = b,\ \langle\!\langle K\rangle\!\rangle\,a = b \vdash \langle\!\langle K\rangle\!\rangle\,ox = oy$

Both sequents can be proved by means of (RK) and identity principles alone; they are thus derivable in any system which includes K. Using them, one can show that intentional indiscriminability is transitive in KT5 in the special case when the subject can identify one or other pair of indiscriminable objects. That is, the following sequents are derivable in KT5:

(2.7a) $\boxed{K}\,ox = a,\ \boxed{K}\,oy = b,\ \langle\!\langle K\rangle\!\rangle\,ox = oy,\ \langle\!\langle K\rangle\!\rangle\,oy = oz \vdash \langle\!\langle K\rangle\!\rangle\,ox = oz$

(2.7b) $\boxed{K}\,oy = b,\ \boxed{K}\,oz = c,\ \langle\!\langle K\rangle\!\rangle\,ox = oy,\ \langle\!\langle K\rangle\!\rangle\,oy = oz \vdash \langle\!\langle K\rangle\!\rangle\,ox = oz$

The proof of (2.7a) is as follows. By (2.6a) the first three premises yield $\langle\!\langle K\rangle\!\rangle\,a = b$, from which $a = b$ follows in KT5 by (2.5); $\langle\!\langle K\rangle\!\rangle\,oy = b$ and $\langle\!\langle K\rangle\!\rangle\,oy = oz$ give $\langle\!\langle K\rangle\!\rangle\,b = oz$, from which $\langle\!\langle K\rangle\!\rangle\,a = oz$ follows by $a = b$, and thence the conclusion by $\boxed{K}\,ox = a$. The proof of (2.7b) is parallel. Thus the non-derivability of the transitivity of intentional indiscriminability in KT5 depends on the absence of a guarantee that premises such as $\boxed{K}\,ox = a$ hold. In the proof that (2.3o) is not derivable, this fact was expressed by the way in which the function interpreting o mapped a given presentation to different objects at different worlds. These worlds represented epistemic possibilities rather than metaphysical ones, of course: it is irrelevant whether a presentation could in fact have presented an object other than the one it actually presents (compare Hintikka 1972).

Thus far we have been considering the first response to the proof in KT5 that non-intentional indiscriminability is transitive: the retreat to intentional indiscriminability. We now turn to the second response: the retreat to systems weaker than KT5, in particular to KT4 and its subsystems. We shall work with non-intentional indiscriminability, since we already know that the intentional variety cannot be proved transitive in such systems.

In KT4, the rejection of the (S5) schema is tantamount to the rejection of the so-called Brouwerian principle:

(B) $A \vdash \boxed{K} \Diamondblack A$

For the addition of (B) to KT4 yields KT5. In terms of the possible worlds model theory, (B) expresses the symmetry of the accessibility relation between worlds. Thus it is no longer maintained that if it is the case that A then the subject is able to activate the knowledge that the subject is unable to activate the knowledge that it is not the case that A. That does not seem to be much of a loss. Consider its equivalent form $\sim A \vdash \boxed{K} \sim \boxed{K} A$, and its instance $\sim a = b \vdash \boxed{K} \sim \boxed{K} a = b$; if Tweedledum and Tweedledee conspire to keep me uncertain as to whether they are the same person, I am in no position to rule out the supposition that rigorous inquiries will show them to be identical.

We can proceed somewhat as in the previous case. What is needed is a proof that (2.3), the transitivity of non-intentional indiscriminability, is not derivable in KT4. In fact, something stronger will be proved: that the *only* constraints imposed by KT4 on $\Diamondblack a = b$ as a relation between a and b are reflexivity and symmetry ((2.1) and (2.2)). The proof will again use the possible worlds model theory.

Let R be any reflexive symmetric relation on a set X; we ignore the trivial case in which X is empty. The idea is to produce a possible worlds model of KT4 in which R is the extension of the formula $\diamondsuit a = b$, thus showing that KT4 imposes no further constraints. The worlds will simply be those unordered pairs $\{i, j\}$ of members of X between which R holds, together with an extra world w^*. Every world is accessible from itself, w^* and no other world; this is a reflexive and transitive relation, so the schemata (T) and (S4) are satisfied. Since we are not concerned with presentations, we can ignore their domain and the function f, interpreting o. The domain of objects is X. If $\{i, j\}$ is a world other than w^*, the equivalence relation $E_{\{i, j\}}$, interpreting identity in that world, has as equivalence classes $\{i, j\}$ and the singleton set of every other member of X; E_{w^*} is simply identity. This fulfils the requirement that if a world $w+$ is accessible from a world w, and E_w holds between two objects, then so does E_{w+}. Thus all derivable sequents of KT4 are valid in such a model. Let i and j be any members of X; one can show that any assignment which maps the variables a and b to i and j respectively satisfies the formula $\diamondsuit a = b$ at the world w^* if and only if R holds between i and j. Thus the extension of $\diamondsuit a = b$ at that world is precisely R. By reasoning like that in the earlier proof, it follows that (2.3) is not a derivable sequent of KT4, nor of any of its subsystems.[8]

The failure of non-intentional indiscriminability to be transitive in KT4 can be traced to the subject's inability to tell that two objects are indiscriminable. For when the subject can activate the knowledge that a and b are indiscriminable, it follows that a and b are not involved in any breakdown of transitivity. That is, the following sequents are derivable in KT4:

(2.8a) $\boxed{\text{K}}\diamondsuit a = b, \diamondsuit b = c \vdash \diamondsuit a = c$

(2.8b) $\boxed{\text{K}}\diamondsuit a = b, \diamondsuit a = c \vdash \diamondsuit b = c$

(2.8a) can be proved as follows, using a rule which is a consequence of (RK): if $A, B \vdash C$ is derivable, then so is $\boxed{\text{K}} A, \diamondsuit B \vdash \diamondsuit C$. (LL) gives us $\diamondsuit a = b, b = c \vdash \diamondsuit a = c$, which yields $\boxed{\text{K}} \diamondsuit a = b$, $\diamondsuit b = c \vdash \diamondsuit \diamondsuit a = c$ by the rule; but we have $\diamondsuit \diamondsuit a = c \vdash \diamondsuit a = c$ from (S4), giving (2.8a). The proof of (2.8b) is parallel. Thus the non-derivability of the transitivity of non-intentional indiscriminability in KT4 depends on the failure of a specific instance of (S5):

(2.9) $\diamondsuit a = b \vdash \boxed{\text{K}}\diamondsuit a = b$

In the proof that (2.3) is not derivable, this fact was expressed by the accessibility from the world w* both of worlds at which $a = b$ was true and of worlds from which no such world was accessible. Again, these worlds represented epistemic possibilities rather than metaphysical ones; it is not suggested that distinct objects could in fact have been identical.

The addition of (2.9) to KT4 would lead to the derivability of (2.3), the transitivity of non-intentional indiscriminability. However, it does not lead to the collapse of non-intentional indiscriminability into identity ((2.5)) in contrast to the addition of the full (S5) schema. This can be seen by considering a model with just two worlds, w and w+, and two objects, i and j. Let w+ be accessible from both worlds and w only from itself; E_{w+} holds between i and j but E_w does not. It is easy to check that this yields a model of both KT4 and (2.9). However, an assignment mapping the variables a and b to i and j respectively satisfies $\Diamond\!\!\!\!\raisebox{0.3pt}{\scriptsize K} \, a = b$ but not $a = b$ at the world w; thus (2.5) is not valid in the model.

A more general point can be extracted from this discussion. In the proof of (2.8a), the only use of principles not already available in the weak system K was the appeal to an instance of (S4), $\Diamond\!\!\!\!\raisebox{0.3pt}{\scriptsize K} \, \Diamond\!\!\!\!\raisebox{0.3pt}{\scriptsize K} \, a = c \vdash \Diamond\!\!\!\!\raisebox{0.3pt}{\scriptsize K} \, a = c$. That sequent is interderivable with:

$$(2.10) \quad \sim\!\Diamond\!\!\!\!\raisebox{0.3pt}{\scriptsize K} \, a = b \vdash \boxed{\text{K}} \sim\!\Diamond\!\!\!\!\raisebox{0.3pt}{\scriptsize K} \, a = b$$

Consider the system which results from the addition of (2.9) and (2.10) to K. By what has just been noted it yields (2.8a), from which (2.9) gives (2.3). Thus the transitivity of non-intentional indiscriminability is derivable in the system. What (2.9) and (2.10) together say is that the subject can always tell whether or not objects are indiscriminable. The underlying idea is then that if a is indiscriminable from b but not from c, the subject can reflect on this difference between b and c, thereby discriminating between them. Thus in K the decidability of non-intentional indiscriminability entails its transitivity. Note that the argument made heavy use of the rule (RK), the closure of activatable knowledge under logical consequence; it therefore does not apply to non-inferential knowledge.

The relation between a and b symbolized by $\boxed{\text{K}} \Diamond\!\!\!\!\raisebox{0.3pt}{\scriptsize K} \, a = b$ is of some interest in KT4. Objects between which it holds are indiscriminable from exactly the same objects, by (2.8a,b). It is an equivalence relation, for it is easy to prove the following sequents in KT4:

(2.11) $\vdash \boxed{K} \diamondsuit a = a$

(2.12) $\boxed{K} \diamondsuit a = b \vdash \boxed{K} \diamondsuit b = a$

(2.13) $\boxed{K} \diamondsuit a = b, \boxed{K} \diamondsuit b = c \vdash \boxed{K} \diamondsuit a = c$

(2.11) and (2.12) follow from (2.1) and (2.2) respectively by (RK); (2.13) follows from (2.8a) by (RK) and (S4). Yet the relation does not collapse into identity; if it did, (2.9) would yield (2.5), which it has been seen not to do. Thus $\boxed{K} \diamondsuit a = b$ has much in common with the equivalence relation of indiscriminability from the same things, which was discussed in the previous chapter and can be symbolized with the introduction of a universal quantifier as $\forall c (\diamondsuit a = c \leftrightarrow \diamondsuit b = c)$. The latter relation is a consequence of the former, and they share the formal properties of reflexivity, symmetry and transitivity. Both relations can be thought of as tighter forms of indiscriminability than $\diamondsuit a = b : \forall c (\diamondsuit a = c \leftrightarrow \diamondsuit b = c)$ requires the impossibility of indirect discrimination between a and b, mediated by c; $\boxed{K} \diamondsuit a = b$ requires the possibility of reflective knowledge of the indiscriminability of a and b. An inquiry into the connections between these two forms of indiscriminability might be fruitful, but will not be attempted here.

These remarks do not extend to the intentional equivalent of reflective indiscriminability, symbolized by the formula $\boxed{K} \diamondsuit ox = oy$. For the equivalent of transitivity fails:

(2.13o)* $\boxed{K} \diamondsuit ox = oy, \boxed{K} \diamondsuit oy = oz \vdash \boxed{K} \diamondsuit ox = oz$

(2.13o) is not a derivable sequent even in KT5; if it were, so would be (2.3o), the transitivity of intentional indiscriminability, since $\boxed{K} \diamondsuit$ reduces to $\diamondsuit$ in KT5. A *fortiori*, (2.13o) is not derivable in KT4 or any other subsystem of KT5.

The upshot of these investigations is that the non-transitivity of indiscriminability is a complex and over-determined phenomenon. Forms of knowledge can give rise to it in at least three different ways: by not being inferential, by not being transparent and by not being reflective. That is not quite to say that a form of knowledge can give rise to a transitive indiscriminability relation only if it is inferential, transparent and reflective, for even when one or more of these fails transitivity may hold in a special case for a special reason. Rather, non-transitivity, when it does occur, may be understood by being subsumed under any one of these cognitive limitations, as an instance of that more general phenomenon. In fact, there are three overlapping general phenomena.

There is an underlying point about the explanation of failure. The occurrence of error in our beliefs about the volumes of objects can be understood by being subsumed under any one of several more general phenomena – errors of perception, errors of calculation and so on. That is not quite to say that, as a matter of logical necessity, any creature which is always right about the volumes of objects will make no errors of perception or calculation at all; doubtless a situation could be rigged in which the kind of errors of perception or calculation it made would not result in erroneous beliefs about volumes. Nevertheless, it is only to be expected that a creature which makes errors of perception or calculation will also make errors about volumes; the latter phenomenon is no more puzzling than the former. Each individual error about volume requires an individual explanation too, of course; sometimes it may be traced back to an error of perception, sometimes to an error of calculation, sometimes both. Similarly, it is only to be expected – although not logically necessary – that a non-inferential, non-transparent or non-reflective form of knowledge will give rise to a non-transitive indiscriminability relation; the latter phenomenon is no more puzzling than the former. Each individual instance of non-transitivity requires an individual explanation too, of course; sometimes it may be traced back to a failure of inferential closure, sometimes to a failure of transparency, sometimes to a failure of reflectiveness, sometimes to a combination of two or all three of these. These conclusions were informally adumbrated in the previous chapter; the point of the formal apparatus was to explore the interconnections of the three factors in a more precise and perspicuous way.

3

Paradoxes of Indiscriminability

The formal apparatus of the previous chapter can be used to investigate a claim at the heart of some current controversy about sorites paradoxes. There is supposed to be a class of *observational predicates* which are applicable on the sufficient and exhaustive basis of observation. The claim is then made that if an observational predicate applies to an object, it also applies to anything indiscriminable from that object; for if its proper application depended on an unobservable difference, observation would not supply an adequate basis for that application. In brief, the claim is that indiscriminability is *congruent with* observational predicates. The standard example is the predicate 'is red', although sometimes there is a retreat to 'looks red'. We can tell whether an object is or at least looks red just by looking at it; if we cannot see any difference between two objects, we are not entitled to apply the predicate to one and deny it to the other. Since a chain of visually indiscriminable objects can lead from one which clearly is and looks red to one which clearly is and looks not red, sorites paradoxes ensue. They will be discussed in more detail in later chapters. The concern of this section is only with the claim that indiscriminability is congruent with observational predicates.[1]

The notion of observation is of course a difficult one: how can a line be drawn between the observed and the inferred? Fortunately, such questions need not be pursued here. For indiscriminability is being understood relative to a kind of cognition; we can simply understand observationality relative to the same kind of cognition, whatever that is. The key idea is then that that kind of cognition is all we need to apply an observational predicate where it is properly applicable and to deny it where it is not. More formally, a predicate F is observational just in case the following conditions hold: if an object a is F, then knowledge of the appropriate kind can be activated that a is F; if a is not F, then knowledge of the

Identity and Discrimination: Reissued and Updated Edition. Timothy Williamson.
© 2013 Timothy Williamson. Published 2013 by Blackwell Publishing Ltd.

appropriate kind can be activated that a is not F. If we add the predicate F to the formal language, we can symbolize these conditions by the following sequents:

(3.1a) $Fa \vdash \boxed{\text{K}} \, Fa$

(3.1b) $\sim Fa \vdash \boxed{\text{K}} \sim Fa$

If those who speak of observational predicates do not mean that, it is up to them to say what they do mean.

A welcome consequence of the definition of observationality by means of (3.1a,b) is that any truth-function of observational predicates is itself observational; this can already be proved in K. In KT the application of $\boxed{\text{K}}$ or $\Diamond\!\!\!\!\Diamond$ to an observational predicate also yields an observational predicate, simply because it is redundant; given (3.1a,b), $\boxed{\text{K}} \, Fa$ and $\Diamond\!\!\!\!\Diamond \, Fa$ are equivalent to Fa (this is not so in K, which yields $\boxed{\text{K}} \, Fa \vdash \boxed{\text{K}} \boxed{\text{K}} \, Fa$ but not $\sim \boxed{\text{K}} \, Fa \vdash \boxed{\text{K}} \sim \boxed{\text{K}} \, Fa$ from those conditions).

The claim that indiscriminability is congruent with the predicate F can be symbolized by the following sequent:[2]

(3.2) $\Diamond\!\!\!\!\Diamond \, a = b, Fa \vdash Fb$

Thus the claim that indiscriminability is congruent with observational predicates becomes the claim that (3.2) is a consequence of (3.1a,b) on the intended interpretation.

The claim can be proved in K as follows. (LL) gives $a = b, Fa \vdash Fb$ and thus $Fa, \sim Fb \vdash \sim a = b$, which by (RK) yields $\boxed{\text{K}} \, Fa, \boxed{\text{K}} \sim Fb \vdash \boxed{\text{K}} \sim a = b$; (3.1a,b) reduces this to $Fa, \sim Fb \vdash \boxed{\text{K}} \sim a = b$, from which (3.2) follows by contraposition. Thus we seem to have vindicated the idea that indiscriminability is congruent with observational predicates using minimal resources of epistemic modal logic and exploiting the account of indiscriminability in terms of identity.

It can be shown that (3.2) is not derivable from either (3.1a) or (3.1b) alone, even in KT4. That is what one would expect. A crude example: if when I am awake I know that I am awake, but when I am not awake I do not know that I am not awake, then I may be unable to discriminate between being awake and not being awake (compare Humberstone 1988). Matters are different in KT5, where (2.5) is derivable, for (3.2) is equivalent to $a = b$,

$Fa \vdash Fb$, an instance of (LL), and is thus derivable independently of both (3.1a) and (3.1b). However, that is just because KT5 does not permit an interesting notion of non-intentional indiscriminability.

The question in any case arises of whether the proof of the congruence claim for non-intentional indiscriminability can be extended to the intentional version. The corresponding sequent would be:

(3.2o) $\diamondsuit ox = oy, Fox \vdash Foy$

It can be shown not to follow from (3.1a,b) even in KT5. Consider a model with two possible worlds, w and w+, both accessible from both. Let the two-membered domain of presentations be {i, j} and the two-membered domain of objects be {m, n}; f(w, i), f(w+, i) and f(w+, j) are m while f(w, j) is n, where f interprets o; = is interpreted as identity; the extension of F is {m} in both worlds. Then (3.1a,b) hold whether m or n is assigned to the variable a, since the extension of F does not vary from world to world, but (3.2o) is not valid, since an assignment of i and j to the variables x and y respectively satisfies $\diamondsuit ox = oy$ and Fox but not Foy at w.

However, it might be suggested that we should seek to derive (3.2o) not from (3.1a,b) but from the corresponding sequents which advert to presentations:

(3.1ao) $Fox \vdash \boxed{K} Fox$

(3.1bo) $\sim Fox \vdash \boxed{K} \sim Fox$

The proof of (3.2) from (3.1a,b) can indeed be turned into a parallel proof of (3.2o) from (3.1ao, bo). It is crucial here that F is a predicate, not simply any context for a singular term. For instance, if one took $F \ldots$ to be $\diamondsuit oz = \ldots$ then (3.2o) would become (2.3o) (apart from a permutation of variables), the transitivity principle which is not derivable even in KT5. However, this reading of F would invalidate the first step of the argument, the instance $ox = oy, Fox \vdash Foy$ of (LL), for it would become the sequent $ox = oy, \diamondsuit oz = ox \vdash \diamondsuit oz = oy$, which cannot be derived from (LL) since it involves an illicit substitution of definite descriptions in a modal context. In contrast, the extension of a predicate is not presentation-sensitive in this way, and $ox = oy$, $Fox \vdash Foy$ is a valid instance of (LL) when F is a predicate.

Two notions of observationality are now in play, symbolized by (3.1a,b) and (3.1ao, bo) respectively. They are not equivalent, for if the former entailed the latter they would also entail (3.2o), which they have been seen not to do. (3.1ao), for example, makes the strong claim that if an object is F then for any presentation of that object it is possible to activate knowledge that the object as so presented is F; for by (LL) it yields the sequent Foy, $ox = oy \vdash \boxed{\text{K}}\, Fox$. In contrast, (3.1a) says only that if an object is F then it is possible to know that it is F. (3.1ao, bo) may well express far too strong a notion of observationality, perhaps applicable to no predicates at all; surely the reasonable demand is for knowledge under some presentation, not under all. But this point severely qualifies the claim that indiscriminability is congruent with observational predicates, for in the case of intentional indiscriminability the claim is not a consequence of the preferred account of observationality; (3.2o) does not follow from (3.1a,b). Nevertheless, it has emerged that there is some substance to the claim, at least enough to account for its intuitive plausibility; (3.2) does follow from (3.1a,b). What does not follow from this, of course, is that any predicates meet the demands on observationality which (3.1a,b) impose.[3]

It is sometimes denied that the sorites-susceptibility of monadic observational predicates extends to polyadic ones.[4] However, the arguments just considered do extend to polyadic predicates. The generalizations of (3.1a,b) to an n-adic predicate F are obvious:

(3.1a+) $Fa_1 \ldots a_n \vdash \boxed{\text{K}}\, Fa_1 \ldots a_n$

(3.1b+) $\sim Fa_1 \ldots a_n \vdash \boxed{\text{K}} \sim Fa_1 \ldots a_n$

Similarly, (3.2) becomes:

(3.2+) $\diamondsuit a_1 = b_1, \ldots, \diamondsuit a_n = b_n, Fa_1 \ldots a_n \vdash Fb_1 \ldots b_n.$

Now for any i between 1 and n we can derive the sequent $\diamondsuit a_i = b_i$, $Fa_1 \ldots a_i b_{i+i} \ldots b_n \vdash Fa_1 \ldots a_{i-1} b_i \ldots b_n$ from (3.1a+, b+) in just the way that (3.2) was derived from (3.1a,b); all places except the ith are treated as parametric. When these sequents are chained together they yield (3.2+), from which it is easy to construct a sorites paradox. A parallel argument can be given in terms of objects under presentations.

We still have a sorites paradox on our hands for non-intentional indiscriminability. (3.2) is derivable in K when F is observational. The derivation appealed to the rule (RK), the closure of activatable knowledge under logical consequence, in moving from $Fa, \sim Fb \vdash \sim a = b$ to $\boxed{\text{K}}\, Fa, \boxed{\text{K}} \sim Fb \vdash \boxed{\text{K}} \sim a = b$. However, it is hard to see this move as the source of the trouble. For the paradox can arise for a perfectly logical subject who draws all available inferences but happens to have bad eyesight. The subtler objection to (RK) – that a subject can have *de re* knowledge of an object under distinct presentations without knowing them to present the same object – is also irrelevant, for it applies only to sequents whose premises may be satisfied by the assignment of the same object to variables in distinct occurrences; this cannot happen to Fa and $\sim Fb$. The fault lies not with the argument from (3.1a,b) to (3.2) but with its interpretation. In some cases the predicates we take to be observational may not really be so; in others the relation of indiscriminability may behave in unexpected ways. The following chapters are concerned with a case of the latter kind, although it is only the third of them which returns to the problem of sorites arguments.

4

Concepts of Phenomenal Character

Things of most kinds have depth; they can be indiscriminable without being identical. It is nevertheless tempting to believe that things of some kinds are purely superficial; for them, indiscriminability and identity would coincide. Some such things are, more precisely, qualities. The look, sound, feel, taste and smell of a physical object may be examples. If so, however, they are complicated examples, for an object may present its sensory qualities in some circumstances (day) but not in others (night), or to some observers (gourmets) but not to others (gourmands). This chapter and the next two will focus on a different example, involving qualities of experiences rather than of bodies.

In what follows, experiences will be treated as particular in the sense of unrepeatable; each is tied to a specific subject in whose life it forms an episode at a specific place and time. The qualities in question will be called *phenomenal characters*, or characters for short. The character of an experience is what it was, is or will be like to have that experience, the maximally specific quality it would share with any experience which was, is or will be the same way for its subject (Nagel 1974). Since characters are maximally specific, each experience has at most one of them, for if it had two their conjunction would be a quality of the same kind more specific than either of them, contradicting their maximal specificity.

For two experiences to be the same in the relevant sense is for them to be exactly similar in a certain respect. This relation of exact similarity can in turn be derived from a relation of comparative similarity in the same respect, two experiences being exactly similar just in case one is as similar to the other as it is to itself. We can grasp this respect of similarity as that which has to do with experiences qua experienced (compare Shoemaker 1975). Thus

Identity and Discrimination: Reissued and Updated Edition. Timothy Williamson.
© 2013 Timothy Williamson. Published 2013 by Blackwell Publishing Ltd.

characters stand to experiences as types of tokens, with respect to a certain mode of classification. Since each experience is exactly similar to itself in the relevant respect, it has exactly one character.

An experience may have many qualities wholly unknown to its subject; for instance, it may be a particular physical event with various neurophysiological qualities. Its character, however, is not supposed to be one of these, but on the contrary to be wholly known to the subject, being exhausted by those features of the experience of which the subject is aware. In particular, characters indiscriminable from the point of view of the subject should be identical, for any difference between them would be a hidden one, and nothing is hidden in a character. The sort of discrimination at issue will not be the most articulate, since one can have experiences without being disposed or even able to think about their phenomenal character (whether under that description or any other), but one will still be sensitive to differences between experiences in phenomenal character, and discrimination of this inarticulate sort was already contemplated in section 1.1. Since identical characters are *a fortiori* indiscriminable, indiscriminability and identity coincide for characters. Or so the story goes.

A kind of quality for which indiscriminability and identity coincide will be called *subjective*; it will not be assumed to be subjective in any sense other than the one just given. Qualities will be assumed to be maximally specific of their kind; that is, the term 'quality' will be restricted to determinates, excluding determinables. In this sense the length of a stick is a quality, but not its being between five and eight inches long.

For more than one reason it may be doubted that there are any subjective kinds of quality. This chapter is concerned with only one threat to their existence: the fact that indiscriminability, unlike identity, is not a transitive relation (e.g. Armstrong 1961 pp. 42–4). In order to test whether this problem can be overcome, it will provisionally be assumed that the character of an experience is a subjective kind of quality. The argument from non-transitivity against this assumption eventually turns out to fail, for it neglects the presentation-sensitivity of discriminability considered in chapter 1; a given character may be presented by many different experiences, each of which it characterizes (section 4.1). Once proper account is taken of presentation-sensitivity, it can plausibly be maintained that indiscriminability, as a relation between characters, is transitive, and indeed coincides with identity (section 4.2). The phenomena to which the non-transitivity argument alludes are compatible with the existence of subjective kinds of quality – characters, for instance. Some positive principles survive the discussion; they entail a necessary and sufficient condition for the identity of characters in terms of presentation-sensitive indiscriminability (section 4.3).

4.1   Presentations of Characters

Characters certainly appear not to be immune to the non-transitivity of indiscriminability. Each twinge of pain may feel exactly like the one before, and yet after an hour the pain is appreciably less. I cannot see the moon moving, but I can see that it has moved. In such cases there may be no time t at which the subject can discriminate his experience at t from his experience one second before t in character; yet for some large enough number n the subject can discriminate his experience at some time t from his experience n seconds before t in character. Since experiences are particular, the subject may also discriminate between them by the times at which they occur, but these are not discriminations in *character* – in what it is like to have the experiences; the qualification 'in character' will often be left tacit but understood in what follows. In a case like those above, consider a number n such that the subject could sometimes discriminate between experiences $2n$ seconds apart, but could not discriminate between any two of the experiences which were much less than $2n$ seconds apart. Since n will be much less than $2n$, there can be a time t such that the experience at t was indiscriminable from the experience n seconds after t, and the latter was indiscriminable from the experience $2n$ seconds after t, but the experience at t was not indiscriminable from the experience $2n$ seconds after t. Since 'indiscriminable' here means indiscriminable in character, indiscriminability appears not to be a transitive relation on characters.

Let a, b and c be characters such that a is indiscriminable from b, and b from c, but not a from c. If characters were subjective qualities, indiscriminability here would be sufficient for identity;

a would be *b*, *b* would be *c*, and so *a* would be *c* by the transitivity of identity – but they are discriminable and therefore distinct. Thus indiscriminability is insufficient here for identity (it is of course necessary, being reflexive), and characters are not subjective.

Someone might concede that characters are not a subjective kind, but claim that other kinds are subjective; the transitivity of indiscriminability would fail for the former but not the latter. This seems a rather desperate move. If what was given as a paradigmatic subjective kind turns out not to be subjective, we have good reason to suspect that there are no subjective kinds.

This chapter explores a different objection to the argument. If it works it will provide a defence for the claim that characters are a subjective kind, by showing that apparent examples of the non-transitivity of indiscriminability for characters do not really exhibit any such thing.

Chapter 1 laid emphasis on the sensitivity of discrimination to differences between presentations of its objects. The objects of discrimination now at issue are supposed to be qualities of a subjective kind. Can we make anything of the idea that there can be different presentations of such a quality? The objection begins with a development of that idea in the case of characters, provisionally treated as a subjective kind.

There is no contradiction in two experiences having exactly the same character; they may be experiences of a single subject at different times, or experiences of different subjects: one type, several tokens. Each experience may be considered as presenting its character to its subject. Perhaps the *mode* of presentation was the same on all occasions, but even so the distinct experiences were distinct presentations of a single character. More generally, to have a quality of a subjective kind is to present it. Conversely, to present such a quality is to have it, in the relevant sense of 'present', for the sort of indiscriminability supposed to coincide with identity for subjective kinds is indiscriminability on the basis of things which have those qualities. The things which have a quality will be called its *instances*. Thus the instances of a certain length are objects that long, not lengths in the supposed sense in which the length of this stick exactly six inches long is a Stoutian abstract particular distinct from the length of that other stick exactly six inches long. In particular, the presentations of a quality of a subjective kind are its instances.

In the supposed examples of the non-transitivity of indiscriminability for characters, the subject's experience at t was indiscriminable in
character from his experience n seconds after t, and the latter from
his experience $2n$ seconds after t, but his experience at t was discriminable in character from his experience $2n$ seconds after t. Let his
experiences at t, n seconds after t and $2n$ seconds after t be x, y and
z respectively. There is a sense in which the character of x is indiscriminable from the character of y, and the character of y from the
character of z, while the character of x is discriminable from the character of z. Let the characters of x, y and z be a, b and c respectively.
By the previous paragraph, x presents a, y presents b and z presents
c. What such an example clearly shows is that a as presented by x
is indiscriminable from b as presented by y, that b as presented by y
is indiscriminable from c as presented by z, and that a as presented
by x is discriminable from c as presented by z. However, the notion
of indiscriminability in play here is the intentional one discussed in
chapter 1; there is no *logical* guarantee that if a as presented by x is
indiscriminable from b as presented by y then a as presented by some
other experience x' is indiscriminable from b as presented by some y'.
If there are counter-examples to that conditional, only non-intentional
indiscriminability has a chance of coinciding with the non-intentional
relation of identity over a subjective kind. What such an example had
better show, and does not clearly show, is that a is indiscriminable
from b, that b is indiscriminable from c, and that a is discriminable
from c. If the example is to make the intended point, some link needs
to be established between the intentional and non-intentional notions
of indiscriminability.

There is a prima facie distinction between the discriminability
of experiences in character and the discriminability of their characters. That is, it should not be assumed without argument that
the discriminability of the character a as presented by the experience x from the character b as presented by the experience y is
equivalent to the discriminability of a from b. For it is certainly
false that discriminating two experiences in character is equivalent
to discriminating their characters. It is plausible enough that if I
discriminate experiences in character, I thereby discriminate their
characters, but this point undermines its converse: I can discriminate characters without discriminating a given pair of experiences

with those characters, by discriminating a different pair of experiences with those characters. More formally, if x and x' are distinct experiences of character a, and y and y' are distinct experiences of character b, then although discriminating a as presented by x from b as presented by y may be sufficient for discriminating a from b, it is not necessary, for I can do the latter without doing the former by discriminating a as presented by x' from b as presented by y'. However, our concern is the supposed non-transitivity of indiscriminability, and therefore with what *can* be discriminated rather than with what *is* discriminated. The crucial question is whether the discriminability of a character a as presented by an experience x from a character b as presented by an experience y is equivalent to the discriminability of a from b.

As already noted, it is plausible that discrimination of a as presented by x from b as presented by y is *ipso facto* discrimination of a from b, at least in the case of characters as presented by experiences. It would follow that the discriminability of a as presented by x from b as presented by y is sufficient for the discriminability of a from b. Thus, in the examples above, the character of the subject's experience at t would be discriminable from the character of his experience at $t+2n$ in the non-intentional sense, since they are discriminable in the intentional sense. In what follows, the sufficiency claim will not be challenged. That is, the following principle is conceded:

(4.1)   If x is an instance of the character a, y is an instance of the character b, and a as presented by x is discriminable from b as presented by y, then a is discriminable from b.

If (4.1) were denied, the argument from non-transitivity would have little chance anyway, for it would then be open to the defender of characters as a subjective kind to claim that no pair of characters in the supposed examples of non-transitivity were discriminable in the non-intentional sense. Thus a critique of the argument may legitimately assume (4.1) to be correct. Moreover, it is a good hypothesis on its own merits, and one which later developments will do nothing to undermine and something to support.

The crux of the argument against characters as a subjective

kind is thus the converse of (4.1):

(4.2)   If x is an instance of the character a, y is an instance of the character b, and a is discriminable from b, then a as presented by x is discriminable from b as presented by y.

Between them, (4.1) and (4.2) would have the intentional and non-intentional notions of discriminability coincide, and therefore do the same for indiscriminability. As a result, they have the following consequence:

(4.3)   If x and x' are instances of the character a, and y and y' are instances of the character b, then a as presented by x is discriminable from b as presented by y if and only if a as presented by x' is discriminable from b as presented by y'.

For by (4.1) and (4.2) each side of the 'if and only if' is equivalent to the discriminability of a from b *tout court*. (4.1) and (4.2) would thus suffice to rebut the presentation-sensitivity objection to the argument against characters as a subjective kind. Conversely, denial of (4.2) would undermine the argument, for the defender of characters as a subjective kind can maintain that all three characters in the supposed examples of non-transitivity are discriminable from each other in the non-intentional sense, because they are discriminable in the intentional sense under suitably different presentations. Given the other assumptions now in play, the truth of (4.2) is thus necessary and sufficient for the soundness of the argument in question against characters as a subjective kind.

4.2   Presentation-Sensitivity

How plausible is (4.2)? Unlike (4.1), it cannot be justified by appeal to the analogous principle in which 'discriminated' replaces 'discriminable', for we have already seen that whereas the analogue of (4.1) is probably true, the analogue of (4.2) is certainly false. However, less direct arguments suggest themselves.

It may be claimed that if characters were a subjective kind then (4.1), (4.2) and (4.3) would all be inevitable constraints on what it is for things to instantiate characters, the idea being that qualities of a subjective kind are precisely those which do not have different modes of presentation. This idea does not obviously follow from the operative definition of a subjective kind, as one for which indiscriminability and identity coincide; that definition says nothing explicit about the relevant notion of intentional indiscriminability. However, the suggestion might be that the only reasons for thinking of characters as a subjective kind are also reasons for thinking of them as presentable in only one way. In the present case, the defender of characters as a subjective kind would then be obliged to uphold the very premises required for the argument that characters are *not* a subjective kind. That would suffice for the argument to work as a *reductio ad absurdum* of its target; it would not matter whether the premises were plausible from the standpoint of those who deny that characters are a subjective kind.

Someone who claims that characters are a subjective kind is under pressure to accept (4.2). The pressure might be expressed as follows. 'The only reason to think of characters as a subjective kind lies in the idea that the subject of an experience must know its character, more precisely, that if the character of an experience x is a, then the subject of x knows that the character of x is a, although not usually in an articulate way. In that case, consider a subject who can discriminate between the characters a and b, and has the experiences x and y, instances of a and b respectively. By hypothesis, the subject knows that the character of x is a and that the character of y is b. Since the subject can discriminate between a and b, she can discriminate between a as presented by x and b as presented by y. But that is just what (4.2) requires. A similar argument could be given for (4.1).' In terms of the formal apparatus of chapter 2, the point would be the equivalence of $\boxed{\text{K}} \sim a = b$ (discriminability of a from b) and $\boxed{\text{K}} \sim ox = oy$ (discriminability of what x presents as such from what y presents as such) in the presence of the assumptions $\boxed{\text{K}}\, ox = a$ and $\boxed{\text{K}}\, oy = b$ (the subject's ability to activate the knowledge that x presents a and that y presents b).

The only special feature of experience to which the above argument appeals is the subject's knowledge of which character her experience has. However, this no doubt true premise cannot bear the weight thus imposed on it. For it still does not answer the question: why should a subject not know a single pair of characters under different pairs of presentations, some of which enable her to discriminate and some of which do not? Lack of *de re* acquaintance with the relevant objects is not the only obstacle to discrimination. Consider an example involving discrimination of bodies rather than qualities. I am presented with a bundle of sticks to look at and touch; however, they are so tightly bound together that I cannot always tell whether a given stick poking out at the left end of the bundle is the same as a given stick poking out at the right end of the bundle. Nevertheless, when I see and touch the end of a stick in these circumstances, I know of a certain stick that it is what I am seeing and touching; I have the kind of acquaintance with it which allows me to think singular thoughts about it such as 'This stick is oak'. Let x and z be two ends poking out at the left of the bundle, and y an end poking out at the right; since I can see that the sticks are reasonably straight, I can tell that x and z are not two ends of one stick; I cannot tell whether x or z or neither is on the same stick as y, but as a matter of fact x and y are the two ends of a stick a and z is an end of a different stick b. Thus I can discriminate a as presented by x from b as presented by z, but I cannot discriminate a as presented by y from b as presented by z. Discriminability here is presentation-sensitive, even though all the presentations (stick-ends) give *de re* knowledge of what they present. In terms of the formal apparatus of chapter 2, the point amounts to the non-closure of epistemic necessity under logical consequence when different occurrences of a free variable are involved, however rational the subject. I may know that this stick (presented by x) is thick at one end, and that that stick (presented by y) is thin at one end, and thereby know both that a is thick at one end and that a is thin at one end, without being in any position to work out that some stick varies in thickness. In particular, the move by (RK) from the correct sequent, $\sim a = b, ox = a, oy = b \vdash \sim ox = oy$ to the sequent $\boxed{\text{K}} \sim a = b, \boxed{\text{K}} ox = a, \boxed{\text{K}} oy = b \vdash \boxed{\text{K}} \sim ox = oy$ is fallacious, and the latter sequent incorrect, on the intended interpretation.

The argument for (4.2) thus requires more of the subject than merely enough acquaintance with the character of her experience to enable her to think singular thoughts about it; something more like *total acquaintance* is needed. One can think singular thoughts about a stick given sight and touch of only one end, but – the idea would be – what a subject has with the character of her experience is the equivalent of sight and touch of the whole stick.

Now the concept of character seems to meet this further requirement. For the character of an experience is nothing more than the experience presents. Indeed, if two experiences present the same character, they must do so in exactly the same way; for any difference in the way they presented it would *ipso facto* be a difference in character between them, in which case they would not present, and therefore have, the same character. As presentations of a given character, experiences differ numerically but not qualitatively. From here, one could argue for the presentation-insensitivity of discriminability for characters by appeal to the further claim that the ways in which x presents a and y presents a distinct character b determine the discriminability of a as presented by x from b as presented by y. However, this further claim is false. Examples will be given which refute both it and (4.2) and (4.3). In doing so they also undermine arguments for (4.1) from presentation-insensitivity, but they do nothing to undermine (4.1) itself, nor the independent argument for it already given.

The first kind of example reads the variables 'x' and 'y' in (4.2) as ranging over the experiences of more than one subject. Surely you and I can have experiences of exactly the same character; they will therefore present that character in exactly the same way.[1] In such a case let your experience be x and mine be y; their shared character is a. Let z be an experience of yours with a somewhat different character b, which you can discriminate from a when both are presented to you. However, your experiences x and z may be too similar for us to be able to tell by normal means (such as talking to each other) which of them, if either, has the same character as my experience y. For instance, x and y might be experiences of a certain kind of pain, and z of a different kind of pain. There is naturally no question of whether x, y and z could have been discriminated as experienced by another subject; they are token experiences, of which occurrence to the given subject is an essential property. Discrimination by neurophysiological means is also not at issue. Thus, for the relevant subjects, x and y are indiscriminable in character, as are y and z, but x and z are discriminable in character. So a as presented by x is discriminable from b as presented by z, but a as presented by y is not discriminable from b as presented by z. This is a direct counter-example to (4.3), and with it to the claim that discriminability of characters depends only on the qualitative ways in which they are presented.

Not surprisingly, when more than one subject is at issue discrimination also depends on *which* subjects the characters are presented to. Since (4.1) and (4.2) entail (4.3), the example can also be used to refute (4.2), if (4.1) is assumed. To be explicit, the discriminability of a as presented by x from b as presented by z yields the discriminability of a from b by (4.1); (4.2) would then require the discriminability of a as presented by y from b as presented by z, and be disappointed. Formally, the argument could be twisted against (4.1), with (4.2) taken as a premise, but the resultant view would have little plausibility: instead of affirming the possibility of discrimination between the characters on the grounds that they are discriminable as presented to the same person, it would deny the possibility of discrimination between them on the grounds that they are indiscriminable when presented to different people. On the latter principle it is not clear that any two characters are discriminable. In contrast, the test of discriminability of characters as presented to the same person seems a fair one. As previously noted, we also have an independent argument for (4.1) not matched by an independent argument for (4.2); simply put, the actuality of discrimination entails its possibility, but its non-actuality does not entail its impossibility. The counter-example to (4.3) shows that either (4.1) or (4.2) is false; given the choice, (4.2) is clearly the one to reject.

'But wasn't it always understood that we were talking about experiences of the same subject?' The reader was never asked to enter into such an understanding. If such a thing is needed to protect (4.3), the latter should begin to lose any air of obviousness it might have had. The asymmetry between (4.1) and (4.2) has moreover been sharpened, if the latter should be rejected in favour of the former except when a special qualification is met. In any case, the appeal to a plurality of subjects is dispensable. The same effect can be achieved by considering the experiences of a single subject at different times.

Surely I can have experiences of exactly the same character at different times; they will therefore present that character in exactly the same way. In such a case let my experience last week be x and my experience today be y; their shared character is a. Let z be an experience of mine today with a somewhat different character b, which I can discriminate from a when both are presented at the same time. Suppose that today's experiences x and z are not very different, and my memory of last week's experience y rather hazy; I cannot tell whether x or z or neither has the same character as y. As before, x and y might be experiences of a certain kind of pain, and z of a different kind of pain. There is naturally no question of whether x, y and z could have been discriminated differently as experienced at another time; they are token experiences, of which occurrence at the given time is an essential property. Discrimination by neurophysiological means is also not at issue. Thus x and y are indiscriminable in character, as are y and z, but x and z are discriminable in character. From here the argument proceeds as before against (4.2), (4.3) and the claim that the discriminability of characters depends only on the ways in which they are presented. Not surprisingly, when more than one time is at issue discrimination also depends on *when* the characters are presented.

'But wasn't it always understood that we were talking about experiences at the same time?' Not only was the reader never asked, however implicitly, to enter into any such understanding: it would rule out many of the kinds of discrimination in which we are most interested. Consider discrimination between the characters of experiences caused by orchestras, light conditions or smells; in standard cases the experiences occur consecutively, not simultaneously. However, even when the experiences can occur simultaneously, this may require some sort of phenomenal space for them to do so in; such a space will ground a new version of the argument, directed against the restriction of (4.2) and (4.3) to simultaneous experiences; in contrast, (4.1) needs no such restriction.

Obvious examples involve experiences in different parts of the visual field. If visual experience cannot be divided in this way, then the restriction to simultaneous experiences is hopelessly narrow in any case. I look at a painting in which two contiguous patches of crimson of just discriminably different shades are separated by other colours from another patch of crimson some distance away. If my experiences of the contiguous patches are x and z and my experience of the third patch y, it seems quite possible that x and y should have the same character. If they have different characters simply in virtue of occurring at different parts of my visual field, the restriction to simultaneous experiences is again hopelessly narrow. Thus x and y may be assumed to have the same character a, while z has a distinct character b. The contiguity of x and z allows me to discriminate between their characters; their distance from y may prevent me from discriminating their characters from its. There is naturally no question of whether x, y and z could have been discriminated differently as experienced elsewhere in my visual field; they are token experiences, of which occurrence at a given part of my visual field is an essential property. The argument proceeds as before. Thus the restriction to simultaneous experiences is either hopelessly narrow or incapable of blocking the argument against (4.2) and (4.3).

The point underlying the examples is quite general. The discriminability of a pair of characters as presented by a pair of experiences depends on non-qualitative relations between the experiences – relations not fixed by the way in which the experiences present their characters – which facilitate or hinder discrimination; such relations are sameness of subject and nearness in time or the visual field. Thus the fact that each character is presentable in only one way does not entail that the discriminability of characters is insensitive to their presentations. The strategy is then to find two instances x and y of a character a, and an instance z of another character b, such that the non-qualitative relations between x and z facilitate discrimination more than do those between y and z. This can yield a situation in which a as presented by x, but not as presented by y, is discriminable from b as presented by z, thereby refuting (4.3). It is hard to envisage a reasonable conception of character that would be immune to this strategy. (4.3) will therefore be assumed to be false; for reasons already rehearsed, its falsehood should be blamed on (4.2), not on (4.1). This vindicates the appeal to the presentation-sensitivity of discriminability in defence of characters as a subjective kind.

How should one describe the purported examples of non-transitive indiscriminability for characters, if the latter are a subjective kind? In such a case, it is uncontroversial that a as presented by x is indiscriminable from b as presented by y, which is in turn indiscriminable from c as presented by z, and that a as presented by x is discriminable from c as presented by z. Since (4.2) has been rejected, it can no longer be inferred that a is indiscriminable from b, or that b is indiscriminable from c. Since (4.1) still stands, it can be inferred that a is discriminable from c. If characters are a subjective kind, indiscriminability is an equivalence relation for them; thus either a is discriminable from b, or b from c, or both. Such discriminations cannot be made under the presentations just considered, but it is required that they can be made somehow. That is presumably to say that they can be made under *other* presentations, for we are concerned with the subject's discriminations between characters as they are experienced. Thus if a is discriminable from b, there could be instances x' and y' of a and b respectively such that a as presented by x' is discriminable from b as presented by y'; we know that x' and y' are not x and y. If no such x' and y' could exist, the claim of discriminability between a and b would be empty. However, there is no reason why such a pair of presentations could not exist to uphold the discriminability of a from b (or of b from c).

Examples of the types recently considered involve only two characters, so that either a is indiscriminable from b or b is indiscriminable from c, but the present approach does not require that. I watch the hour hand of a clock; I can discriminate between the character a of my experience x two minutes ago and the character c of my experience z now, but not between either of these and the character b of my experience y one minute ago. The description of the case is quite compatible with a, b and c being three distinct characters. My failure to discriminate between a and b, and between b and c, could be explained by appeal to the plausible claim that a resembles b, and b resembles c, more than a resembles c. On the present approach distinctness entails discriminability for characters; thus a could be discriminated from b, and b from c, on presentation by appropriate instances, perhaps to the same subject when more alert (alertness not always being a property of the character itself), or even to a different subject.

It is not obligatory to think of a, b and c as distinct characters in the case just considered. Suppose, for example, that a is b. Since a is not c, it follows that c is not b; although this asymmetry between a and c with respect to b seems surprising, there was obviously no guarantee that the relations between characters would be as it were proportional to the relations between the physical causes of the experiences which instantiate them. Nevertheless, it needs to be explained why c as presented by z should be discriminable from a $(=b)$ as presented by x but not as presented by y. Memory problems would make the difference harder to explain here, in contrast with an earlier case; discrimination succeeds when the time gap is two minutes long, and fails when it is only one minute long. However, once it has been established that relations between experiences can affect discrimination between the characters they present without affecting the characters themselves, new relations may be sought to do the explanatory work. It may be argued that token experiences have physical properties, and that token experiences with the same character may differ in their physical properties; thus different physical differences can underlie the same difference of character; some of these physical differences will facilitate discrimination between the characters more than others do. In this case, my visual system may take in more information than is present to consciousness, information which affects the physical basis of the experience but not its character. Thus the physical basis of my experience x of the clock hand two minutes ago may be more different than the physical basis of my experience y of it one minute ago from the physical basis of my experience z of it now. Even if x and y have the same character, the difference between it and the character of z may be easier to notice when the difference between the physical bases of the presenting experiences is greater. Discrimination between the characters of experiences depends on the physical bases of the latter, even though the physical bases are not what is being discriminated; this is really no stranger than the fact that discrimination depends on the times at which the experiences occur, even though the times are not what is being discriminated.

The example of the clock has a more standard structure than those considered earlier. Whether it is taken to involve three characters or two, it can be handled on the present approach. A positive account can be given of the supposed examples of the non-transitivity of indiscriminability for characters on which indiscriminability for characters coincides with identity, and is transitive. The argument to the contrary fallaciously ignores presentation-sensitivity; (4.2) and (4.3) are to be rejected.

4.3   The Identity of Characters

Discriminable characters need not be discriminable under all presentations. Nevertheless, as noted earlier, if the character a is discriminable from the character b, there could be instances x of a

and y of b such that a as presented by x is discriminable from b as presented by y. That is not to say that the actual discriminability of a and b requires the actual existence of such an x and y; a and b might have no instances at all or – if that is not a coherent supposition – the only instances of a might chance not to be comparable with the only instances of b, occurring to different subjects or at different times. However, these modal considerations would add distracting complexities to issues which are complex enough without them; one thing at a time. Clarity will be served if we work under the simplifying assumption that discriminable characters have (rather than could have) presentations under which they are discriminable:

(4.4)   If the character a is discriminable from the character b, then for some instances x of a and y of b, a as presented by x is discriminable from b as presented by y.

One can finesse the modal objection to (4.4) in one of at least two ways: by treating the quantifier 'some' as ranging over possible as well as actual instances, or by dealing with the somewhat idealized case in which actuality contains an adequate supply of instances of the characters at issue.[2] The reader is asked to pick one or the other way according to taste.

The experiences quantified over in (4.4) need not be restricted to those of a single subject or at a single time. If (4.4) is true for a restricted domain, it is true for any less restricted one. However, the more restricted the domain, the more informative (4.4) is. The reader has interpretative latitude in this respect too.

What (4.4) provides is a necessary condition for non-intentional discriminability in terms of intentional discriminability. A parallel sufficient condition would be:

(4.5)   If for all instances x of the character a and y of the character b, a as presented by x is discriminable from b as presented by y, then a is discriminable from b.

Like (4.4), (4.5) would give anomalous results for uninstantiated characters. However, all characters have instances on the simplifying assumption of the previous paragraph, and in that case (4.5) easily follows from (4.1), which has already been granted. (4.4) follows in the same way from (4.2), but (4.2) has been rejected. (4.5), unlike (4.4), is not an additional assumption. Conversely, in the presence of (4.3), (4.4) and (4.5) would entail (4.2) and (4.1) respectively, but (4.3) has been rejected.

The two main theses to survive the preceding discussion are (4.1) and (4.4). They have provided the basis for a defence of the view that characters are subjective qualities, but they provide the view with more than that: a non-trivial necessary and sufficient condition for the identity of characters. This comes about as follows. By (4.4), if characters are discriminable then they are discriminable under some presentations. By (4.1), the converse is also true. Thus characters are indiscriminable if and only if they are indiscriminable under all presentations. If characters are a subjective kind, they are indiscriminable if and only if they are identical. It follows that they are identical if and only if they are indiscriminable under all presentations. More formally:

(4.6)   The character a is the character b if and only if for all instances x of a and y of b, a as presented by x is indiscriminable from b as presented by y.

It is natural to conjecture that this account can be generalized to all subjective kinds:

(4.6a)   The quality a of a subjective kind is the quality b of the same subjective kind if and only if for all instances x of a and y of b, a as presented by x is indiscriminable from b as presented by y.

An argument for (4.6 a) could be constructed formally parallel to that for (4.6). However, it is outside the scope of this book to support its premises in detail; (4.6 a) must be left as a conjecture.

(4.6) is the basis for a positive account of what identity comes to for phenomenal characters as a subjective kind. The next chapter will unfold its consequences; they turn out to give an unexpectedly complex picture.

5

Logics of Phenomenal Character

The previous chapter concluded with a necessary and sufficient condition for identity of phenomenal character, (4.6): characters are identical if and only if they are indiscriminable under all presentations.

Characters are presented to us by experiences, and the primary way of thinking of a character is as the character of some experience, in the sense in which qualities are presented to us by their instances, and the primary way of thinking of a quality is as the quality of some instance. Lengths are presented to us by things that are long, for instance, and the primary way of thinking of a length is as the length of something. A theory of length will largely be a theory of certain relations between things which have length. In the same way, a theory of phenomenal character will largely be a theory of certain relations between experiences, the things which have character. (4.6) enables such a theory to be developed.

Section 5.1 develops the technical concept of a maximal M-relation, and shows the content of (4.6) to be precisely that sameness in character is a maximal M-relation. However, there are many maximal M-relations. Does this mean that we do not know which of them sameness in character is, or that it is indeterminate which of them it is? Section 5.2 discusses the question, and dismisses the somewhat different idea that characters might be vague objects. Section 5.3 compares this account of sameness in character with the common suggestion that experiences have the same character just in case they match the same experiences.

5.1   Maximal M-Relations

Some symbols will help to abbreviate the arguments which follow. As usual, the variables u, v, x, ... range over experiences, and the

Identity and Discrimination: Reissued and Updated Edition. Timothy Williamson.
© 2013 Timothy Williamson. Published 2013 by Blackwell Publishing Ltd.

variables $a, b, c, \ldots$ over characters. The character of the experience x is ox. The indiscriminability of ox as presented by x from oy as presented by y can be considered as a relation M of *matching* between the experiences x and y. Experiences match when and only when they are indiscriminable in character. As already discussed, matching is reflexive, symmetric and non-transitive; it is the non-intentional indiscriminability relation between characters that is transitive.

(4.6) can now be symbolized as follows:

$$(5.1a) \quad \forall a \forall b (a = b \leftrightarrow \forall x \forall y ((ox = a \,\&\, oy = b) \to Mxy))$$

As an analysis of the identity of characters, (5.1a) would be blatantly circular, since both occurrences of the identity sign on the right-hand side are flanked by terms for characters. Nevertheless, (5.1a) is far from uninformative, as will now be shown.

Our interest in the identity of characters is primarily an interest in the question 'When do two experiences have the same character?', that is, in the relation of *sameness in character* between experiences u and v, symbolized as $ou = ov$. (5.1a) evidently entails the following constraint on this relation:

$$(5.1b) \quad \forall u \forall v (ou = ov \leftrightarrow \forall x \forall y ((ox = ou \,\&\, oy = ov) \to Mxy))$$

Given that every character is instantiated by some experience ($\forall a \exists x \; ox = a$), (5.1b) is indeed equivalent to (5.1a). It says that sameness in character is a relation E of which this holds:

$$(5.1c) \quad \forall u \forall v (Euv \leftrightarrow \forall x \forall y ((Exu \,\&\, Eyv) \to Mxy))$$

The advantage of (5.1c) is that it makes no explicit reference to characters; it speaks only of experiences and their relations. Of course, the 'Mxy' means that the character of x as presented by x is indiscriminable from the character of y as presented by y, but what matters is that one can have a good grasp of the extension of M prior to having a good grasp of the extension of E. This was evident in the clock example in the previous chapter, where it was clear which pairs of experiences matched (presented their characters in a discriminable way), but unclear which of the experiences were the same in character – for it was not even clear whether three characters were involved, or only two. Since matching can have this kind of epistemological priority over sameness in character, there is a point to the project of characterizing the latter in terms of the former. This point does not require the *conceptual* priority of matching over sameness in character, and thus is not vulnerable to the objection that sameness in character is conceptually prior to matching, or at least coeval with it. Similarly, there is no need to insist that one can grasp what it is for something to be an experience prior to grasping what it is for it to have a character. Moreover, matching – qualitative indiscriminability – may be *realized* by an independently identifiable relation M^* between experiences. If M^* is extensionally equivalent to M, (5.1c) can then be read as a constraint on E in terms of M^*.

We know that sameness in character, E, is to be an equivalence relation, for we must be able to regard it as $ou = ov$, and identity is an equivalence relation. What more information about E does (5.1c) add? Its left-to-right direction tells us that M is necessary for E, $\forall u \forall v (Euv \rightarrow Muv)$, for we have Euu & Evv by the reflexivity of E; but it tells us no more than that, since Euv, Exu and Eyv together yield Exy by the symmetry and transitivity of E. Thus sameness in character entails matching, which is hardly a surprise.

The interesting direction of (5.1c) is from right to left. It can be understood in terms of the way in which E, as an equivalence relation, partitions the class of experiences into mutually exclusive and jointly exhaustive equivalence classes, where the equivalence class of an experience is the set of experiences to which it bears E. What the right-to-left direction does is to rule out the situation in which every member of one equivalence class matches every member of a different equivalence class. For if every member of the equivalence class of x matches every member of the equivalence class of y, it requires E to hold between x and y, in which case their equivalence classes are identical. This constraint tells us, for example, that E is not identity: if it were, the matching of x and y would entail that whatever had E to x matched whatever had E to y, and thus the identity of x and y; but distinct experiences can match each other. Provided that E has no two equivalence classes every member of which matches every member of the other, the right-to-left direction of (5.1c) is satisfied.

The import of (5.1c) can be put in a different way. It will help to think of relations in extension, as sets of ordered pairs, so that we can speak of one relation as included in another when the latter holds wherever the former does. Let us call any equivalence relation included in M – that is, which relates only matching experiences – an *M-relation*. A *maximal M-relation* is any M-relation not included in any larger M-relation, that is, which includes any M-relation in which it is included. We can now prove that the equivalence relations which satisfy (5.1c) are precisely the maximal M-relations.

To prove that all equivalence relations which satisfy (5.1c) are maximal M-relations, let E be any equivalence relation which satisfies (5.1c). By the left-to-right direction of (5.1c), E is an M-relation. Now let F be any M-relation which includes E; what we need to show is that E includes F. Let u and v be any experiences for which Fuv holds, and suppose that we have Exu and Eyv; since F includes E we therefore have Fxu and Fyv; Fxy follows because F is an equivalence relation; Mxy follows because M includes F. The right-hand side of (5.1c) is therefore satisfied, giving Euv. Thus E includes F. It follows that E is a maximal M-relation.

We must now prove the converse, that all maximal M-relations are equivalence relations which satisfy (5.1c). Let E be any maximal M-relation. Since E is an M-relation it is an equivalence relation which satisfies the left-to-right direction of (5.1c). Suppose that u and v satisfy the right-hand side of (5.1c). Let F be the equivalence relation whose equivalence classes are just like those of E except that if the equivalence classes of u and v differ under E F merges them into a single one. It is easy to check that F is an M-relation and includes E. Since E is a maximal M-relation, it includes F. Thus Euv holds, because Fuv does, giving the left-hand side of (5.1c). This completes the proof that E satisfies (5.1c).

As an account of sameness in character, (5.1c) tells us precisely that it is a maximal M-relation. In a certain sense this means that sameness in character approximates as well as it possibly can to matching. If there is a crude intuition that sameness in character should be a relation between experiences for which matching is necessary and sufficient, then on our account it fully satisfies the intuition of necessity, and comes as close to satisfying the intuition of sufficiency as is consistent with satisfaction of the former intuition – that is, no relation which satisfies the intuition of necessity comes closer to satisfying the intuition of sufficiency (where relative closeness is measured by set-theoretic inclusion).

Our account of sameness in character as a maximal M-relation faces an obvious question of consistency. Given a domain and some relation M on it, which may be assumed to be reflexive, symmetric and non-transitive, under what conditions – if any – is there a maximal M-relation?[1] If one cannot exist, our account is incoherent; nothing could fit its description of sameness in character. If one need not exist, what reason is there to suppose that one exists in the special case where M is the matching relation on the domain of experiences?

In attempting to prove the existence of a maximal M-relation, the obvious strategy is to start with the equivalence classes of the M-relation of identity. Wherever one finds two equivalence classes all of whose members bear M to each other, one merges them; the result is a more inclusive M-relation. One continues this process of lumping together equivalence classes until one reaches an M-relation which does not have two equivalence classes all of whose members bear M to each other; it must be a maximal M-relation. All that is easier said than done; the domain may be infinite, even uncountable. However, the strategy can be generalized to these cases by means of the Axiom of Choice. To be precise, one can prove the following:

(5.2)   If M is reflexive, there is a maximal M-relation

(See Appendix). Thus the account of sameness in character as a maximal M-relation is at least consistent: the description it gives is guaranteed to fit something. In one respect the appeal to the Axiom of Choice poses no problem, for if standard set theory without the Axiom is consistent, so is standard set theory with the Axiom; thus it is inconsistent to postulate a maximal M-relation only if standard set theory is inconsistent.

It can be shown that the use of the Axiom of Choice is ineliminable, for (5.2) (for variable M) is in fact equivalent to the Axiom. This in turn suggests that in some cases a maximal M-relation will be a rather unnatural, gerrymandered relation, if it takes the Axiom of Choice to prove its existence. However, it does not follow that these cases comprise the one in which M is matching; after all, there we have independent reason to believe that a maximal M-relation exists: the philosophical argument for (4.6), which entails that sameness in character is a maximal M-relation.

Given the existence of maximal M-relations, the next question concerns their uniqueness. Does (5.1c) determine a single value of E for a given value of M, so that sameness in character is extensionally definable in terms of matching, or does a fixed value of M allow a variety of maximal M-relations? To answer this question, we first relativize (5.2) to relations which include a given M-relation:

(5.3) If M is reflexive and R is an M-relation, some maximal M-relation includes R.

(5.2) is the special case of (5.3) where R is the M-relation of identity. (5.3) is provable in the same way as (5.2), using the Axiom of Choice, except that the process of merging equivalence classes starts with the equivalence classes of R rather than with those of identity (see Appendix). Since (5.3) entails (5.2), this use of the Axiom is also ineliminable. In effect, (5.3) says that any set of positive judgements of sameness in character of the form 'x is the same in character as y' is consistent with the assumption that sameness in character is a maximal M-relation, provided only that no non-matching experiences are linked by a chain of experiences judged to be the same in character (let the equivalence class of x under R be the least set to contain x and anything judged to be the same in character as anything it contains). Not surprisingly, therefore, (5.3) entails that (5.1c) does not determine sameness in character uniquely in terms of matching.

The precise result is the following:

(5.4) If M is reflexive, symmetric and non-transitive, there are non-equivalent maximal M-relations.

To prove (5.4), consider any case in which M fails to be transitive: thus we have Mxy and Myz without Mxz. Let R_1 be the equivalence relation whose equivalence classes are $\{x, y\}$ and the singleton sets of all other members of the domain; let R_2 be the equivalence relation whose equivalence classes are $\{y, z\}$ and the singleton sets of all other members of the domain. By Mxy and the reflexivity and symmetry of M, R_1 is an M-relation; thus by (5.3), some maximal M-relation E_1 includes R_1, giving E_1xy. Similarly, some maximal M-relation E_2 includes R_2, giving E_2yz. If E_1 and E_2 were equivalent, we should have E_1yz, and therefore E_1xz by transitivity

(*M*-relations are equivalence relations); but that is impossible, for Mxz fails (*M*-relations are included in *M*). Thus E_1 and E_2 are non-equivalent maximal *M*-relations, which was to be proved.

There would be a unique maximal *M*-relation if *M* were transitive as well as symmetric and reflexive, since then *M* itself would be an *M*-relation, and therefore the only maximal one, but this special case is of no use to us, since *M* has already been seen to be non-transitive.

One can gain a better sense of the position by working through some schematic examples. The smallest domain in which *M* fails to be transitive is a set $\{x, y, z\}$ of three experiences, for which as usual we have Mxy and Myz without Mxz. This may be represented by a diagram:

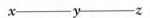

It will be easiest to think of equivalence relations in terms of the partitions of the domain into equivalence classes which they induce. Five partitions are possible here; arranged by relative fineness they are:

$$\{\{x\}, \{y\}, \{z\}\}$$

$$\{\{x, y\}, \{z\}\} \qquad \{\{x, z\}, \{y\}\} \qquad \{\{x\}, \{y, z\}\}$$

$$\{\{x, y, z\}\}$$

Of these, only $\{\{x, z\}, \{y\}\}$ and $\{\{x, y, z\}\}$ are not *M*-relations, for they are the ones which put the two experiences unrelated by *M*, x and z, in the same equivalence class. Of the three *M*-relations, just the first is not maximal, for it cuts finer than either of the other two. Thus the two maximal *M*-relations are $\{\{x, y\}, \{z\}\}$ and $\{\{x\}, \{y, z\}\}$. In this case it is clearly impossible to secure uniqueness by imposing some further formal constraint in terms of *M* which one but not the other maximal *M*-relation would meet, for the set-up is quite symmetrical between them. More precisely, the interchange of x and z leaves *M* invariant while interchanging the two maximal *M*-relations; thus any sentence whose only non-logical terms are *E* and *M* is true in this domain when *E* stands for one maximal *M*-relation if and only if it is true when *E* stands for the other *(M* having its intended interpretation).

Symmetry between different maximal *M*-relations is not an inevitable consequence of non-transitivity, however. Consider a four-membered domain structured by *M* as follows:

Of the fifteen partitions of this domain, the five *M*-relations are arranged by relative fineness as follows:

$$\{\{w\}, \{x\}, \{y\}, \{z\}\}$$

$$\{\{w\}, \{x, y\}, \{z\}\} \qquad \{\{w, x\}, \{y\}, \{z\}\} \qquad \{\{w\}, \{x\}, \{y, z\}\}$$

$$\{\{w, x\}, \{y, z\}\}$$

Thus there are just two maximal *M*-relations, $\{\{w\}, \{x, y\}, \{z\}\}$ and $\{\{w, x\}, \{y, z\}\}$. They are by no means symmetrical in respect of each other, in spite of the underlying symmetry in the pattern of *M* in the domain (interchange *w* and *x* with *z* and *y* respectively). One partition contains three equivalence classes, the other only two. Thus here one could single out a unique maximal *M*-relation by a formal constraint in terms of *M*: that the maximal *M*-relation should partition the domain into no more equivalence classes than any maximal *M*-relation does. Call this the *Minimality Constraint.*

It is at least consistent to add the claim that sameness in character satisfies the Minimality Constraint to the principle that it is a maximal *M*-relation. For consider the class of cardinal numbers each of which is the number of equivalence classes into which some maximal *M*-relation partitions the domain; this class is non-empty on the assumption that the equivalence classes of some such relation can be numbered. It therefore has a least member, because every non-empty class of cardinals has (by the Axiom of Choice), and by hypothesis the least member is the number of equivalence classes into which some maximal *M*-relation partitions the domain. Thus some maximal *M*-relation obeys the Minimality Constraint.

The intuitive effect of the Minimality Constraint is often to sift the sensible maximal M-relations from the silly ones. Consider, for instance, a domain consisting of the experiences $x_0, \ldots, x_{1000}$, where x_i matches x_j just in case the difference between i and j is no more than 500. Since x_0 does not match x_{1000}, any M-relation involves at least two equivalence classes. Just two partitions of the domain into exactly two equivalence classes do yield M-relations: $\{\{x_0, \ldots, x_{499}\}, \{x_{500}, \ldots, x_{1000}\}\}$ and $\{\{x_0, \ldots, x_{500}\}, \{x_{501}, \ldots, x_{1000}\}\}$. These are therefore the maximal M-relations which obey the Minimality Constraint. In contrast, some other maximal M-relations partition the domain into many more equivalence classes. An example is the partition $\{\{x_0, x_{500}\}, \{x_1, x_{501}\}, \ldots, \{x_{499}, x_{999}\}, \{x_{1000}\}\}$, which involves five hundred and one equivalence classes. This maximal M-relation seems to be a far less plausible candidate for sameness in character than are those which obey the Minimality Constraint: why classify x_0 but not x_1 with x_{500}?

Should we simply impose the Minimality Constraint? One's attitude to the suggestion should depend on one's view of certain issues about the status of the present inquiry; they are the topic of the next section.

5.2 Ignorance and Indeterminacy

Sameness in character is a maximal M-relation, it has been argued, but there are many maximal M-relations. Which of them is sameness in character? Two quite different views can be taken of this question. The naive view – although not on that account the wrong one – is that the phrase 'sameness in character' in its present use determinately picks out a certain relation between experiences, a relation which can be correctly but not completely described by saying that it is a maximal M-relation. This description is epistemologically useful to us, since we know more about the extension of matching (M) than we do about the extension of sameness in character. The latter relation may or may not obey the Minimality Constraint; it is not up to us whether it does, and thus there is no question of *imposing* the Minimality Constraint on it, although we can propose the hypothesis that sameness in character satisfies the constraint. In contrast, the sophisticated view – although not on that account the right one – is that the phrase 'sameness in character' in its present use fails to pick out a unique relation between experiences; perhaps no more is determinate than that it is to stand for some maximal M-relation or other. The latter condition might itself be determinate, for the term 'matching' may be tied down to an extensionally unique relation M by its links to specific acts of discrimination in a way inapplicable to 'sameness in character'. On this view there might be room to impose the Minimality Constraint by stipulation as part of an attempt to give the latter phrase a more precise sense, so that it would come closer to picking out a single relation.

The strength of the naive view is its refusal to make things more difficult than they seem; why postulate indeterminacy when we know perfectly well what relation sameness in character is by reflection on the nature of experience? The strength of the sophisticated view is its refusal to treat one of two apparently quite symmetrical alternatives as correct and the other as incorrect, where one maximal M-relation is the mirror image of another. The naive view asserts, while the sophisticated view denies, that facts about sameness and difference in character, and therefore about the indiscriminability and discriminability of characters, transcend facts about the matching and non-matching of the experiences which have those characters.

The difference between the two views has metaphysical and epistemological ramifications. If sameness in character is isomorphic to some other maximal M-relation, there will be two experiences which are the same in character but not related by the other maximal M-relation; knowledge of their sameness in character would involve a knowledge-based preference for one of the isomorphic relations over the other, and it is not clear where this knowledge could come from. We have no better way of comparing characters than by comparing them as they are presented by experiences which instantiate them: how could such comparisons give knowledge of what goes essentially beyond the matching and non-matching of experiences? The naive view may therefore be committed to the existence of unknowable truths about sameness in character, truths which not even the subject of the experiences can know, even though the subject knows what their character is. Such consequences do not amount to a *reductio ad absurdum* of the naive view, but they should give one pause.

The plausibility of the two views may vary from the inter-subjective to the intra-subjective case. Experiences match when they are indiscriminable in character; this relation is more revealing when the experiences belong to the same subject, who can make the comparison. It might be felt that facts about identity in character can transcend facts about matching in the former case but not the latter, giving inter-subjective ignorance and intra-subjective indeterminacy (although the latter will presumably infect the former too). However, a good night's sleep can form an epistemological barrier to comparison of the same subject's experiences not altogether different from the barrier to inter-subjective comparison. It is not easy to hold a line between ignorance in some cases and indeterminacy in others. The problem resembles that of spectrum inversion (Shoemaker 1981).[2]

This chapter will leave the choice of ignorance or indeterminacy open; the next will suggest that the ignorance view has more explanatory power than might be supposed. Any final settlement of the issue would far exceed the scope of this monograph. Fortunately, there is much common ground between the two views. For both supply a notion of a pair of experiences being *uncontroversially* the same in character: that is, being related by *every* maximal M-relation. Experiences are uncontroversially the same in character just in case they satisfy the dyadic predicate 'x is the same in character as y' whichever maximal M-relation it is interpreted by. Similarly, both views supply a notion of a pair of experiences being uncontroversially different in character: that is, being related by *no* maximal M-relation. The naive view treats uncontroversialness as an epistemological matter while the sophisticated treats it as a semantic one, but for many purposes the effect is the same. The idea can be used to give a partial account of sameness in character which is neutral between the two views of its status.

When are two experiences uncontroversially the same in character? When are they uncontroversially different? The latter question has a simpler answer than the former. If two experiences do not match, they bear no M-relation to each other, and thus are uncontroversially different in character. Conversely, if they do match each other, they bear that M-relation to each other whose equivalence classes are the pair of them and the singletons of all other members of the domain; it follows by (5.3) that they bear some maximal M-relation to each other, and are therefore not uncontroversially different in character. We thus have:

(5.5)   Experiences x and y are uncontroversially different in character if and only if x does not match y.

The corresponding equivalence for sameness in character is:

(5.6)   Experiences x and y are uncontroversially the same in character
if and only if either x is y or every experience which matches x
matches every experience which matches y.

The 'if' direction of (5.6) will be proved first. If x is y the point is trivial.
If every experience which matches x matches every experience which
matches y, then given any M-relation which does not relate x and y we
can merge the equivalence classes of x and y to form a new M-relation,
which will properly include the old one, showing the latter not to be
maximal; thus any maximal M-relation relates x and y. To prove the
'only if' direction, suppose that x is not y and some experience x^*
which matches x does not match some experience y^* which matches
y. It is easy to show that the sets $\{x, x^*\}$ and $\{y, y^*\}$ are disjoint.
Consider the M-relation whose equivalence classes are $\{x, x^*\}$, $\{y, y^*\}$
and the singletons of all other members of the domain. By (5.3), that
M-relation is included in some maximal M-relation E, giving Exx^*
and Eyy^*. We cannot have Exy, for that would entail Ex^*y^*, which is
impossible since x^* does not match y^*; thus some maximal M-relation
does not relate x and y. By contraposition, if every such relation
relates x and y then either x is y or every experience which matches x
matches every experience which matches y. This completes the proof
of (5.6).

All non-matching experiences are uncontroversially different in
character, but it may be quite rare for matching experiences to be
uncontroversially the same in character. It is easy to check that
no two experiences in the worked examples from the previous section are uncontroversially the same in character. Most pairs of
matching experiences may be neither uncontroversially the same
nor uncontroversially different in character, but simply controversial. One could liberalize the notions by incorporating the Minimality Constraint; thus experiences would be uncontroversially the
same (or different) in the new sense just in case they were related
by every (or no) maximal M-relation which obeyed the Minimality
Constraint. Whatever was uncontroversial under the old definitions
would be uncontroversial under the new ones, but much would be
uncontroversial under the latter that was not so under the former.

However, the new definitions will not be adopted. Not only is the status of the Minimality Constraint uncertain; nothing like (5.5) or (5.6) could be found as substitutes for them. More precisely, the uncontroversial sameness (or difference) in character of x and y would not be equivalent to any local facts about the matching of x, y and what matches them; indeed, it would not be equivalent to any first-order formula in x and y whose only non-logical predicate was matching.[3]

The notion of uncontroversialness can be generalized. Consider any first-order formula whose only non-logical symbols are the dyadic predicates E and M; it is uncontroversially true (false) relative to an assignment of values to variables if and only if it is true (false) relative to that assignment whenever E is interpreted by a maximal M-relation and M by matching, and the domain of quantification is taken to be the relevant class of experiences. A formula is uncontroversially true (false) if and only if it is uncontroversially true (false) relative to all assignments. These notions will be rendered into English in obvious ways, reading E as sameness in character. Thus it is uncontroversially true that some maximal M-relation is sameness in character, but it is not uncontroversially true of some maximal M-relation that it is sameness in character.

Uncontroversialness is a thin disguise for the concept of a *supervaluation* (van Fraassen 1971, Fine 1975). Suppose that we have a class of valuations – assignments of semantic values to linguistic items – which are equally legitimate in some respect; then the corresponding supervaluation assigns to a linguistic item that semantic value assigned to it by all the valuations in the class, if such exists, and otherwise assigns it nothing. In particular, the valuations may be classical recursive assignments of values to variables and truth values to formulae; the supervaluation makes a formula true if all the valuations make it true, false if all the valuations make it false, and neither true nor false otherwise. Consider the language described in the previous paragraph, and let the class of valuations comprise those which take the class of experiences as the domain of quantification, the extension of M as that of matching and the extension of E as that of some maximal M-relation; a sentence is true (false) on the corresponding supervaluation just in case it is uncontroversially true (false).

Uncontroversial truth values exhibit the characteristic features of supervaluations. If there is at least one valuation (the qualification 'in the relevant class' being understood), no formula is both true and false on the supervaluation; if a formula is assigned different truth values by different valuations, it is neither true nor false on the supervaluation. Since there are always non-equivalent maximal M-relations, no formula is both true and false on the supervaluation, but some formulae (e.g. Exy) are neither true nor false on the supervaluation, relative to a fixed assignment of values to variables. Bivalent valuations yield a non-bivalent super-valuation. However, even if neither A nor $\sim A$ is true on the supervaluation relative to a given assignment, $A \vee \sim A$ is still true on the supervaluation, since it is true on each valuation, the latter being bivalent. Thus although the supervaluation is not bivalent, it does validate the Law of Excluded Middle, since it can make a disjunction true without making either disjunct true. More generally, on the supervaluation every truth of classical logic is true and every classically valid sequent is truth-preserving.[4] The same points can be made in terms of uncontroversial truth: a disjunction may be uncontroversially true even though neither disjunct is; every truth of classical logic is uncontroversially true, and every classically valid inference preserves uncontroversial truth.

In some ways the present case is particularly well adapted to the method of supervaluations. The class of legitimate valuations can be clearly defined via the class of maximal M-relations. This definition is of course no clearer than the relation of matching (M), but since the problems in which we are interested still arise if matching is completely determinate in extension, but non-transitive, any unclarity about matching is not to the point. In contrast, supervaluations have been used by Kit Fine (1975) to handle vague predicates, the relevant valuations being given by legitimate 'precisifications'. It might be held that the occurrence of second-order vagueness – vagueness in what counts as a borderline case – is central to the problem of vagueness; but then the class of relevant valuations is itself vaguely defined, and it is not clear that supervaluations take us to the heart of the problem, since the meta-language in which they are constructed is itself vague. The present application may avoid this objection, since it concerns an issue which does not breed a second-order copy of itself.

There is nevertheless a reason for speaking of uncontroversial truth rather than truth on a supervaluation. The method of supervaluations is associated with cases, such as that of vagueness, in which there is not supposed to be a uniquely correct valuation; indeed, that is the problem with which it is intended to deal. If sameness in character is genuinely indeterminate between the various maximal M-relations, then the present case is one in point. However, it has not been shown that the present indeterminacy is semantic rather than merely epistemological; if it is the latter, one maximal M-relation gives the uniquely correct valuation on the intended interpretation of the language, even if we do not know which valuation it is. Neutrality on the issue can better be preserved by the terminology of uncontroversial truth values.

The notion of uncontroversial truth values has an important limitation. It has not been defined for formulae with variables for characters as opposed to experiences. One can think of Exy as abbreviating $ox = oy$, but no sense has been given to the idea that the formula $\exists x\ ox = a$ is uncontroversially true (or false) relative to the assignment of an object to the variable a, for no definition of legitimacy has been given either for the domain of quantification for character variables such as a or for interpretations of the function symbol o ('the character of'). If it is assumed that every character is the character of some experience ($\forall a \exists x\ ox = a$) then the interpretation of o will fix the domain of characters, since the domain of experiences is already fixed. Nevertheless, two kinds of variation can be distinguished: variation in the domain of characters, and variation in the mapping from experiences to characters relative to a given domain of characters. When the Minimality Constraint is violated, different maximal M-relations will partition the experiences into different numbers of equivalence classes; on the assumption that every character is the character of some experience, these equivalence classes will be in one-one correspondence with the characters, so that domains of characters of different cardinalities will automatically be involved. Even if the cardinality of the domain is fixed (as it could be by the Minimality Constraint), the domain may still vary. Even if the domain itself is fixed, different mappings will vary the truth value of the formula $ox = a$ relative to a given assignment of members of the relevant domains to x and a; to determine that an object is the character of some experience is not to determine which experience it is the character of.

Suppose that identity in character can be indeterminate. That is, some sentences of the form 'The character of x is the character of y' are indeterminate in truth-value, where 'x' and 'y' are replaced by terms whose reference to particular experiences is determinate. Does it follow that either 'the character of x' or 'the character of y' is indeterminate in reference? Some would claim that it does not, on the grounds that the indeterminacy might lie in the extension of the identity relation rather than the reference of the terms. On this view, the terms might determinately refer to *vague objects*. If they did, there would be a specific pair of characters of which it was neither true nor false that they were identical. Such characters would also have vague boundaries, in the sense that it would be indeterminate what instantiated them: for example, the character of x is supposed to be such that it is neither true nor false that y is an instance of it. However, the most controversial claim is that identity can be indeterminate for some objects.

Gareth Evans and Nathan Salmon have given versions of a now famous argument against the possibility of vague objects.[5] Its gist is as follows. Suppose that a is b. Trivially, b is such that it is determinately true that it is b. By Leibniz's Law a has every property of b, so a is such that it is determinately true that it is b. Thus it is determinately true that a is b (this move is legitimate because 'a' and 'b' are variables). By contraposition, if it is not determinately true that a is b, a is not b. Yet the defender of vague objects in the above sense must sometimes assert the antecedent of this conditional while refusing to assert its consequent; his position is therefore incoherent.

The argument may seem to beg the question.[6] Let it be granted that logical validity is a matter of truth-preservation; then the defender of indeterminacy in truth-value may object to the use of contraposition, on the grounds that a logically valid argument may have an indeterminate premise and a false conclusion, whereas its contraposed version will be invalid, having a true premise and an indeterminate conclusion. However, one should not assume that one knows what one is talking about when one starts to say things of that kind. The premise 'a is b' is acknowledged by the objector to have as a logical consequence the conditional 'If b is determinately b then a is determinately b'; Leibniz's Law is logically valid. The conditional is supposed to be false, for its antecedent is supposed to be true and its consequent false. Yet we are not allowed to deny the premise '*a* is *b*' which logically entails the false conclusion. Something has gone wrong; the condition for correct denial has been set unreasonably high.

Suppose that it is determinate what the truth-condition of a sentence *s* is (which is not to assume that it is determinate whether that condition obtains); then the truth-condition of the negation of *s* is merely that the truth-condition of *s* should not obtain. Even if some people prefer to use the word 'not' in a different way, they should agree that it can quite coherently be used in the way just suggested. It is also agreed to be determinate what the truth-condition of '*a* is *b*' is, when the assignment of reference to '*a*' and '*b*' is determinate; there is no suggestion that the 'is' of identity is indeterminate between several identity relations (an argument against such a suggestion can in any case be found at p. 114 of Williamson 1987/8). So if '*a* is *b*' is not true, its truth-condition does not obtain, and thus the truth-condition of its negation '*a* is not *b*' does obtain; in other words, *a* is not *b*. There is a right answer to the question 'Is *a* *b*?'; it is 'No'. What was presented as the indeterminacy of identity turns out to be merely another way in which things can fail to be identical. More generally, it looks as though a sentence and its negation, properly understood, can both fail to be true only in case of indeterminate truth-*conditions*.[7]

The idea that identity might be indeterminate is the distorted reflection of deviant usage. If identity in character is indeterminate, it is only because the reference of 'the character of *x*' may be indeterminate even when the reference of '*x*' is not; but it has not been shown that identity in character is indeterminate.

Even if it is determinate which experiences are the same in character, it may be indeterminate what the character of an experience is. Frege faced a similar problem in the *Grundlagen*, when he discovered that fixing what it is for two lines to have the same direction (compare $ox = oy$) is not sufficient for fixing what it is for an object to be the direction of a given line (compare $ox = a$); the question 'Is England the same as the direction of the Earth's axis?' remained unanswered (Frege 1884 section 66; Wright 1983 pp. 107–17). In that case there is no issue of ignorance or indeterminacy with respect to the question 'When do two lines have the same direction?', since the answer 'When they are parallel' is clearly correct; nevertheless, the gap between that answer and an answer to the question 'What is the direction of a line?' has an analogue in the present case. Frege dealt with the problem by identifying directions as equivalence classes of parallel lines. The manoeuvre gives an answer to the question 'What are directions?', and at least states the correct conditions for sameness in direction, since two lines are parallel just in case the same lines are parallel to each. The idea is of course quite general, and therefore applicable in the present case. However, its formal adequacy does not guarantee its substantive correctness. If one takes a non-reductive attitude to the character of experience, one may well doubt that characters could be equivalence classes of experiences, on the grounds that a shared character of itself constitutes a genuine similarity between the experiences that share it, whereas joint membership of a class never of itself constitutes a genuine similarity. In order not to rule out such a position, the Fregean identification will not be made.

5.3   Matching the Same Experiences

The preceding sections have sought to describe a transitive notion of indiscriminability in terms of a non-transitive one. There is a much better-known way of doing so, associated with Bertrand Russell (1950 pp. 104–5) and Nelson Goodman (1951 pp. 196–200) and briefly discussed in chapter 1. Given a non-transitive notion of indiscriminability by direct means, we can say that two things are indirectly discriminable if something is indiscriminable from one but not from the other. Indirect indiscriminability can then be shown to be an equivalence relation. The aim of the present section is to show that indirect indiscriminability is no substitute for maximal M-relations when it comes to the character of experience, but also to indicate a partial reconciliation between the two approaches.

    The starting point is the non-transitive relation of matching. Goodman uses the same term, but not quite in its present sense of a relation between token experiences. Matching in Goodman's sense is a relation between qualia, repeatable qualities of experience which have more in common with characters than with experiences. One quale matches another just in case they are not noticeably different. Goodman therefore uses matching as a criterion of identity for qualia: qualia are identical if and only if they match the same qualia. There is no hope for the corresponding principle about experiences, where 'matching' is understood in the sense of this chapter (x matches y just in case the character of x as presented by x is indiscriminable from the character of y as presented by y):

(5.7) $\forall x \forall y (x = y \leftrightarrow \forall z (Mxz \leftrightarrow Myz))$[8]

For two experiences at different times can have exactly the same character, and could match the same experiences. (5.7) would rule that out, absurdly. The obvious emendation to (5.7) is the claim that matching the same experiences is the condition for the characters of the experiences, not the experiences themselves, to be identical:

(5.8) $\forall x \forall y (ox = oy \leftrightarrow \forall z (Mxz \leftrightarrow Myz))$

(5.7) is a 'one level' criterion of identity; its variables range over the items whose identity is in question (compare the Axiom of Extensionality for sets). (5.8) is a 'two level' criterion of identity; its variables range over experiences, but the items whose identity is in question are characters (compare Frege's account of the identity of directions in terms of the parallelism of lines, 1884 section 68, and Dummett 1957 pp. 55–7, Hausman 1967 pp. 86–90, Wright 1987 p. 253–4). It may be compared with (5.1b), one formalization of the idea that sameness in character is a maximal M-relation. (5.8) has one advantage over (5.1b); it determines sameness in character uniquely in terms of matching.

Unfortunately, (5.8) is false, for it denies the presentation-sensitivity of indiscriminability. That is, it entails (4.3); for if x and x' are instances of the character a, and y and y' of the character b, then by the left-to-right direction of (5.8) x matches y if and only if x matches y' and y' matches x if and only if y' matches x', so by the symmetry of matching x matches y if and only if x' matches y' – in other words, a as presented by x is indiscriminable from b as presented by y if and only if a as presented by x' is indiscriminable from b as presented by y'. The counter-examples to (4.3) can just as easily be turned against the left-to-right direction of (5.8); indeed, the two are equivalent. For instance, if two experiences of different subjects or at different times have the same character, a third experience may match one and not the other (in the technical sense in which 'match' is being used) because it occurs to the appropriate subject or at the appropriate time. The arguments of the last chapter need not be repeated here. To put the point in a different way: there is no relation which holds between the character of x and the character of y just in case x matches y, for the assumption that such a relation exists entails (4.3) and therefore the left-to-right direction of (5.8). Conversely, if that direction held, the formula $\forall x \forall y \, ((ox = a \,\&\, oy = b) \to Mxy)$ would define such a relation between the characters a and b.

(5.8) can also be shown to be inconsistent with the principle that sameness in character is a maximal M-relation. The relation of matching the same experiences is an M-relation – if x matches the same experiences as y, it matches y because y matches itself – but it is never maximal when M is non-transitive. For consider its equivalence classes: if x matches y but not z and y matches z then the equivalence classes of x and y are distinct but can be merged to give a larger M-relation, for if u matches the same experiences as x and v matches the same experiences as y, u matches y and therefore v. The argument in fact shows that if sameness in character is a maximal M-relation then the left-to-right direction of (5.8) is false, for this direction entails that sameness in character is a relation contained in the M-relation of matching the same experiences; since the latter is not maximal, neither is the former.

Sameness in character is thus not a matter of matching the same experiences; (5.8) is false. However, all the objections to it have concerned its left-to-right direction, the claim that matching the same experiences is necessary for sameness in character. Could matching the same experiences be sufficient for sameness in character? Perhaps one half of (5.8) could be preserved:

(5.9) $\forall x \forall y (\forall z (Mxz \leftrightarrow Myz) \to ox = oy)$

If two experiences match all the same experiences, what reason could there be for denying that they have the same character? (5.9) seems worth investigating.

If the domain of experiences were a very limited one, (5.9) would not be plausible. Given two matching experiences of different characters, there might chance to be no experience matching one and not the other. However, the discussion of (4.4) has already brought out the need for a domain more representative of the variety of possible experiences, and on this understanding (5.9) looks quite plausible.

It should be emphasized how tight a relation matching the same experiences is (Russell 1950 p. 105, Dummett 1975 pp. 266–8, Peacocke 1986 pp. 4–5). In none of the examples in section 5.1 did it hold between any pair of distinct experiences. It is fine-grained in a way paradoxically insensitive to the subject's powers of discrimination; if experiences form a continuum such that they match just in case they are less than a certain positive distance d apart, matching the same experiences will typically require being located at the same point of the continuum, irrespective of the value of d. (5.9) does not deliver any judgements of sameness in character until one has a universal generalization about matching; in contrast, the other direction of (5.8) delivered judgements of difference in character on the basis of particular statements about matching ('x but not y matches z'). Thus (5.9) would not be very informative; but it might still be true. Indeed, it is automatically true in those examples where its antecedent is equivalent to $x = y$. What needs to be investigated is the general case.

One can easily show that some maximal M-relations make (5.9) true, so that it is at the very least not uncontroversially false that matching the same experiences suffices for sameness in character. For matching the same experiences is an M-relation, and therefore is contained in some maximal M-relation, which verifies (5.9) when used to interpret $ox = oy$. However, some maximal M-relations may make (5.9) false. Consider the following diagram:

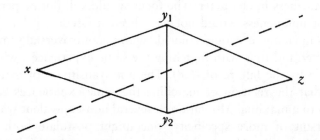

M holds between every two experiences except x and z. Thus y_1

and y_2 match the same experiences, and so are related by every maximal M-relation which verifies (5.9); the corresponding partitions are $\{\{x, y_1, y_2\}, \{z\}\}$ and $\{\{x\}, \{y_1, y_2, z\}\}$. But the partitions $\{\{x, y_1\}, \{y_2, z\}\}$ (as in the diagram) and $\{\{x, y_2\}, \{y_1, z\}\}$ also correspond to maximal M-relations, and these falsify (5.9). There is no logical guarantee that matching the same experiences is uncontroversially sufficient for sameness in character. Equivalently, there is no logical guarantee that matching the same experiences is sufficient for uncontroversial sameness in character.

One positive connection can be made out. Matching the same experiences is *necessary* for uncontroversial sameness in character. For if x and y do not match the same experiences, it can be assumed without loss of generality that x matches an experience z unmatched by y, in which case some maximal M-relation holds between x and z by (5.3) and thus not between x and y, so that they are not uncontroversially the same in character. It does not follow, however, that matching the same experiences is uncontroversially necessary for sameness in character; that is just the untenable left-to-right direction of (5.8). Indeed, matching the same experiences is uncontroversially unnecessary for sameness in character, since it has already been seen not to contain any maximal M-relation.

Matching the same experiences is necessary and almost sufficient for uncontroversial sameness in character. One could bring the two relations fully into line if one could impose (5.9) as an extra constraint on sameness in character, so that the definition of 'uncontroversial' considered only maximal M-relations containing the relation of matching the same experiences. This would give a slightly clearer picture of sameness in character. The focus would still not be perfectly sharp, for uniqueness would not have been secured: if it had been, sameness in character would coincide with uncontroversial sameness in character and thus with matching the same experiences, which is impossible by the failure of (5.8). The non-transitivity of matching ensures that the relation of matching the same experiences can be extended to a maximal M-relation in several non-equivalent ways.

In pursuit of more specificity, one might postulate both (5.9) and the Minimality Constraint. It can be shown that at least one maximal M-relation does satisfy both.[9] On the corresponding definition of 'uncontroversial' matching the same experiences might no longer be necessary for uncontroversial sameness in character, but it would still be sufficient.

If our problem with character is one of indeterminacy, the joint imposition of (5.9) and the Minimality Constraint will at least partially resolve it. If the problem is one of ignorance, neither condition can be imposed, because either may be false; nevertheless, it is not unreasonable to suppose that both are true.

6

Paradoxes of Phenomenal Character

The concept of phenomenal character is closely related to that of a phenomenal quality. Michael Dummett has argued that 'there are no phenomenal qualities, as these have been traditionally understood' (1975, p. 268), because the non-transitivity of indiscriminability leads to sorites paradoxes.[1] If phenomenal characters are just maximally specific phenomenal qualities, it would follow that there are no phenomenal characters either.

There is a not very important equivocation in the term 'phenomenal'. For Dummett, the notion of a phenomenal quality is correlative with that of an observational predicate, in a sense of the latter phrase like that in chapter 3: a predicate decidable on the basis of observation. The supposed non-existence of phenomenal qualities corresponds to the supposed incoherence of observational predicates such as 'red'. Speakers predicate the latter of ordinary material objects, 'moderate-sized specimens of dry goods'; they say that berries and fire engines are red. Such objects would have phenomenal qualities in Dummett's sense if anything had. In contrast, it is an experience which has a phenomenal character, as the latter term has been used here. Phenomenal characters are not the kind of phenomenal quality of which Dummett writes. However, it does not follow that Dummett's arguments pose no threat to the preceding account of phenomenal character. For they can be adapted to its case without much difficulty. No experience is red, but some experiences are sensations of red; experiences can be pleasant or painful too.

Section 6.1 gives reasons for fearing that observational predicates are susceptible to sorites paradoxes, but denies that predicates such as 'painful' are perfectly observational. They are instead *phenomenal*, in a sense developed in section 6.2. The concept of

---

Identity and Discrimination: Reissued and Updated Edition. Timothy Williamson.
© 2013 Timothy Williamson. Published 2013 by Blackwell Publishing Ltd.

uncontroversial truth from the previous chapter is used to explain the resistance of phenomenal predicates to sorites paradoxes. Section 6.3 considers and rejects a final attempt to revive a sorites paradox for 'painful'. Section 6.4 tentatively places these thoughts against a background of a general account of sorites paradoxes, on which they may reflect either speakers' ignorance or semantic indeterminacy or both, depending on the facts of the particular case.

6.1   The Paradox of Observational Predicates

Chapter 3 formalized two notions of an observational predicate, which may be thought of as intentional and non-intentional. A predicate F is non-intentionally observational just in case (a) if something is F it can be observed to be F and (b) if something is not F it can be observed not to be F (this is one reading of (3.1a,b)). It is intentionally observational just in case (a) if something is F as presented in a certain way it can be observed to be F as presented in that way and (b) if something is not F as presented in a certain way it can be observed not to be F as presented in that way (this is one reading of (3.1ao,bo)). If F is non-intentionally observational and a pair of things are non-intentionally indiscriminable by observation, then if the first is F so is the second, for otherwise one could observe the difference between them (compare (3.2)). If F is intentionally observational and a pair of things are intentionally indiscriminable by observation as presented in a certain way, then if the first is F as presented in that way so is the second, for otherwise one could observe the difference between them as presented in those ways (compare (3.2o)). Both of these principles tug in the direction of a sorites paradox, for one will expect something clearly F to be linked to something clearly not F by a series of which each member is indiscriminable from the next, given the non-transitivity of indiscriminability. How do these general considerations apply to the specific case of phenomenal character?

The word 'observe' may not be the happiest for what one does to one's own experience; in the definition of 'observational' it should be replaced by 'feel', standing for the kind of knowledge subjects have of their own experiences. On that understanding, certain predicates such as 'painful' do have a strong claim to count as observational.

As in previous chapters we are concerned with discrimination between phenomenal characters rather than particular experiences, the latter being trivially discriminable through their times of occurrence, although discrimination between the phenomenal characters of two experiences is in effect qualitative discrimination between the two experiences. Thus our first concern will be with predicates of phenomenal characters rather than experiences, although such predicates generate predicates of experience, and the latter will be discussed too.

For phenomenal characters, non-intentional indiscriminability coincides with identity. There is thus no danger of a sorites paradox in the principle about non-intentionally observational predicates, that if a pair of phenomenal characters are non-intentionally indiscriminable then if the first is F so is the second. For it reduces to an instance of Leibniz's Law: if a pair of phenomenal characters are identical then if the first is F so is the second. The previous chapter provided a model of phenomenal character which has this consequence; it therefore cannot render the account incoherent. If one tried to construct a sorites series linking a painful to a painless character, one would look for a series of actual or possible experiences with those characters, each indiscriminable in character from the next; but then one would be open to the charge that the series of characters had a member discriminable from its successor when they were presented by other experiences. The cogency of such a charge was upheld in chapter 4.

The threat to phenomenal character comes from the principle about intentionally observational predicates: if a pair of characters are intentionally indiscriminable as presented by certain experiences, then if the first is F as presented by the appropriate experience so is the second. Even for phenomenal characters intentional indiscriminability is non-transitive (or the intentional equivalent), and does not reduce to identity. One can construct a series of experiences each indiscriminable in phenomenal character from the next whose first member has a painful character and whose last member has a painless one; the characters of neighbouring experiences are intentionally indiscriminable as presented by those experiences. Thus the phenomenal characters form a sorites series, given that 'painful' is an intentionally observational predicate. If any member of the series is painful, so is the next; by the transitivity of material conditionals, if the first member is painful, so is the last – but the first member was chosen to be painful, and the last to be painless. Yet it seems very plausible that 'painful' *is* an intentionally observational predicate: (a) if a phenomenal character is painful as presented by a certain experience it can be felt to be painful as presented by that experience, and (b) if a phenomenal character is not painful as presented by a certain experience it can be felt not to be painful as presented by that experience.

The reference to phenomenal character in the paradox can be minimized. As in the previous chapter, we can say that experiences x and y match (Mxy) just in case they are indiscriminable in character, that is, the phenomenal character of x as presented by x is indiscriminable from the phenomenal character of y as presented by y. We can also say, with harmless ambiguity, that an experience x is painful (Fx) just in case the character of x as presented by x is painful. The intentional observationality of 'painful' for characters then reduces to its non-intentional observationality for experiences: (a) if an experience is painful it can be felt to be painful, and (b) if an experience is not painful it can be felt not to be painful. This conjunction will be referred to simply as the observationality of 'painful'. The principle it seems to entail is that if two experiences match and one is painful then so is the other; in symbols:

(6.1) $\forall x \forall y (Mxy \rightarrow (Fx \leftrightarrow Fy))$

Matching is a non-transitive relation, and (6.1) does generate a sorites paradox.

Could one deny that (6.1) follows from the observationality of 'painful'? Suppose that 'painful' is observational, that an experience x is painful and an experience y is not painful. By (a), x can be felt to be painful. By (b), y can be felt not to be painful. This surely suffices for the discriminability of x and y in phenomenal character; thus x does not match y. By contraposition, if x matches y and x is painful, so is y (note the use of classical logic). By the symmetry of matching, if x matches y and y is painful, so is x. It does not seem plausible to blame the paradox on a gap between the observationality of 'painful' and (6.1) in normal cases.

A different way of escaping from the paradox is by denying the observationality of 'painful'. One can defend the possibility of an experience which either is painful but cannot be felt to be painful or is not painful but cannot be felt not to be painful. That is, an experience might be painful even though its subject was incapable of knowing by having it that it was painful, or it might not be painful even though its subject was incapable of knowing by having it that it was not painful. There is no need to deny that being in pain is a matter of feeling pain, for that sense of 'feel' is not the one it has in 'felt to be painful'; the latter, unlike the former, describes a certain kind of conceptualized knowledge that something is painful, otherwise the argument from the observationality of 'painful' to (6.1) would fail.

A creature without the concept of pain can feel pain, but cannot feel anything to be painful (or not to be painful). Such creatures thus present apparent counter-examples to the observationality of 'painful'. Could one say that a mouse in pain would feel its experience to be painful if it had the requisite concepts? The counterfactual looks shaky; it preserves the observationality of 'painful' only if that very mouse could have had that very experience and applied the concept of painfulness to it. However, it would be unsatisfying to rest a case against the observationality of 'painful' on this kind of example, for the sorites paradox arises just as much for creatures which do have the requisite concepts.

Better cases lie on the borderline between the painful and the non-painful. I may be unsure whether to call my present annoying sensation a pain or an itch. To plump for one rather than the other would be neither the effect nor the cause of knowledge. However, I may not be tempted to plump; what is so far in question is ignorance, not error, on the part of the subject. Given classical logic, either my experience is painful and I cannot know that it is or it is not painful and I cannot know that it is not. In both cases the observationality of 'painful' fails, and with it the argument for (6.1).

There are obvious objections to this view of the matter; they will be confronted in section 6.3, once a positive conception of predicates such as 'painful' has been sketched. The next section begins with a different argument for (6.1), one which does not depend on the notion of observationality. It therefore requires a different response. Although it too will be found wanting, it leaves behind a new notion of a *phenomenal predicate*, which will guide the subsequent discussion of the original argument.

6.2   The Paradox of Phenomenal Predicates

If two experiences match – if they are indiscriminable in phenomenal character – then they feel the same; thus if one feels painful, so does the other. Even if 'feels painful' is to be distinguished from 'is painful', we seem to have validated a reading of (6.1) on which F stands for the former phrase rather than the latter: but then we have a sorites paradox for 'feels painful' on our hands, and that is quite bad enough.

The argument just presented trades on an ambiguity in the phrase 'feel the same'. In one sense, experiences feel the same just in case it feels to the subject that they are the same (in phenomenal character); this sense is not applicable to a pair of experiences of different subjects. When experiences match it may feel to the subject that they are the same (if any comparison is made). However, given that it feels to the subject that x and y are the same and that x feels painful, it does not follow that y feels painful. For the subject may not be sure that x feels painful, and may not be sure that x does not feel painful. To rule out this possibility is just to claim that 'feels painful' is observational, and thus to revert to the argument of the previous section, applied to 'feels painful' rather than to 'is painful'. That argument is dealt with elsewhere.

There is a different sense in which experiences feel the same just in case the way that one of them feels is the same as (identical with) the way the other feels; this sense is applicable to a pair of experiences of different subjects. Since feeling painful is just an aspect of the way an experience feels, it may be granted that if the way x feels is the same as the way y feels and x feels painful then y feels painful. However, the argument now fails at another point: given that two experiences match, it does not follow that the way one feels is the same as the way the other feels. For the way an experience feels is what it is like to have that experience – in other words, its phenomenal character. Thus the argument moves from matching to identity in phenomenal character, or equivalently from intentional to non-intentional indiscriminability; this move was seen to be fallacious in chapter 4.

The argument makes two moves; each is plausible because there is an interpretation on which it is (more or less) correct, but no interpretation has been found on which both are correct. However, the second interpretation did leave behind a residue of positive thought.

A predicate such as 'feels painful' – or, for that matter, 'is painful' – applies to an experience in virtue of the way that experience feels, that is, in virtue of its phenomenal character.[2] For any such predicate, the following principle is correct: if two experiences have the same phenomenal character and the predicate is true of one, then it is true of the other. This can be symbolized:

(6.2) $\forall x \forall y (ox = oy \rightarrow (Fx \leftrightarrow Fy))$

For if F applies to an experience in virtue of a feature G of its phenomenal character, Fx and Fy are equivalent to Gox and Goy respectively, from which (6.2) follows by Leibniz's Law. The mistake in the argument was the identification of identity in phenomenal character with matching:

(6.3) $\forall x \forall y (ox = oy \leftrightarrow Mxy)$

(6.1) is an easy consequence of (6.2) and (6.3). This derivation explains some of the intuitive force behind (6.1), for it is in any case clear that we find (6.3) tempting; it is simply the conflation of intentional indiscriminability, matching, with the non-intentional version, identity in phenomenal character. It would be very surprising if the intuitions favouring (6.1) and (6.3) came from independent sources, given that one obviously follows from the other in the presence of a correct principle about the relevant predicates (6.2). The same confusion is at work in the sorites paradox for 'painful' and the paradox of the apparently non-transitive criterion of identity for phenomenal characters.

Some treatments of sorites arguments for observational predicates rest on the plausible claim that the satisfaction of such a predicate is a matter of degree.[3] In that case, when x matches y, why should the degree to which x satisfies the observational predicate F not be different, but indiscriminably different, from the degree to which y satisfies F? (6.1) would then be almost but not quite true, and the sorites argument would fail. However, such analyses are now visibly inadequate to the present case. For the point behind (6.2) is that the predicate F applies to experiences in virtue of their phenomenal character; thus if two predicates have the same phenomenal character, they should satisfy F to exactly the same degree. Thus (6.2) should be true to the highest degree. What needs to be attacked is (6.3); but it does not contain the observational predicate F. It does contain the binary predicates of identity and indiscriminability in phenomenal character, but we have been given no way of applying the idea of degrees of satisfaction to them. Moreover, (6.3) should be denied outright; thus the appeal to degrees of satisfaction falls away as redundant.

We can say that F is a *phenomenal predicate* just in case (6.2) holds. A phenomenal predicate applies to an experience when a corresponding predicate applies to the phenomenal character of that experience; given (6.2) it is legitimate to define Gox by Fx (thus a truth-function of phenomenal predicates is itself a phenomenal predicate). The notion can be extended to non-monadic predicates; the n-place predicate F is phenomenal just in case the following holds:

$$(6.2+)\quad \forall x_1 \ldots \forall x_n \forall y_1 \ldots \forall y_n((ox_1 = oy_1 \;\&\; \ldots \;\&\; ox_n = oy_n) \rightarrow$$
$$(Fx_1 \ldots x_n \leftrightarrow Fy_1 \ldots y_n))$$

From (6.2+) and (6.3) one can then derive:

$$(6.1+)\quad \forall x_1 \ldots \forall x_n \forall y_1 \ldots \forall y_n((Mx_1 y_1 \;\&\; \ldots \;\&\; Mx_n y_n) \rightarrow$$
$$(Fx_1 \ldots x_n \leftrightarrow Fy_1 \ldots y_n))$$

(6.1+) is just as vulnerable as (6.1) to sorites arguments. Suppose, for instance, that x and y are linked by a long series of experiences, each matching the next, and that Fxy holds, where F is an asymmetric binary relation; (6.1+) will enable one to deduce Fyx. Of course, (6.1+) is also a consequence of the observationality of F.[4]

In what follows it will be taken for granted that (6.3) is false. The new argument for (6.1) and (6.1+) thus disappears. However, (6.2) and (6.2+) remain to define a class of phenomenal predicates. Any observational predicate is phenomenal, for (6.1) and (6.1+) entail (6.2) and (6.2+) respectively (since identity in phenomenal character entails matching), but the idea is that there are virtually no observational predicates; many of the predicates of experiences which were wrongly though plausibly classified as observational are to be reclassified as phenomenal. What matters is that phenomenal predicates should not be observational. They clearly need not be; for example, the predicate 'the same in phenomenal character as one of Savonarola's experiences' is phenomenal but not observational. More needs to be said about the failure of a predicate such as 'painful' to be observational; it will be said in section 6.3. The notion of a phenomenal predicate first requires some exploration.

It seems to be 'part of the meaning' of a predicate such as 'painful' that it should be phenomenal. Nothing beyond the phenomenal character of an experience makes it painful or otherwise; if one has no grasp of that, one does not fully understand the word 'painful'. One might therefore expect it to be *uncontroversially* phenomenal in the sense of the previous chapter. That is, (6.2) should be uncontroversially true when F is read as 'painful'; it should come out true whatever admissible interpretation (maximal M-relation) is given to $ox = oy$. On one view, identity in character is one of these relations, but we do not know which; on another, the concept of identity in character is indeterminate between these relations. Thus the requirement is either that (6.2) should be true within our ken or that it should be determinately true. Whichever view is taken, the requirement looks reasonable. It acts as a constraint on the interpretation of phenomenal predicates in a way that will now be unfolded.

At first sight the uncontroversial truth of (6.2) seems to revive the argument for (6.1), and thereby the paradoxes. For suppose that x matches y. By (5.5) it follows that there is an admissible interpretation of $ox = oy$ on which it is true. Since (6.2) is uncontroversially true, it is true on that interpretation. Thus one can detach the consequent $Fx \leftrightarrow Fy$. So if x matches y, Fx is equivalent to Fy, which is just what (6.1) says. What has gone wrong?

The argument is valid on one condition: that the extension of F does not vary from one admissible interpretation to another. Otherwise $Fx \leftrightarrow Fy$ might be false on some interpretation other than the ones which make $ox = oy$ true; (6.1) would fail on that interpretation. Consider a sequence $x_1 \ldots, x_n$, where Fx_1 is uncontroversially true, Fx_n is uncontroversially false and x_i always matches x_{i+1}. For each biconditional $Fx_i \leftrightarrow Fx_{i+1}$ there is an admissible interpretation on which it is true, but there is no admissible interpretation on which all the biconditionals are true, because $Fx_1 \leftrightarrow Fx_n$ is false on every admissible interpretation and is entailed by the conjunction of the biconditionals. If one takes the biconditionals as the premises of a sorites argument, no premise is uncontroversially false – which helps to explain the argument's appeal – but the conjunction of the premises is uncontroversially false. It is a familiar fact about supervaluations that they can make a conjunction false without making either conjunct false; for example, P & $\sim P$ is false on a supervaluation even if P is true on some valuations and false on others, so that neither P nor $\sim P$ is false on the supervaluation. The account of the sorites paradox in terms of uncontroversial falsehood exploits and relabels that fact.

The moral of the fallacy in the penultimate paragraph is that most uncontroversially phenomenal predicates vary in extension from one admissible interpretation to another.[5] When such a predicate is monadic, for instance, its extension is the union of some equivalence classes of the relation which interprets identity in phenomenal character ($ox = oy$); since these classes vary from interpretation to interpretation, the extension of the predicate varies correspondingly. An experience in the extension of a phenomenal predicate, on some but not all admissible variations, is a *borderline case* for that predicate. On one view, the variation simply means that our ignorance of the extension of identity in character goes with ignorance of the extension of phenomenal predicates; on another view, indeterminacy in the former goes with indeterminacy in the latter. This divergence is reflected in accounts of the sorites paradox: on the ignorance view, some biconditional $Fx_i \leftrightarrow Fx_{i+1}$ is false, but we cannot know which; on the indeterminacy view, some biconditional is indeterminate in truth value. The last section of the chapter will return to this choice of view.

Not every predicate of experiences is a phenomenal predicate, of course. The binary predicate 'matches' is an example: uncontroversially there will be matching experiences u and v which differ in character; by (5.1b) some experience with the same character as u will not match some experience with the same character as v, which falsifies the appropriate instance of (6.2+). However, any predicate of experiences can be 'phenomenalized'. The *inner phenomenalization* F^I of an n-adic predicate F applies to some experiences just in case F applies to all experiences with the same character; in symbols:

$$(6.4) \quad \forall x_1 \ldots \forall x_n (F^I x_1 \ldots x_n \leftrightarrow$$
$$\forall y_1 \ldots \forall y_n ((ox_1 = oy_1 \& \ldots \& ox_n = oy_n) \rightarrow F y_1 \ldots y_n))$$

If F is monadic, F^I is the union of all equivalence classes of identity in character wholly contained in the extension of F. The *outer phenomenalization* F^O of F applies to some experiences just in case F applies to some experiences with the same character; in symbols:

$$(6.5) \quad \forall x_1 \ldots \forall x_n (F^O x_1 \ldots x_n \leftrightarrow$$
$$\exists y_1 \ldots \exists y_n (ox_1 = oy_1 \& \ldots \& ox_n = oy_n \& F y_1 \ldots y_n))$$

If F is monadic, F^O is the union of all equivalence classes of identity in character not wholly excluded from the extension of F. Inner and outer phenomenalizations are dual operations, in the sense that F^I is equivalent to $\sim((\sim F)^O)$ and F^O to $\sim((\sim F)^I)$.

Both inner and outer phenomenalizations are evidently phenomenal predicates, and admissible interpretations of each will vary with admissible interpretations of identity in character, in a way the definitions make explicit. F^I is the best approximation to F by a phenomenal predicate which F contains; F^O is the best approximation to F by a phenomenal predicate which contains F. If F is itself phenomenal, both F^I and F^O are therefore simply F itself. These operations can be used to build up a stock of phenomenal predicates. For example, suppose that we wish to use experiences with a feature F as *paradigms* for a phenomenal predicate; one such predicate would be the outer phenomenalization of F. If we wish to use experiences which lack F as counter-paradigms of a phenomenal predicate – as paradigms of its non-application – then one such predicate would be the inner phenomenalization of F.

A positive account of phenomenal predicates is now in place, on which they need not be observational. However, more needs to be said about the failure of a predicate such as 'painful' to be observational. The next section will begin by considering a further danger of paradox in the use we make of such predicates.

The defusion of this threat leads to an account of their non-observationality.

6.3   The Failure of Observationality

We use words like 'painful' fluently. We apply them without hesitation, calculation or special props. Could such a use be sensitive to indiscriminable differences? If not, new sorites arguments threaten.[6]

We can remember what 'painful' means. We use it on the basis of that memory. Our use cannot involve any difference too slight to be remembered. But how can we remember an indiscriminable difference?

The argument will be easier to follow in schematic form. Suppose that certain experiences (perhaps identified by their causes) are paradigms for the predicate F. Speakers cannot cause new paradigms to occur at will; they are expected – reasonably enough – to remember old ones. A speaker S is prepared to ascribe F to an experience x just in case x matches some paradigm of F – that is, just in case, for S, x is indiscriminable in phenomenal character from some paradigm. Let x and y be matching experiences for S. Suppose that S is prepared to ascribe F to x. For S, then, x matches some paradigm z of F. It may now be claimed that the most perfect memory of z can give no further information than that it felt just like x. In judging whether something is F, S is therefore in no *better* a position if S uses S's memory of z than if S uses x itself as a paradigm. Since S is prepared to ascribe F to anything which matches a paradigm of F, S should be prepared to ascribe F to y, which matches x, the grounds for ascription in this case being as good as memory can provide. Thus a reasonable speaker prepared to ascribe F to one of two matching experiences is prepared to ascribe it to the other. But then if S is reasonable the predicate 'S is prepared to ascribe F to x' succumbs to a sorites paradox; it satisfies (6.1) in place of Fx.

Fortunately, the argument from memory is flawed. It assumes that the information content of the memory of the paradigm z is exhausted by the propositional knowledge that it felt just like x – given the way x feels (one might remember that two experiences felt exactly the same without remembering what either of them felt like); but – one might say – the memory only feels as though its information content were exhausted by its feeling just like x. Suppose that matching experiences x and y occur immediately after the paradigm z, and that x but not y matches z (matching is non-transitive). A reasonable subject will ascribe F to x and withhold it from y, given that y does not match any paradigm of F other than z. A feature of z beyond its feeling just like x is operative here; after what lapse of time does the *a priori* argument take over to show that such features are no longer operative?

The use of the term F does not require speakers to remember the difference between two matching experiences as such; it merely requires their memory of one – in analogue form – to differ (indiscriminably) from a memory of the other – also in analogue form. Why should this requirement not be met? It might be replied that speakers would be open to indiscriminable changes in their memories of the paradigm, but only a sceptic should regard that point as a damaging one. Our language can function quite adequately if the neurophysiology of the brain ensures that our memory impressions do in fact enjoy a certain stability. It is not necessary, just as it is not possible, for an impression to carry a guarantee of this on its face.

If the argument from memory were sound, it would tell equally against ostensively explained predicates of material objects. Speakers remember the paradigms; they do not carry them around. Wittgenstein often insisted that a mental paradigm cannot do *more* than a physical one, but the argument from memory asks us to accept that it cannot even do *as much*. For if speakers did carry a paradigm around with them, they could use it to ascertain which of two indiscriminable objects satisfied a predicate, where one but not the other of them was discriminable from the paradigm. One's memory of the paradigm cannot be shown *a priori* to be so bad – so much worse than present perception – as to be incapable of functioning in the same way. The argument fails for predicates of material objects; it fails equally for predicates of experience.

The same thoughts undermine a different attempt to revive the sorites, by an appeal to utility. It is useful for our language to have predicates by means of which we can classify things *unreflectively*, on the basis of casual observation. In particular, we may need to be able to cry out that we are in pain without going through elaborate and time-consuming cogitation. On such a basis, it might be argued, we could not classify two matching experiences differently with respect to a predicate such as 'painful'. However, it was seen that a reasonable speaker might ascribe a predicate to just those experiences matching one of its paradigms, and might thereby ascribe it to one experience and withhold it from a matching one. Predicates of natural language do not depend on paradigms in so crude a way, but the argument from utility can draw no comfort from that fact, since its strength is supposed to lie in the crudeness of our use. Our more sophisticated recognitional capacities do not commit us to ascribing 'painful' to both or neither of two matching experiences; nor does the thought that 'painful' is a phenomenal predicate. To have called one experience 'painful' may be a reason for calling the other so too, but it is a reason which may be overridden by other considerations.

Suppose that I am given a series of electric shocks of imperceptibly decreasing severity. After each I am asked 'Was it painful?'. When I give an answer, I know it to be correct. I answer 'Yes' to the first question and 'No' to the last. Of the questions to which I answer 'Yes', there is a last one. I assent to the description 'painful' for the experience of that shock, and do not assent to it for the matching experience of the next shock. I have not broken a rule of language, or acted unreasonably. What would be unreasonable would be the reply 'Yes' to one question and 'No' to the next, but that is not what I say. The last 'Yes' is followed by 'I'm not quite sure'.

The utility of unreflective application is quite consistent with the existence of a band of uncertainty, and may even require it. Utility requires only that there should be a broad spectrum of cases in which unreflective application is possible. There is no argument from utility to observationality.

For phenomenal predicates, a band of uncertainty was predictable, since experiences may be neither uncontroversially the same nor uncontroversially different in phenomenal character. The last experience to prompt 'Yes' and the first to prompt 'I'm not quite sure' have the same character if one maximal M-relation is the criterion, but not if another is. On the former criterion, the phenomenality of 'painful' makes it true of both or neither; on the latter, it does not. Whether this is the only source of uncertainty, and whether it is a matter of ignorance or indeterminacy, are further questions.

Sorites paradoxes have been discussed in this chapter only for phenomenal predicates. Many sorites paradoxes do not involve such predicates. How many grain makes a heap? How many inches tall is the least tall tall person? How many natural numbers are small? In examples of this kind, each step of the sorites makes a noticeable difference, but one which seems not large enough to be the difference between the application and non-application of the predicate. The present approach might be undermined if it does not generalize to such cases, but confirmed if it does.

The general approach consists in the use of supervaluations to handle terms whose extension is subject to ignorance or indeterminacy. That idea can be extended to all sorites paradoxes, whatever its other merits or demerits.

The specific approach consists in the use of maximal M-relations. At first sight it does not generalize. The paradox of small numbers seems to have nothing to do with the non-transitivity of indiscriminability (any two natural numbers are discriminable). That impression is a mistake. Just as the paradox of painful experiences concerned the indiscriminability not of experiences but of their phenomenal characters (and of the painfulness which supervenes on the latter), so the paradox of small numbers concerns the indiscriminability not of numbers but of their smallnesses, where two numbers have the same smallness just in case either both are small or neither is. Just as successive experiences in the series were indiscriminable in character, so n and $n+1$ are indiscriminable in smallness. We cannot activate the knowledge that they are distinct in smallness, for in effect that would require us to know that n is small and $n+1$ is not small. Nevertheless, zero and a trillion are discriminable in smallness. For an appropriately colloquial sense of 'small', we are reluctant to allow for hidden facts about which natural numbers are small, so there is pressure to equate indiscriminability and identity for smallnesses; the latter can be regarded as qualities of a subjective kind. The arguments of this chapter and the previous two therefore have parallels for the paradox of small numbers. If M is the non-transitive relation on numbers of indiscriminability in smallness, the equivalence relation of having the same smallness would then be a maximal M-relation. In place of the Minimality Constraint, one can use a special constraint dictated by the sense of 'small': if $n+1$ is small then n is small. The only partitions of the natural numbers to be considered will therefore have the form $\{\{0,\ldots, n\}, \{n+1, n+2,\ldots\}\}$. The upshot is an orthodox supervaluational treatment of the paradox of small numbers. Other cases can be handled by a similar trick; details are left to the interested reader. The apparatus of maximal M-relations can thus be generalized: but its full complexity is required only for examples with a richer structure, as in the case of phenomenal predicates.

The preceding account has been neutral between the claims of ignorance and indeterminacy as sources of paradox. Although the rest of the book does not depend on an adjudication between them, the final section makes some remarks towards one. It suggests that both can generate a paradox; the allocation of blame in a particular case depends on one's view of the underlying metaphysics.

6.4   Sorites Arguments and Necessary Ignorance

Some true propositions cannot be known to be true. Either 'The number of books in TW's room on 1 July 1989 is even and no one will ever know that it is' or 'The number of books in TW's room on 1 July 1989 is odd and no one will ever know that it is' expresses an example.[7] It is in some ways an attractive suggestion that sorites paradoxes turn on unknowably true propositions giving the whereabouts of a cut-off point. Such a view has been defended by James Cargile (1969, 1979 pp. 108–13) and Roy Sorensen (1988 pp. 239–46).

Let $x_1,\ldots, x_n$ be a sorites series for the predicate F: x_1 is clearly F, x_n is clearly not F, and for no value of i is there any reason to assert that x_i is F while x_{i+1} is not. The idea is that some proposition of the form 'x_i is F and x_{i+1} is not F' is true, but cannot be known to be true. We can know that some such proposition is true, but we cannot know which it is. Because of our tendency to assume that true propositions are knowable, we are tempted to infer from the fact that no proposition of the form 'x_i is F and x_{i+1} is not F' is knowable that no such proposition is true – hence the paradox. One advantage of this account is that it involves no interference with classical logic or semantics whatsoever.

Just about any vague predicate gives rise to a sorites series. The suggestion is therefore that vagueness is a matter of necessary ignorance rather than of semantic indeterminacy. We may follow Sorensen in calling this *the epistemic theory of vagueness*.

Sorensen claims that resistance to the epistemic theory of vagueness 'can only be motivated by a prior resolve to allow no unknowable truths' (1988 p. 245). That is not the case. One can be happy to accept the existence of unknowably true propositions in general, while being unable to see how they could include a proposition of the form 'A novel i words long is a short novel but a novel i+1 words long is not a short novel'. For if such a proposition is true, what is the *obstacle* to our knowing it to be true? In the case of examples like 'The number of books in TW's room on 1 July 1989 is even and no one will ever know that it is', the obstacle lies in the structure of the proposition. In other cases, our ability to refer to natural kinds without knowing their real essences may enable us to formulate unknowably true propositions. Neither of these factors is useful in dissolving sorites paradoxes. Some propositions with the structure 'x_i is F and x_{i+1} is not F' can be known to be true, and 'short novel' is not a natural kind term. Nor would the provision of complete statistics about the length of every novel ever published make much difference. The problem is not that different speakers have different speech dispositions; it would arise even if they did not (and knew it). We are not ignorant of the meaning of the term 'a short novel'; we know that it means a short novel. If one cannot find any barrier to knowledge of a proposition, it is not unreasonable to conclude that it falls outside the class of unknowable truths.

However, one line of thought may rescue the epistemic theory of vagueness. Consider again the sorites series $x_1, \ldots, x_n$ for the vague predicate F. In order to know a proposition, one must at least be reliably right about it. Thus knowing that x_i is F entails being reliably right in taking x_i to be F. The main idea is that reliability here involves a certain *margin for error*. One has a margin for error in taking x_i to be F only if things sufficiently close to x_i are also F (where the appropriate dimension of closeness depends on F). The intervals in a sorites series are in effect chosen to make successive members sufficiently close. So one has a margin for error in taking x_i to be F only if x_{i-1} and x_{i+1} are F. Putting the pieces together, one has the following principle about the series (for all i):

(6.6)   If x_i is known to be F then x_{i+1} is F.

It can be used to explain the difficulty of knowing the conjunction: 'x_i is F and x_{i+1} is not F'. In knowing the conjunction, one knows its first conjunct.[8] By (6.6), if one knows the first conjunct then the second conjunct is false. If the second conjunct is false, the whole conjunction is and is therefore not known (knowledge entails truth). Thus (6.6) rules out knowledge of the conjunction.

    (6.6) should not be confused with two other principles: 'If x_i is F then x_{i+1} is F' and 'If x_i is known to be F then x_{i+1} is known to be F'. Both of these validate sorites arguments to false conclusions, the former to 'If x_1 is F then x_n is F' and the latter to 'If x_1 is known to be F then x_n is known to be F'. (6.6) generates no such conclusion, for the predicate of x_i in its antecedent differs from the predicate of x_{i+1} in its consequent.[9]

    On this account, the difficulty in knowing 'x_i is F and x_{i+1} is not F' closely resembles the difficulty in knowing 'The number of books in TW's room on 1 July 1989 is even and no-one will ever know that it is'. In both cases, knowledge of the first conjunct is incompatible with the truth of the second. In the latter case, the incompatibility is a matter of logic; in the former, it follows from the margin for error principle, given the circumstances.

    In order to uphold (6.6), it is not enough to point out that x_i and x_{i+1} are indiscriminable in respect of F. I can know that this glass ($= x_i$) contains H_2O, even if I could not discriminate it from a glass ($= x_{i+1}$) full of XYZ, provided that the latter is far away on Twin Earth. The point is rather that sorites paradoxes are so arranged as to ensure the truth of (6.6). But why is that possible for some predicates and not for others?

    The key to the account is the claim that reliability in applying a vague predicate involves a margin for error. It needs to be examined more carefully. Since $x_1, \ldots, x_n$ is a sorites series, there are several values of i for which it is neither part of standard practice to take x_i to be F nor part of standard practice to take x_i not to be F; such an x_i is a hard case. Suppose that x_i is F but that x_{i+1} is not; it may be assumed that both x_i and x_{i+1} are hard cases.

What is to stop me from finding out that x_i is F? If I take x_i to be F, it is no part of standard practice to do so, but it does not follow that I am using 'F' with a new extension (otherwise the defence of (6.6) would be easier than it actually is); I might simply be making a discovery. What determines the extension of 'F' is the standard practice in its context; theoretical standards or explicit rulings are not there to help in the respects in which it is vague. If the standard practice with 'F' had been slightly different, its extension would have been slightly different; for example, it might have included x_{i-1} but not x_i. But standard practice with a vague predicate 'F' could very easily have been different in that way; only a small shift in speech dispositions along the relevant dimension is needed. Moreover, if standard practice had been different in that way, I might still have applied 'F' to x_i, for my doing so is no part of standard practice. But then I would have been in error, for x_i falls outside the extension 'F' would have had in those circumstances. It may not even be necessary to invoke counterfactual circumstances, for the extension of most vague predicates is constantly shifting with change of context. In any case, my actual application of 'F' to x_i is unreliable; my taking x_i to be F does not manifest a reliable disposition to get things right – which is just what is needed to support (6.6). Vagueness is a matter of our unreliability in locating arbitrarily and tacitly drawn lines.

The argument just given is far from watertight. It does not rule out the possibility that my application of 'F' to x_i, although no part of standard practice, is so sensitive to it that it would not have occurred if standard practice had differed in the envisaged way. However, there is no need for the argument to explain the absolute impossibility of knowledge that x_i is F and x_{i+1} is not, for it is not a datum that such knowledge is absolutely impossible. The datum is that we have no idea how to obtain such knowledge; since we have no idea how to make applications of 'F' beyond the standard practice sensitive to that practice to the required degree, the argument explains all that it needs to explain.

Precious little has been said about the way in which standard practice determines extension for vague predicates. That is not an objection to the argument. For precious little is understood about that determination even in the non-borderline cases. A standard practice of applying 'F' to x is not in general sufficient for x to be F; why should it be necessary? We have little to gain from the suggestion that speakers would not have bothered to lay down a precise line between 'painful' and 'not painful' when we lack a clear sense in which they have 'bothered' to lay down a vague line between them. No extant theory of the relation between standard practice and extension provides a sound basis for dismissing the possibility that standard practice with vague predicates determines precise extensions.

One can have an epistemic theory of vagueness without holding that all vague predicates are semantically determinate. Indeed, it is hard to deny that semantic indeterminacy can occur. I might introduce the term 'dommal' by making only the following stipulations: (a) all dogs are dommals; (b) all dommals are mammals. Surely 'dommal' is semantically indeterminate; the sentence 'All cats are dommals' lacks a truth-value. If words introduced by stipulation can suffer this kind of indeterminacy, why not other words? At least some vague predicates may be subject to this kind of indeterminacy. The point behind the epistemic theory is that such indeterminacy is not the root of all vagueness.

Consider a series of colour samples running from red to yellow, each indiscriminable to the naked eye from the next. Suppose that the problem in applying the term 'red' to some of these samples is not essentially one of ignorance. It presumably follows that there could be a speaker of English who knew every fact relevant to this problem and meant what we mean by 'red'. We could talk to this speaker. She may be assumed to be truthful and informative. Of each sample, we could ask her 'Is it red?'. To the first question she would answer 'Yes', to the last 'No'. Uncertainty would never cause her to hesitate; she would never answer 'I don't know'. To some questions she might answer neither 'Yes' nor 'No'. Nevertheless, there would be a last question to which she answered 'Yes', and a first to which she answered 'No'. Given her omniscience and her use of 'red' in our sense, these points would reveal unexpected sharp boundaries in the correct application of our word 'red'. If 'red' is semantically determinate, it has only one such boundary. If it is semantically indeterminate, it has several. That issue seems to be a subsidiary one. When ignorance is removed, sharp boundaries emerge.[10]

Once the existence of hidden sharp boundaries is acknowledged, there is less need to find vague predicates indeterminate. Moreover, justice can be done to such indeterminacy as remains by means of supervaluational techniques. The main objection to them is that they presuppose sharp second-order boundaries, such as that between the determinately true and the not determinately true. Such boundaries have been seen to exist; they are manifest in the speech of our omniscient interlocutor.

Perhaps sharp boundaries for 'red' could not emerge. If so, that is not because the removal of ignorance is insufficient to enable them to emerge, but because the removal of ignorance is impossible – which is the point of the epistemic theory of vagueness.

Ignorance can generate a sorites paradox: but so can indeterminacy. None of the foregoing remarks goes any way towards showing the expression 'same in phenomenal character' to be referentially determinate. If it is not, phenomenal predicates such as 'painful' will be referentially indeterminate too, for reasons explained in section 6.2. On some views, phenomenal characters are explanatorily and ontologically basic properties; we can refer to them as we can refer to other natural kinds, with no special problems of indeterminacy. On other views, phenomenal characters must be reduced to physical properties; since different maximal M-relations lead to different but equally good reductions, indeterminacy is inevitable. The paradoxes of phenomenal character can arise on either view. The choice between them (and many other views) depends in part on the metaphysics of mind and body. In the case of other sorites paradoxes, the choice between ignorance and indeterminacy as culprits will be equally sensitive to metaphysical issues. No doubt some paradoxes are caused by ignorance, some by indeterminacy, and many by both. Fortunately, the notion of uncontroversial truth was introduced to allow the use of maximal M-relations in all those cases.

7
Generalizations

Much of the argument in preceding chapters has been visibly formal. The formulae were read as about experiences, discrimination and phenomenal character, but that was not required for the validity of the inferences. Generalizations therefore come readily, prescinding from that interpretation. What need to be found are generalizations with worthwhile instances, beyond those already considered. This chapter makes a start with both tasks. Section 7.1 abstracts a formal schema from the preceding discussion: when a supposed criterion of identity M for objects of some kind turns out to be non-transitive, but is still held to be a necessary condition, the best approximation to the original criterion is a maximal M-relation. Section 7.2 applies the schema to operationally defined quantities, species, and non-Cantorian cardinal numbers; section 7.3 applies it in more detail to persons. Section 7.4 considers the case in which M is held to be a sufficient condition rather than a necessary one. Section 7.5 analyses the relevant concept of a best approximation.

7.1 Maximal M-Relations as Minimal Revisions

There is a conception of phenomenal character on which it is shared by experiences just in case they match:

(7.1) $\forall x \forall y(ox = oy \leftrightarrow Mxy)$

The conception cannot be wholly correct as it stands, for sameness in phenomenal character is what matching turns out not to be, a transitive relation. However, it may also not be wholly incorrect.

A first move is the decomposition of (7.1) into the claim that

Identity and Discrimination: Reissued and Updated Edition. Timothy Williamson.
© 2013 Timothy Williamson. Published 2013 by Blackwell Publishing Ltd.

matching is necessary for sameness in phenomenal character and the claim that it is sufficient:

(7.2) $\forall x \forall y (ox = oy \rightarrow Mxy)$

(7.3) $\forall x \forall y (Mxy \rightarrow ox = oy)$

The non-transitivity of matching shows (7.2) and (7.3) not to be both true, but it does not show them both to be false. Indeed, critical reflection suggested that matching is necessary, and therefore not sufficient, for sameness in phenomenal character. One half of the original conception was saved at the expense of the other. (7.2) is true and (7.3) false; but more of (7.3) was preserved in earlier chapters than that remark suggests. For while (7.2) was wholly accepted, (7.3) was not wholly rejected.

In the terminology of previous chapters, (7.2) makes sameness in phenomenal character an M-relation: an equivalence relation included in matching. It was argued that sameness in phenomenal character is in fact a maximal M-relation: an M-relation which includes any M-relation in which it is included. This account concedes as much of (7.3) as is consistent with conceding all of (7.2), given the purely logical requirement that sameness in phenomenal character be an equivalence relation, inheriting its reflexivity, symmetry and transitivity from the corresponding features of identity. To describe sameness in phenomenal character as a maximal M-relation is to make it an equivalence relation for which matching is necessary and – given that – as nearly as possible one for which it is sufficient.

The point can be argued as follows. (a) If E is a maximal M-relation then it is an equivalence relation for which matching is necessary and – given that – as nearly as possible one for which it is sufficient. For any M-relation is an equivalence relation for which matching is necessary; what needs to be shown is that E is as nearly as possible one for which it is sufficient. If it were not, there would be an equivalence relation F for which matching was necessary and more nearly sufficient than for E. Could that occur? If F includes E, E includes F because E is a maximal M-relation and F an M-relation; thus E and F are equivalent, and matching cannot be more nearly sufficient for one than for the other. If F

does not include E, there can be experiences x and y related by E but not by F; since E is an M-relation, x matches y, so the sufficiency of matching fails in this case for F but not for E; in no clear sense would matching be more nearly sufficient for F than for E. Thus no such relation F exists. (b) Conversely, if E is an equivalence relation for which matching is necessary and – given that – as nearly as possible one for which it is sufficient then E is a maximal M-relation. For the necessity of matching makes E an M-relation; it is maximal because it would otherwise not include some M-relation F in which it was included – but then F would be an equivalence relation for which matching was necessary and more nearly sufficient than for E, contrary to hypothesis.

On the account of sameness in phenomenal character as a maximal M-relation, a good sense has been provided in which the original conception (7.1) is as near to the truth as *it* possibly could have been – that is, in which the truth comes as near as possible to (7.1). The main point here does not depend on the correctness of the account: it is that, given the non-transitivity of matching and the priority of the left-to-right over the right-to-left direction of (7.1), (7.1) is as nearly true as it could be if and only if sameness in phenomenal character is a maximal M-relation. Whether (7.1) *is* as nearly true as it could be is a different question. What has been identified is thus the natural fall-back position from (7.1), the minimum revision needed to overcome the non-transitivity problem. But the argument for this connection between maximal M-relations and the failure of (7.1) does not essentially rely on the interpretation of 'M' as matching; it is therefore open to generalization.

Suppose that there is a conception of entities of some kind on which a necessary and sufficient condition for their identity is a relation M, which turns out not to be transitive. Suppose also that critical reflection gives priority to the necessity of M over its sufficiency. Then the original conception is as nearly true as it could be, given the non-transitivity of M, if and only if sameness in the relevant respect is a maximal M-relation. The natural fallback position from the original conception, the minimum revision needed to overcome the non-transitivity problem, is an account of sameness in the relevant respect as a maximal M-relation. One may either accept such an account, concluding that the original conception is as nearly true as it could be, given the non-transitivity of M, or reject the account, concluding that there is more wrong with the original conception than the non-transitivity problem reveals. What we have is a technique for surgically removing a certain kind of false consequence from theories of the form (7.1) with minimum mutilation; such an operation cannot be guaranteed to cure all ailments.

The generalization applies to theories of the form (7.1), but more needs to be said about what that form is. For (7.1) is rich in logical structure. It requires a domain of entities over which the relation M is to be defined and the variables 'x' and 'y' can range, but these entities are to be mapped into a possibly distinct domain by the function o. On the original reading the domains are indeed distinct; the former contains experiences (tokens), the latter phenomenal characters (types). It is the values of o, not its arguments, whose identity is at issue. In what follows the values of o will simply be called *objects* and its arguments *locations*; o maps a location to the object *at* that location.[1] This terminology is not intended to have spatial implications; the object at a location might be the phenomenal character of an experience. Equally, objects need not stand to locations as types to tokens. 'Location' and 'object' are schematic variables, fully interpreted only with respect to a particular reading of (7.1). If the objects at locations x and y are identical ($ox = oy$), x and y will be said to *present the same object*. The relation of presenting the same object generalizes sameness in phenomenal character; it is of course an equivalence relation, but an equivalence relation between locations rather than objects, and it is not that of identity (except in the very special case where o is a one-one function).

Why should discussion of the identity of objects involve locations at all? Questions of identity arise because the same object can be presented in different ways. The apparatus of locations is a means of being explicit about these differences. However, that is not the whole story, for not all modes of presentation are relevant. The issues discussed under the rubric 'the identity of artifacts', for instance, seem to be more directly raised by the question 'Is the ship made of these planks the ship that was made of those ones?' than by the question 'Is the tallest ship the longest ship?'. It looks as though some notion of a *canonical* mode of presentation of an object is at work, but it is hard to explain such a notion clearly. The final chapter will return to these issues.

The general form of (7.1) is the claim that locations present the same object just in case they are M-related. When M turns out not to be transitive, and (7.2) is given priority over (7.3), the minimum mutilation of (7.1) will be an account of presenting the same object as a maximal M-relation.

Earlier mathematical results about maximal M-relations in no way depend on the interpretation of 'M' as matching. Thus the Axiom of Choice entails quite generally that there is at least one maximal M-relation, and that since M is non-transitive there are at least two (M will be assumed to be reflexive and symmetric). The plurality of maximal M-relations will present many of the problems that it did in the case of phenomenal character. Does it make for indeterminacy in the reference of 'presenting the same object', and of 'object' itself? If – as some theories suggest – the reference of these terms is determined by what best fits our basic beliefs in which they figure, and the relevant beliefs boil down to the conception (7.1), then their reference may indeed be indeterminate between different maximal M-relations. On other views their reference will be determinate, and the account of presenting the same object merely incomplete – there is more truth to be told.

Either of the above views allows a notion of uncontroversial truth value to be defined, where (roughly speaking) a sentence has a given truth value uncontroversially just in case it has that truth value whichever maximal M-relation is used to interpret 'presenting the same object'. The sentence 'These locations present the same object' proves as before to be uncontroversially false if and only if the locations referred to are not M-related. This point provides an account of the sorites paradox embryonic in any non-transitivity of M. If M relates x to y and y to z but not x to z, then by (7.1) x presents the same object as y and y presents the same object as z but x does not present the same object as z – which is incoherent, since each location presents only one object. It turns out that x has some maximal M-relation to y and y has some maximal M-relation to z but x has no maximal M-relation to z; thus it is uncontroversially false that x presents the same object as z but neither uncontroversially false that x presents the same object as y nor uncontroversially false that y presents the same object as z.

As before, formal constraints such as Minimality can be used to reduce but not wholly eliminate the variety of maximal M-relations.

However, the meaning of this variety depends on the particular kind of objects and locations at issue. More examples are needed.

7.2   Examples

Previous chapters discussed the case of phenomenal characters. The problem arose because they are supposed to be a subjective kind, for which identity and indiscriminability coincide. An obvious generalization is thus to other subjective kinds, to which many secondary qualities may belong. For instance, one might take locations to be material things, the object at a location as the specific shade of colour of that material thing, and the relation M as the impossibility of direct discrimination in colour by the naked eye (matching). (7.1) would then be read as the tempting claim that material things have the same shade of colour just in case they match. Alternatively, one could relativize a material thing's shade of colour to a perceiver, point of view, time, lighting conditions or the like by taking a location as an ordered pair of a material object and an appropriate index. In either case matching threatens to be non-transitive, and is harder to give up as a necessary condition for sameness of shade than as a sufficient one. From here the discussion might proceed on lines parallel to those of the earlier one.

Other examples of subjective kinds may be found in operationally defined physical quantities, which are to be measured by instruments of limited precision: these kinds are supposed to be subjective in the sense that such quantities are identical if and only if they are indiscriminable by means of the relevant instruments. One material thing has the relation M to another just in case they cannot be discriminated by these means in respect of the relevant quantity. Limited precision will make M a non-transitive relation: think, for instance, of balancing on a given pair of scales as a condition for sameness of operationalist weight (Suppes 1969 pp. 44–5). As before, such a relation is harder to give up as a necessary condition for sameness than as a sufficient one. However, it will be more interesting to look at examples in which the relation M is not one of indiscriminability at all.

One standard definition of a species is as a group 'of actually or potentially interbreeding natural populations reproductively isolated from other such groups'. Cases are known of a synchronic sequence of natural populations, where each population is geographically adjacent to the next and actually or potentially interbreeds with it, but where the first and the last populations in the sequence do not actually or potentially interbreed; the distribution may even be circular, so that the first and the last are geographically adjacent (Minkoff 1983, pp. 251–4). Actual or potential interbreeding is a reflexive, symmetric but non-transitive relation on natural populations. Such cases cause considerable problems for the practice of classification into species. They exemplify the problem schema of the previous section if one takes locations as natural populations, the object at a location as the species to which that natural population belongs and the relation M as actual or potential interbreeding. The quoted definition of a species seems to imply that natural populations belong to the same species if and only if they actually or potentially interbreed, the appropriate reading of (7.1). Given this principle, cases of the kind described generate a sorites paradox for species: the principle rules that the species to which any given member of the sequence belongs is the same as the species to which the next member belongs, but that the species to which the first member belongs is not the species to which the last member belongs.

If one sticks to the necessity of actual or potential interbreeding for sameness of species (as not all taxonomic systems do), and therefore gives up its sufficiency, the minimum mutilation of the concept of a species is the view that belonging to the same species is a maximal M-relation on natural populations. If one is determined – perhaps on pragmatic grounds – to classify natural populations into as few species as possible, short of classifying together populations incapable of interbreeding, then what one needs is a maximal M-relation which satisfies the Minimality Constraint (it has no more equivalence classes than any maximal M-relation has); such a relation has been proved to exist. It seems plausible here that the plurality of maximal M-relations reflects some indeterminacy in our concept of a species, rather than our ignorance of the true boundaries in nature.[2]

A more frivolous example involves the attempt to construct a non-Cantorian concept of cardinality for sets, on which every set has more members than any of its proper subsets (compare section

21 of Bolzano 1851). On the now orthodox view, sets have the same number of members just in case they can be put in one-one correspondence, which allows an infinite set (such as the integers) to have the same number of members as one of its proper subsets (such as the even integers). This result violated a naive intuition to the effect that the part cannot be equal in size to the whole. One might try to develop a concept of cardinality in harmony with that intuition. If the result is to be of the same generality as the orthodox concept, no particular mathematical structure should be presupposed in the sets to be numbered. A first try would be to say that sets x and y have the same non-Cantorian cardinality just in case the members of x which are not in y can be put in one-one correspondence with the members of y which are not in x. If that relation is M, locations are sets and the object at a location is the non-Cantorian cardinality of that set, we have an instance of (7.1). However, although M is reflexive and symmetric, it is not transitive; the even integers have M to the odd integers, and the odd integers have M to the integers divisible by 4, but the even integers do not have M to the integers divisible by 4. If M were taken as sufficient for sameness of cardinality, we should still have the result, which we were trying to avoid, that there are no more even integers than integers divisible by 4. Rather, M should be taken as necessary but not sufficient for sameness of non-Cantorian cardinality. The minimal mutilation of the original proposal would then have sameness of non-Cantorian cardinality as a maximal M-relation. The plurality of maximal M-relations shows the non-Cantorian concept to be in need of further determination. Even if that could be supplied, there is of course no prospect that the result would be anything like as useful as the orthodox concept.

7.3   Necessary Conditions for Personal Identity

This section is not an attempt to develop a theory of personal identity. Its aim is to use the concept of a maximal M-relation to discover one kind of pattern in arguments about personal identity. For the sake of generality, theories and examples will be characterized in a deliberately schematic way. None of them is endorsed, except for the sake of argument.

The best-known examples of the non-transitivity problem concern personal identity. Many accounts find it hard to accommodate the conceptual possibility that people might undergo certain
kinds of fission or fusion, as illustrated in thought-experiments about
amoeba-like behaviour, teletransportation and the separating and
transplanting of the brain's two hemispheres. Personal identity has
been equated with various kinds of physical and/or psychological
connectedness and/or continuity which would obtain between the pre-
fission person and each of the post-fission people but not between one
post-fission person and another, or between the post-fusion person
and each of the pre-fusion people but not between one pre-fusion
person and another. Such a relation may be necessarily reflexive and
symmetric; it is transitive in all ordinary circumstances, but not with
respect to these conceptual possibilities; it cannot therefore be conceptually both necessary and sufficient for personal identity.[3] It is in
fact clear that such a relation cannot be sufficient for personal identity, for otherwise the post-fission (or pre-fusion) people would be
identical with each other, since all would satisfy a sufficient condition
for identity with the pre-fission (or post-fusion) person and identity is
an equivalence relation: but this is a grossly counter-intuitive result in
itself, even if the relation were not a universally necessary condition
of personal identity. Once the claim of sufficiency is withdrawn, the
cases of fission or fusion present no obstacle to the claim of necessity,
and some of the considerations which motivated the original account
can no doubt be marshalled in its favour. The minimum revision of
that account to accommodate the problem cases therefore seems to
be the view that personal identity is a maximal M-relation, where M
is the relation of physical and/or psychological connectedness and/or
continuity to which the account appealed.

   In one respect the claims in the last paragraph are premature.
For nothing has been said about what the relation M relates.
In terms of the schema of objects and locations, the objects are
clearly persons, but what are the locations? Some discussions of
personal identity start with person-stages, temporal slices of people, and seek a relation between them necessary and sufficient for
them to be stages of the same person (Perry 1975 pp. 7–12, D. K.
Lewis 1976). One might thus interpret locations as person-stages,
the object at a location as the person of whom it was a stage and

M as a relation of physical and/or psychological connectedness and/or continuity between stages. However, it is quite doubtful that a person-stage exists as anything other than an artificial logical construction out of a person, such as an ordered pair of the person and a temporal interval. But if so it is hard to see what person-stages contribute to the discussion of personal identity; why not simply say that person-stages are stages of the same person if and only if they have the same first element (compare Wiggins 1980 at p. 169)? Issues of personal identity are usefully formulated in terms of person-stages only if the latter have a more controversially robust existence than that.

A more neutral choice is to interpret locations literally – as quadruples of spatio-temporal co-ordinates – and the object at a location as the person at that place at that time.[4] Spatio-temporal location provides an important mode of reference to persons on any reasonable view, and persons are not built into locations in the way in which they are arguably built into stages. No particular spatio-temporal location is essential to a person, although possession of some such location may be. There might be an illuminating account of the circumstances in which the person at spatio-temporal location x is the person at spatio-temporal location y, perhaps even an account not presupposing the concept of a person.

The reference to time only makes explicit the widespread assumption that the problem of personal identity is the problem of personal identity over time. The statement '$a = b$' raises a problem of identity only if the singular terms 'a' and 'b' differ in sense, whether or not their reference is the same; discussions of personal identity are characteristically concerned with examples in which 'a' and 'b' refer to persons by adverting to distinct times in their lives (contrast 'George Eliot = Marian Evans', which does not raise the philosopher's question). If one is to refer to a person by a time, one needs to specify which person one intends of all those who existed at that time, and that can naturally and uniformly be achieved by reference to the place where that person was at that time. On some but not all views of personal identity there is a deeper need than that for reference to places, for existence in space is held to be as integral a part of the concept of a person as existence in time, and the problem is conceived as one of distinguishing possible from impossible paths for a person through space over time. Whether or not that is so, the reference to spatio-temporal location articulates structure already implicit in philosophical discussions of personal identity.

There may be good reason to formulate issues about personal identity in the way just described. Gareth Evans suggests one line of thought: 'as we conceive of persons, they are distinguished from one another by fundamental grounds of difference of the same kind as those which distinguish other physical things, and [...] a fundamental identification of a person involves a consideration of him as the person occupying such-and-such a spatio-temporal location' (1982 p. 211). However, the idea of a fundamental ground of difference is elusive, and its pursuit would take the present discussion too far afield; it will recur in the final chapter. It is enough for present purposes that the issues can be formulated in the way described, whether or not they must be.

The phrase 'personal identity' can henceforth be used for the relation which the spatio-temporal location x has to the spatio-temporal location y just in case the person at x is the person at y. Speaking strictly in this technical sense, personal identity is neither a relation between persons nor a species of identity.

The position is now as follows. We start with a conception of persons on which a relation M is necessary and sufficient for personal identity. M is a matter of physical and/or psychological connectedness and/or continuity in what is going on at x, y and points between. Conceptual possibilities emerge in which M is neither transitive nor sufficient for personal identity. With respect to them, the nearest the original conception could be to the truth is that personal identity might be a maximal M-relation.

There are several maximal M-relations, if M is non-transitive; which of them is necessary and sufficient for personal identity? It might be held that the original conception is implicit in our concept of a person, and that whatever it best describes is *ipso facto* personal identity. Since the original conception describes several maximal M-relations equally well, and better than anything else, the concept of personal identity might be held to be indeterminate between these relations. That could lead to something like Derek Parfit's view (1984), on which questions about personal identity may have no right answer.

Consider a case of fission; let x be a spatio-temporal location of the pre-fission person, y and z locations of the two post-fission persons, A the statement that the person at x is the person at y, B the statement that the person at x is the person at z and C the statement that the person at y is the person at z. Suppose that M relates x to y and to z, but not y to z. Some maximal M-relation relates x to y and some relates x to z, but none does both, and none relates y to z. Thus A and B are neither uncontroversially true nor uncontroversially false, but their conjunction and its consequence C are uncontroversially false. On the envisaged view, 'uncontroversially' here means *determinately*. If there are no other fissions or fusions, every maximal M-relation may relate x to either y or z, in which case the disjunction of A and B would be determinately true – perhaps a less Parfitian result. But there is no prospect of making one of the disjuncts true by imposing extra formal constraints on the maximal M-relations, for many proposed cases of fission are symmetrical between y and z with respect to x. A question to ponder: does this indeterminacy manifest indeterminacy in the reference of 'person' itself?

On a different view, personal identity is determinate. We make theories about it, but they have no role in fixing the reference of our concepts. Our original theory proved to be false, but the evidence in its favour also supports a revised theory – that some maximal M-relation is necessary and sufficient for personal identity. The revised theory does not say which maximal M-relation is necessary and sufficient, and it may be impossible for us ever to know in cases such as symmetrical fission. On this view, 'uncontroversially' should be reinterpreted to mean *knowably*. That could lead to something like Roderick Chisholm's view (1970), on which questions about personal identity may have unknowably right answers.

No attempt will be made here to adjudicate between indeterminacy and ignorance. Instead, comparison will be made with a problem for some accounts of personal identity which does not lead to that dilemma. If we take a relation M to be necessary and sufficient for personal identity, and then discover it to be non-transitive, we may give up either the necessity or the sufficiency. So far only cases of the former kind have been considered. The next section deals with cases of the latter kind.

7.4   Sufficient Conditions

Locke proposed memory as a criterion of personal identity. One such view can be formulated by means of the relation M, which holds between spatio-temporal locations x and y if and only if either there is a memory at x of being at y or there is a memory at y of being at x or x is y. The definition ensures that M is both reflexive and symmetric. The claim might be that the person at x is the same as the person at y just in case x has M to y. There are several well-known objections to this view, but for the purposes of clarity it is best to ignore all but one. The relation M is not transitive, a point made by Berkeley in *Alciphron* (Seventh Dialogue, section 8) and later dramatized in Reid's *Essays on the Intellectual Powers of Man*:

> Suppose a brave officer to have been flogged when a boy at school for robbing an orchard, to have taken a standard from the enemy in his first campaign, and to have been made a general in advanced life: suppose, also, which must be admitted to be possible, that, when he took the standard, he was conscious of his having been flogged at school, and that, when made a general, he was conscious of his taking the standard, but had absolutely lost the consciousness of his flogging. (Reprinted on p. 114 of Perry 1975)

Let x, y and z be the spatio-temporal locations of the flogging, the taking of the standard and the promotion to general; M relates x to y and y to z but not x to z. The example shows not just that M is not both necessary and sufficient for personal identity, but that it is not necessary, for the person at z was clearly at x too. Moreover, M remains plausible as a sufficient condition for identity; the person at x cannot have a memory of being at y without having been there.[5]

What is the least change in the original, conception that would reconcile it with the example? Given that M is sufficient for personal identity, how nearly necessary could it be? As classes of ordered pairs, personal identity properly includes M. The instances in which M fails to be necessary for personal identity are those ordered pairs in personal identity but not in M; the fewer such pairs, the nearer M is to being necessary. Thus the minimum revision is one in which personal identity is as restrictive as possible for an equivalence relation that includes M. What is the smallest equivalence relation to include M?

The concept we need is that of an *ancestral*. The ancestral M^* of M is that relation which x has to y just in case there is a finite sequence $z_0, \ldots, z_n$ such that z_0 is x, z_n is y and each z_{i-1} has M to z_i. M^* is automatically transitive; it inherits reflexivity and symmetry from M.[6] Thus M^* is an equivalence relation that includes M. Moreover, it is the smallest such relation. For let E be any equivalence relation that includes M. Since E is transitive, it also includes M^*; thus E is at least as large as M^*. M^* is an equivalence relation that includes M and is included in any equivalence relation that includes M. It is obviously unique in having this property, in the sense that any pair of relations which have it are included in each other.

If the original conception is adjusted to the non-transitivity of M in the most conservative way possible, the result is the claim that M^* is necessary and sufficient for personal identity. On one such view, the person at x is the person at y if and only if there is a finite sequence of spatio-temporal locations $z_0, \ldots, z_n$ such that z_0 is x, z_n is y and, for each i, either there is a memory at z_i of being at z_{i-1} or there is a memory at z_{i-1} of being at z_i or z_{i-1} is z_i. Reassuringly, the standard response to Berkeley/Reid examples has indeed been a move to the ancestral of the relation (Grice 1941, Quinton 1962, Perry 1975 pp. 16–20, Mackie 1976 pp. 179–81, Wiggins 1980 pp. 154–5).

The equation of personal identity with the ancestral of a relation is pointful only if, as here, the phrase 'personal identity' is not used for a species of identity. For suppose that identity itself (as restricted to persons) is equivalent to the ancestral R^* of a relation R. It follows that R is transitive. For if x has R to y and y has R to z, y has R^* to z, so y and z are identical, so by Leibniz's Law x has R to z. Since R is transitive, it is equivalent to R^*. Thus identity is equivalent to R itself, any apparent examples of its non-transitivity are spurious and talk of its ancestral gains nothing. The move to the ancestral achieves something only if personal identity is not a species of identity, and therefore is presumably a relation between non-persons – such as spatio-temporal locations.

There is a striking difference between the failure of a necessary condition for personal identity to be sufficient and the failure of a sufficient condition to be necessary. If one conservatively modifies the theory that M is both necessary and sufficient in the light of such a failure, the former replaces M by a plurality of maximal M-relations, the latter by its unique ancestral M^*. The difference has nothing to do with personal identity in particular; it is a matter of the logic of equivalence relations and necessary and sufficient conditions. The final section explains the difference, and gives a more rigorous and general account of the notion of minimum mutilation at work in this chapter.

7.5   Close Relations

This chapter has concerned problems in which one is given a non-transitive relation M and seeks an equivalence relation as close to it as possible. Such an equivalence relation may then be claimed to be necessary and sufficient for the identity of corresponding objects of some kind, as a conservative revision of an original, incoherent conception that M is necessary and sufficient. For this to work, a concept of relative closeness for relations is needed.

Similarity in some respects is irrelevant. As relations, love has much in common with hate, and eating with being eaten. That is not what is wanted here. All that matters for present purposes is the extent to which the relations coincide in extension. The area over which the dyadic relations R and S coincide is the extension of $Rxy \leftrightarrow Sxy$ over the relevant domain. In effect, the idea has been that R is at least as close to S as T is to U just in case the area of coincidence between R and S includes that between T and U. More formally:

(7.4) R is at least as close to S as T is to U $=_{\text{df}}$
$\forall x \forall y ((Txy \leftrightarrow Uxy) \rightarrow (Rxy \leftrightarrow Sxy))$

What (7.4) does not allow is for a large area of coincidence between R and S but not between T and U to compensate for a small area of coincidence between T and U but not between R and S (compare Pareto optimality in welfare economics). In order to do so, one would have to count the ordered pairs in those areas, or something of the kind. That would lead to complications. It is better to start with a crude but simple standard, such as (7.4).

Closeness, as defined by (7.4), has the formal properties that one would expect of a relation of comparative similarity (Williamson 1988b). R is at least as close to R as S is to T. If R is at least as close to S as T is to itself then R is equivalent to S. R is at least as close to S as S is to R, and as R is to S. If R is at least as close to S

as T is to U, and T is at least as close to U as V is to W, then R is at least as close to S as V is to W.

We are interested in relations as close as possible to M. As usual, M is assumed to be reflexive, symmetric and non-transitive. We can say that R is *as close as* S if R is at least as close to M as S is to M, and that R is *closer than* S if R is as close as S but S is not as close as R. 'As close as' expresses a reflexive, anti-symmetric and transitive relation, 'closer than' an irreflexive, asymmetric and transitive one. If M includes both R and S, R is as close as S just in case R includes S. If both R and S include M, R is as close as S just in case S includes R. Suppose that C is a class of relations, and that R is a member of C. R satisfies the *strong constraint* with respect to C if and only if R is as close as any member of C. R satisfies the *weak constraint* with respect to C if and only if no member of C is closer than R. Satisfaction of the strong constraint entails satisfaction of the weak constraint, but not *vice versa*. If a relation satisfies the strong constraint, it is (in extension) the only one to do so; moreover, it is the only relation to satisfy the weak constraint. On the other hand, several non-equivalent relations may satisfy the weak constraint, provided that none satisfies the strong. If C is the class of equivalence relations included in M, the relations which satisfy the weak constraint are the maximal M-relations; no relation satisfies the strong constraint. If C is the class of equivalence relations which include M, the ancestral M^* satisfies both constraints and no other relation satisfies either. Thus the preceding work can be subsumed under a general account of comparative closeness for relations.

Why the asymmetry between necessary and sufficient conditions? Why is the strong constraint satisfiable for equivalence relations which include M, but not for equivalence relations which M includes? In the former case, one seeks an equivalence relation which includes M and is included in all relations with that property. Such a relation would have to be the intersection of all equivalence relations which include M. Now the conjunction (i.e. intersection) of some equivalence relations is always itself an equivalence relation, so the required equivalence relation exists. We have simply described the ancestral M^* in an impredicative way. In the latter case, one seeks an equivalence relation included in M and which includes all relations with that property. Such a relation would have to be the union of all equivalence relations included in M.

But the disjunction (i.e. union) of some equivalence relations is not always itself an equivalence relation, so the required equivalence relation may not exist. 'London' either begins or ends with the same letter as 'Leicester', and 'Leicester' either begins or ends with the same letter as 'Chester', but 'London' does not begin or end with the same letter as 'Chester'. The union of all equivalence relations included in M is in fact simply M itself, which is not an equivalence relation. This book balances on that point of logic.

8

Modal and Temporal Paradoxes

How different could things have been, still being those things? How different could *they* have been? We can make sense of such questions if we take them in limited doses. A table or a planet could have been originally made of slightly different material from its actual original material; it could not have been originally made of utterly different material, although such material could have made up another table or planet. However, many slight differences can amount to an utter difference; if the transitive relation of identity is preserved through the former, how can it fail through the latter? Sorites paradoxes threaten identity across possible worlds, as Roderick Chisholm pointed out some time ago (Chisholm 1967). This chapter develops one such paradox, arguing that it formally resembles the problems discussed in previous chapters, and can be resolved by means of the apparatus developed there (section 8.1). Lest it be thought that the paradox depends on the special nature of possibility, similar paradoxes are sketched for identity over time (section 8.2). Both modal and temporal versions involve the identity of artifacts. Treatments of closely related problems by Graeme Forbes and Nathan Salmon do not generalize in the same way (section 8.3).

8.1   A Modal Paradox

A typical paradox of cross-world identity begins with an artifact x originally made of material m_0 in the actual world w_0. It is urged that since x could have been originally made of slightly different material, there is a possible world w_1 in which x is originally made of material m_1, 99 per cent of which is part of m_0. By parity of reasoning, there is a possible world w_2 in which x is originally made of material m_2, 99 per cent of which is part of m_1 but only 98

Identity and Discrimination: Reissued and Updated Edition. Timothy Williamson.
© 2013 Timothy Williamson. Published 2013 by Blackwell Publishing Ltd.

per cent of which is part of m_0. The argument finally arrives at a world w_{100} in which x is originally made of material m_{100}, none of which is part of m_0, violating the intuition that that very artifact x could not have been originally made of utterly different material. The intuition may be sharpened by the occurrence in w_{100} of an artifact originally made of m_0, the actual original material of x, and having the actual form of x; m_0 seems to have a better claim than m_{100} to constitute x.

What has gone wrong? The style of argument involves a chain of worlds $w_1, w_2, \ldots, w_{100}$ receding from the actual one w_0; it tempts one to think of possibility as somehow being lost in the course of the series. That embryonic idea can be developed in various ways. Salmon proposes that although w_1 is possible from the standpoint of w_0, and w_2 from the standpoint of w_1, so that w_2 is possibly possible from the standpoint of w_0, it does not follow that w_2 is possible from the standpoint of w_0; relative possibility is a non-transitive relation, and – contrary to the S4 axiom in modal logic – what is possibly possible need not be possible (Salmon 1981 Appendix I, 1986, 1989). On Forbes's view, a version of counterpart theory, the material m_{i+1} put together in world w_{i+1} is slightly less of a possibility for x than the material m_i put together in world w_i; the material m_{100} in w_{100} may be utterly impossible for x (Forbes 1983, 1984, 1985 chapter 7). However, similar paradoxes can be developed from a different perspective, in which the series of worlds is viewed not from one end but from the standpoint of a world outside the series, from which all its members are equally possible. The idea of diminishing possibility does little to alleviate the latter kind of paradox. Something more like the apparatus of previous chapters seems to be required. Since that apparatus can handle the former kind of paradox too, there is no clear need of the specifically modal claims invoked by Salmon, Forbes and others.

The new version of the paradox refers to merely possible objects. That is a hard achievement to understand, but it is one we frequently bring off. A factory mass-produces clocks from a blueprint which numbers each part. Assume that there are at least as many clocks now on the production line as parts on the blueprint, and consider the first part of the first clock now on the production line, the second part of the second clock, ... No actual clock consists of those parts, but such a clock could easily have been assembled. Moreover, *being a clock originally made of those parts according to that blueprint by a specified worker at a specified time and place* is not a property that fits one object in one possible world and a different object in some equally possible world, in the way that *winning the lottery* may do. Rather, something like this is true: there is one and only one possible object x such that x would have been a clock with those parts if they had been assembled in those circumstances. The identity of the parts and the details of their assemblage fix the identity of the clock. One could say 'Let Chronos be the possible clock whose parts these would have been had they been assembled together' and use 'Chronos' like a name; one might believe that Chronos would have been more robust than any clock now on the production line actually will. Much remains to be understood about *how* we can refer to the merely possible, but in assuming *that* we can do so the argument relies on what a future semantic theory will explain (Williamson 1989 sketches a metaphysical view which helps to make such reference intelligible).

One new version of the paradox involves a fantasy about the manufacture of a certain kind of ear-ring. The craftsman turns a patterned metal disc with rotational symmetry on a lathe, and then cuts it along a diameter into matching halves, the two ear-rings, with a device that simultaneously punches an attachment for the ear out of each half. Once the disc is lying ready to be cut, the only remaining uncertainty in the manufacture concerns the diameter along which the cut will be made; the story can fix the craftsman, the time, the place and other such details. In the actual world of the story, the craftsman is struck dead before he can cut the disc; had he not been, he would have chosen a diameter at random.

For any diameter d, the craftsman might have cut along d; he would thereby have made one and only one pair of ear-rings. Something more is true: there is one and only one possible pair of ear-rings which in the circumstances he would have made by cutting along d. For if there were two possible pairs of ear-rings either of which in the circumstances he might equally well have made by cutting along d, a curious kind of indeterminism would follow: the same process in the same circumstances could lead to the creation of either pair of ear-rings, and nothing in the period up to the moment of creation would determine which pair was created. Indeterminism does not come so cheap. Even if each of several pairs is a *logically possible* outcome of cutting along *d* in the circumstances, surely there is only one possible pair which *would have been* the outcome; uniqueness holds for nearby worlds if not for all. Thus we can talk about the possible pair of ear-rings the craftsman would have made had he cut along *d*.

It will be convenient to have a system for denoting the possible ear-rings made by different cuts. Let P be a point on the circumference of the circular upper surface of the disc. For any real number r, let P_r be the point reached by travelling r degrees clockwise round the circumference; thus P_{r+180} is diametrically opposite P_r and P_{r+360} is P_r. A cut along the diameter from P_r to P_{r+180} makes two ear-rings, whose curved edges run clockwise from P_r to P_{r+180} and from P_{r+180} to P_r respectively; let the former be $o(r)$ and the latter $o(r+180)$[1]. Clearly, $o(r)$ and $o(r+180)$ are distinct possible ear-rings. With harmless ambiguity, 'r' will also be treated as denoting the material that would constitute $o(r)$.

An angle of one degree is slight (if it is not slight enough, divide it by a large enough integer k). The difference between cuts along the diameters $P_r P_{r+180}$ and $P_{r+1} P_{r+181}$ is minuscule. One cut produces the ear-rings $o(r)$ and $o(r+180)$, the other the ear-rings $o(r+1)$ and $o(r+181)$, but are these distinct pairs? The metal which would constitute $o(r)$ on a cut along $P_r P_{r+180}$ is almost exactly the same as the metal which would constitute $o(r+1)$ on a cut along $P_{r+1} P_{r+181}$; the other circumstances of manufacture are exactly the same. Intuitively, the differences between these two processes of manufacture are too slight to amount to the distinctness of their products. The very same ear-rings would be made in both cases, but out of marginally different material. An imperceptible tremor of the craftsman's hand would not cause an ear-ring to appear in the workshop that would otherwise never have been there. The underlying intuition feels the same as that which gives plausibility to somewhat different principles such as Salmon's:

> If a wooden table x is the only table originally formed from a hunk of matter y according to a certain plan P, and y' is any (possibly scattered) hunk of matter that sufficiently overlaps y and has exactly the same mass, volume, and chemical composition as y, then x is such that it might have been the only table originally formed according to the same plan P from y' instead of from y. (Salmon 1986, p. 77)

Thus $o(r)$ and $o(r+1)$ may be assumed to be the same possible ear-ring, for an arbitrary value of 'r'.

The last two paragraphs constitute a paradox. The latter gives:

$$o(0) = o(1)$$
$$o(1) = o(2)$$
$$\cdot$$
$$\cdot$$
$$\cdot$$
$$o(179) = o(180)$$

The former gives:

$$\sim o(0) = o(180)$$

Identity is a transitive relation.

The possible ear-rings $o(0)$ and $o(180)$ are quite clearly not identical; if they were made, someone could wear one on the right ear and one on the left. Thus the fault lies with one of the identities between $o(i)$ and $o(i + 1)$. But if any of them is at fault, they presumably all are, for the disc is symmetrical about its centre; it would be wholly arbitrary to suppose that $o(i)$ and $o(i + 1)$ were identical but $o(j)$ and $o(j + 1)$ distinct. In any case, the failure of at least one identity means that the almost exact similarity of processes of manufacture is insufficient for the identity of their products.

The smaller the angle between the cuts, the more strongly one feels their products to be identical; the intuition varies in degree. However, this is not the source of the paradox. For even if the direct intuitive plausibility of the claim $o(r) = o(r + s)$ were maximal for any s in [0, 180] less than some positive constant c, and minimal for any s not less than c, the paradox would proceed just as before (cp. Salmon 1979 pp. 724–5, 1981 pp. 241 and 250–52, Gupta 1980 p. 103, Forbes 1985 p. 166n). Thus one does not compromise the main issue by assuming that the intuition does have a sharp cut-off point c.

There is in fact a salient value for c: 90. For if s is less than 90, the material of $o(r)$ on a cut along $P_rP_{r + 180}$ at least has more overlap with the material of $o(r + s)$ than with that of the latter's other half $o(r + s + 180)$ on a cut along $P_{r + s}P_{r + s + 180}$, so that the identification of $o(r)$ with $o(r + s)$ has some point, which is not the case if s is not less than 90. Certainly, if one is to identify the unordered pairs of ear-rings $\{o(r), o(r + 180)\}$ and $\{o(r + s), o(r + s + 180)\}$, $o(r)$ is more reasonably identified with $o(r + s)$ if s is less than 90 and with $o(r + s + 180)$ if s is greater than 90; if s is exactly 90, either identification would be arbitrary. In other words, there is something to be said for the identity $o(x) = o(y)$ if and only if the difference between the real numbers x and y is less than 90 (modulo 360); the latter condition may be abbreviated as 'Mxy'[2]. M is evidently reflexive and symmetric. It is fairly clear that Mxy is a necessary condition for $o(x) = o(y)$, since when it fails $o(x)$ would be $o(y + 180)$ rather than $o(y)$, if either. For the sake of simplicity, our intuition will be represented as holding that Mxy is also a sufficient condition for $o(x) = o(y)$; a more complex representation would not jeopardize the main lines of the following treatment. The intuition leads to paradox because M is not a transitive relation: 0 has M to 60, and 60 has M to 120, but 0 does not have M to 120 (where '0', '60' and '120' may be treated as naming the portions of metal that would constitute $o(0)$, $o(60)$ and $o(120)$ respectively).

The apparatus of maximal M-relations can now be applied; the conditions for its use identified in the previous chapter have been met. The question is 'Which processes produce the same product?'. For the special process described it becomes 'Which portions of metal would constitute the same ear-rings?'. An appropriate answer is an equivalence relation between portions of metal; the correct answer may be called *ear-ring identity* (although it is of course restricted to one very special process of ear-ring manufacture). The original conception incoherently identified ear-ring identity with the non-transitive relation M. On critical reflection, M turns out to be necessary and therefore not sufficient for ear-ring identity. The conservative response to the problem is a retreat to the view that ear-ring identity is an equivalence relation for which M is necessary and, given that, as nearly as possible sufficient; in other words, ear-ring identity is a maximal M-relation.

Less conservative responses are also possible, of course. It might be argued that any difference, however slight, in material gives what is strictly speaking a distinct artifact, although it is often convenient to speak loosely as though that were not the case. It is not necessary to go to such extremes. The concern of this chapter is to see how much of the original conception can be saved; maximal M-relations provide the appropriate technique.

Since M is non-transitive, there is more than one maximal M-relation. Our interest is naturally confined to maximal M-relations which always hold between x and $x + 360$, for they represent the same material; thus we need only look at the behaviour of these relations on the interval [0,360), from which the rest can be extrapolated[3]. One such maximal M-relation induces the partition into equivalence classes {[0,90), [90,180), [180,270), [270,360)}; another induces the partition {[0,60), [60,120), [120,180), [180,240), [240,300), [300,360)}. However, the result of rotating any maximal M-relation through any angle is also a maximal M-relation. Thus clockwise rotation through 5 degrees transforms those partitions into {[5,95), [95,185), [185,275), [275,360) ∪ [0,5)} and {[5,65), [65,125), [125,185), [185,245), [245,305), [305,360) ∪ [0,5)} respectively, both of which also correspond to maximal M-relations.

One might reduce the variation by means of the Minimality Constraint, which countenances only maximal M-relations with the least possible number of equivalence classes. In this case that number is clearly four: 0, 90, 180 and 270 must go into separate equivalence classes, since no two of them are M-related, and a partition into four classes is possible, {[0,90), [90,180), [180,270), [270,360)} being an example. However, not all the variation can be eliminated, for the result of rotating any maximal M-relation obeying the Minimality Constraint through any angle is also a maximal M-relation obeying the Minimality Constraint. The rotational symmetry of the original disc makes the same true of any other formal constraint. In fact the maximal M-relations obeying the Minimality Constraint correspond precisely to the divisions of a circle into four quadrants[4]. Since any two of these are isomorphic, there is no reasonable way of choosing between them; any two partitions of the possible halves that are maximal M-relations obeying the Minimality Constraint could have been represented by a single partition of the real numbers [0,360) given different choices of the origin P[5]. Now any two points on the circumference of a circle subtending less than a right-angle at its centre fall in the same quadrant according to some partitions and not others. Thus if x and y are distinct but M-related, they are related by some maximal M-relations obeying all reasonable constraints and not by others.

The upshot of the preceding discussion is that the possible ear-rings which would result from different material are never uncontroversially the same, but are also not uncontroversially distinct when more than half the material is shared. Thus each of the premises $o(0) = o(1)$, $o(1) = o(2), \ldots, o(179) = o(180)$ of the original paradox is neither uncontroversially true nor uncontroversially false, but their conjuction is uncontroversially false, because its consequence $o(0) = o(180)$ is; $\sim o(0) = o(180)$ is uncontroversially true. Each of the other premises is plausible because it is not uncontroversially false.

It may even be possible to develop a notion of degree of controversy in this case, for there is a sense in which a randomly chosen partition of a circle into quadrants will put two points into the same quadrant with probability 89/90 if they subtend an angle of 1 degree at the centre, and with probability 1/90 if they subtend an angle of 89 degrees. Thus the use of the relation M as a cut-off point is consistent with the way in which our intuitions vary in strength.

Does controversy here reflect indeterminacy or ignorance? The symmetry of the original disc makes ignorance a scarcely credible option; what invisible lines could dictate that one pair of cuts a degree apart would yield the same ear-rings, while another pair a degree apart would yield distinct ear-rings? It is far more plausible to suppose that judgements without uncontroversial truth-values are indeterminate in truth-value. Thus the judgements $o(r) = o(r + 1)$ are neither determinately true nor determinately false. It has already been argued that identity is a determinate relation; the source of the indeterminacy must therefore lie in the reference of the singular terms. Such a term '$o(r)$' denotes the possible ear-ring that would result from a certain process. As already argued, there seems to be no relevant indeterminacy in what would happen if the process were carried out. Thus the indeterminacy of reference would not have been resolved even if the process had been carried out. 'That ear-ring' would still have failed of perfectly determinate reference. Any purported mapping o from ostended materials to the ear-rings they would constitute is inconsistent with at least one maximal M-relation E which obeys the Minimality Constraint, in the sense that $o(x) = o(y)$ is not equivalent to Exy. Since our concept of an ear-ring is neutral between such maximal M-relations, it does not fully determine what object falls under the concept of the ear-ring constituted of given material. The indeterminacy does not matter for practical purposes, but it is there.

It would be incautious to conclude that the general term 'earring' is itself indeterminate in reference. For it might pick out a determinate class of objects, even if the constitution relation in which their materials stand to them is undetermined. Each candidate constitution relation can be thought of as a mapping o from materials to objects such that the equivalence relation $o(x) = o(y)$ is a maximal M-relation obeying the Minimality Constraint. The equivalence relation varies from mapping to mapping, but the mappings might all be onto the same class of objects. If so, the equivalence relations should all have the same number of equivalence classes: but the Minimality Constraint ensures precisely that. This view may or may not be stable under metaphysical reflection. If not, intended reference to ear-rings in general is as indeterminate as intended reference to particular ear-rings.

Could the context in which 'that ear-ring' is uttered resolve the indeterminacy in 'ear-ring'?[6] Perhaps the term has an indexical component; when we point in the direction of material m and say 'that ear-ring', we should be interpreted by means of a maximal M-relation on which the equivalence class of m is as large a similarity sphere as possible centred on m, so that no slight change of material would have made a different ear-ring in the relevant sense. Let m' be slightly different material at the margin of that equivalence class; if m' had been in the direction of our pointing, we should instead have been interpreted by means of a different maximal M-relation on which m' is at the centre of its equivalence class. Such constraints certainly reduce the indeterminacy. They cannot be expected wholly to resolve it, for two reasons. First, to fix the equivalence class of m is not to fix all the other equivalence classes. Second, the equivalence class of m may not itself have been fixed, both because for any maximal M-relation that puts m at the centre of a sphere some other maximal M-relation may put it at the centre of a larger sphere, and because there may be incompatible but equally good ways of cashing out the geometric metaphor. Moreover, the paradox in this section was told from the standpoint of a world in which no division of the material was made and none was salient; that context of utterance for 'ear-ring' does not single out a value of 'm'. The idea of context-dependence is helpful nevertheless, for it suggests a psychological mechanism by which each step of the sorites becomes plausible in turn. In using words to describe hypothetical situations, it is easy to slip from their actual content to the contents they would have had in those situations; thus in discussing a hypothetical division of the material we focus on the content that 'ear-ring' would have had in the context of that division, and thus on the maximal M-relations with respect to which the corresponding sorites step judgement is correct.

The preceding treatment can be generalized to other modal paradoxes of identity, especially of artifacts. Some mathematical structure will be lost, but it was not essential to the approach. It is sometimes important to allow for the possibility that the same material may constitute different artifacts in different circumstances; that can be achieved by taking ordered triples of places, times and worlds as the locations which are to be mapped to objects. No special claims about modality – such as Salmon's denial of the S4 axiom or Forbes's counterpart theory – need be invoked. Techniques evolved in response to non-modal paradoxes apply equally well to modal variants. The next section will underline the point of a uniform approach by sketching temporal analogues of modal paradoxes about artifact identity.

8.2   Two Temporal Paradoxes

Not every modal paradox about identity has a straightforward temporal analogue. For nothing in the modal case perfectly corresponds to the way in which considerations of spatio-temporal continuity permit one to keep track of ordinary physical objects as they change their materials over time. The paradox of the ear-rings is an example. A perfect temporal analogue would involve a story about two ear-rings whose constituent materials are swopped, little by little, over a long period. At the end of the process each ear-ring would be constituted of precisely the material that had constituted the other ear-ring at the beginning. Now the inductive step in this new argument is indeed plausible: surely the continuance of two ear-rings is quite consistent with the exchange of a small quantity of their material. However, the conclusion of the argument

is not clearly paradoxical. The identity of the artifacts has not followed the identity of their materials, but so what? The final episodes
in the history of each ear-ring are related to the initial ones by a kind
of spatio-temporal continuity which is standardly sufficient for successive episodes to be episodes in the history of the same ear-ring.
Unless one is a materialist of the grossest sort, why should one find
the case puzzling?

The temporal paradox of the ear-rings may have been dismissed
rather glibly; it is not clearly unparadoxical.[7] Fortunately, that issue
can be left hanging. Not all kinds of artifact have the same conditions
for persistence through time. In some cases spatio-temporal continuity
is clearly insufficient; they provide clearer analogues of the modal
paradoxes. Two cases will be considered, *drawings* and *languages*
(the latter being artifacts in an extended sense).

In order to avoid controversies about the nature of works of art,
one can focus on drawings made for practical rather than aesthetic
purposes: for example, a drawing of a courtroom scene, intended
to illustrate a newspaper report. A drawing can go through many
stages. Lines are inserted, lengthened, shortened, darkened, lightened,
widened, narrowed or rubbed out. At a different level of description,
the direction and point of view may be varied; one person is shown in a
new posture, others are added or subtracted. These may all be stages
of the same drawing. Although an illustrator may destroy several
hundred drawings in producing one, that is not the usual procedure,
and there is no good reason to think that it is what the process just
described involves. When the illustrator asks her editor 'Will you
publish this drawing?', there is clearly a difference between being told
'Yes, but first put in the judge' and 'No, do another with the judge
in and I'll publish that'. However, not everything goes. A series of
small changes of the kind just described could alter the drawing out
of all recognition; it could show different figures to a different scale
from a different point of view in a different style. A panorama of the
courtroom in which no witness appeared could eventually become a
study of a witness's face. That would not be a different stage of the
same drawing, but a different drawing. The illustrator could carry
out her editor's instruction to do a new drawing by making such
a series of changes, if the result were far enough from the starting
point. Moreover, matters can certainly be arranged so that at any
moment during the process there is one and only one drawing on the

paper. These points yield all that is needed in order to construct a fairly straightforward sorites paradox. Suppose that the drawing on the paper at time t_0 is a panorama of the courtroom, the drawing on the paper at time t_n is a close-up of the witness, and for each i just one small change is made to the drawing in the interval between t_{i-1} and t_i. Our criteria for the persistence of drawings seem to require that for each i the drawing on the paper at t_{i-1} is the same as the drawing on the paper at t_i, but that the drawing on the paper at t_0 is not the same as the drawing on the paper at t_n.

The case of languages is similar. The concept of a language in use here is the ordinary one, on which a language can change over time: both Shakespeare and Dr Johnson spoke English, but the meaning of certain words in English was different in 1750 from what it had been in 1600. Philosophers of language often find it convenient to use the word 'language' in a different sense, in which a language is a function from expressions to intensions, or something of the kind; in this technical sense, Shakespeare and Dr Johnson spoke different languages. The present claim is not that the technical sense is unreal or useless: only that the nontechnical sense is real and useful too, and different from the technical one. A language in the non-technical sense can persist through a small semantic, syntactic or phonetic change. However, not everything goes. A series of such changes could alter the language out of all recognition, so that speakers at the beginning of the process and those at its end would find as much difficulty in communicating with each other as do speakers of English and Chinese. They would be speaking not different stages of the same language, but different languages. When we say that Latin and Italian are not the same language, we surely do not mean to imply that the evolution of one into the other was not of this gradual kind (whatever the actual facts of linguistic history). Consider, for example, the process by which Rome was transformed from a city of Latin-speakers into a city of Italian-speakers. We can simplify history and suppose that at any moment during the process one and only one language was the language current in Rome. These points yield all that is needed in order to construct a fairly straightforward sorites paradox. Suppose that the language current in Rome at time t_0 is Latin, the language current in Rome at time t_n is Italian, and for each i just one small change befell the language in the interval between t_{i-1} and t_i. Our criteria for the persistence of languages seem to require that for each i the language current in Rome at t_{i-1} is the same as the language current there at t_i, but that the language current at t_0 is not the same as the language current at t_n.

Three points about these examples are worth noting.

(1)   In neither case is the paradoxical criterion for persistence merely adventitious. It is a natural idea that sameness of language should be necessary and sufficient for linguistic communication (at least where a causal link between the languages of the kind above is given), and it leads directly to a criterion on which languages can persist through minute but not through massive change. The criterion for the persistence of drawings has a similar basis in the purposes for which they are used. The paradoxes result not from unsupported intuitions but from intuitions too strongly determined by practical convenience.

(2)   In both cases, although it is probably indeterminate just how much variation can be tolerated, the paradox in no way trades on this fact. Our concepts do not exactly fix a point at which there is a new drawing or language rather than an old one in a new state, they do not specify how much is too much: but even if they did, the paradox would remain. Enough small changes still make a large one when 'large' and 'small' are given precise values (of course, much arbitrariness would be involved in constructing a scale for measuring the degree of change in drawings or languages, but that is another issue). The paradoxes may depend on vagueness, but not on this vagueness.

(3)   Although both cases could be described in terms of the concept of a temporal stage or slice, that is not essential to the paradox. In one case, the crucial question had the form: is the drawing on the paper at time t the same as the drawing on the paper at time t'? It was to be answered in terms of some relations of causality and resemblance. Although one could think of these as relating temporal stages of drawings, there is no evident need to do so. The argument still runs smoothly into contradiction if one thinks of them as relating the paper at t to the paper at t' in virtue of the physical states of its surface, where the paper at t or t' is simply the ordered pair of the paper and a time. In the other case the crucial question had a similar form: is the language current in Rome at time t the same as the language current in Rome at time t'? It was to be answered in terms of some relations

of causality and resemblance. Although one could think of these as relating temporal stages of languages, there is no evident need to do so. The argument still runs smoothly into contradiction if one thinks of them as relating Rome at t to Rome at t' in virtue of the capacities of its inhabitants, where Rome at t or t' is simply the ordered pair of Rome and a time. Think of drawings or languages as enduring continuants, wholly present at any time at which they are present at all because their parts are lines or words or the like, not temporal stages; the paradoxes are not thereby resolved.

Points 1–3 have analogues for the modal paradoxes. Moreover, the source of the difficulty seems to be the same: principles of tolerance governing variation in the constituents of artifacts (in a broad sense of the latter term). The paradox of the ear-rings does have a more elaborate structure than those above; it exploits the circular ordering of some possible worlds by similarity to make vivid the distinctness of the beginning and end of the sorites series. That device has no temporal analogue, for time does not order any moments into a circle. However, the distinctness of the drawings or languages at each end of the sorites series is clear for other reasons; the disanalogy is not pertinent. One should therefore expect a good treatment of the modal paradoxes to generalize to the temporal ones, and *vice versa*. Is that true of maximal M-relations?

By point 3 above, the temporal paradoxes can be stated in terms of a function o from times to objects. In one case, ot would be the drawing on the paper at time t; in another, the language current in Rome at that time. A more comprehensive treatment might use a single function from triples of places, times and worlds to artifacts of all kinds, but the present simplified definition is enough for purposes of illustration. On the original conception of drawings or languages, a necessary and sufficient condition for the identity of ot and ot' is some sort of roughly continuous evolution in the artifact from the earlier time to the later not involving change out of all recognition. This condition can be treated as a well-defined relation M between the times t and t'; point 2 above makes this idealization legitimate. M is symmetric, and reflexive for the relevant times. However, it is not transitive. The paradoxes exploit a sequence of times $t_0, \ldots, t_n$ in which M clearly holds between each time and the next, but clearly fails to hold between the first time and the last. The necessary and sufficient condition would then yield:

$$ot_0 = ot_1$$
$$ot_1 = ot_2$$
$$.$$
$$.$$
$$.$$
$$ot_{n-1} = ot_n$$
$$\sim ot_0 = ot_n$$

The relation M thus cannot be both necessary and sufficient for the identity of the artifacts. Indeed, it seems fairly clear that M cannot be sufficient for their identity, no matter how slight the change it permitted. For if it were, transitivity would ensure that the artifacts could persist through any amount of change: an implausible result. But once M is allowed to be insufficient for the identity of the artifacts, the paradoxes offer no reason to deny that it is necessary. The conservative response is thus a retreat to the view that the identity of the artifacts is an equivalence relation for which M is necessary and, given that, as nearly as possible one for which it is sufficient – in other words, a maximal M-relation. Less conservative responses are also possible, but they are not the concern of this chapter. The practical concerns mentioned under 1 above provide some justification for the conservative response.

As usual, there will be many maximal M-relations. The variation might be reduced by further constraints, such as Minimality, but since their effect depends on the details of the case at hand they will not be discussed here. Now any two times t_{i-1} and t_i in the sorites series are related by M, and therefore by some maximal M-relation. Thus none of the judgements $ot_0 = ot_1$, $ot_1 = ot_2$, . . . , $ot_{n-1} = ot_n$ is uncontroversially false, which helps to explain their plausibility. However, their conjunction is uncontroversially false, because its consequence $ot_0 = ot_n$ is; t_0 and t_n are not related by M, and therefore not by any maximal M-relation, so $\sim ot_0 = ot_n$ is uncontroversially true.

Does controversy here reflect indeterminacy or ignorance? The former seems more likely, as in the modal case. It is hard to believe that a smooth process of evolution is punctuated by unidentifiable instants at which one drawing or language ceases and another begins. Thus none of the judgements $ot_{i-1} = ot_i$ is determinately false. Since their conjunction is determinately false, at least one of them is not determinately true; the smoothness of the series makes it implausible that some but not others are determinately true, so none of them is determinately true. Since identity is a determinate relation, the source of the indeterminacy lies in the reference of the singular terms. Thus even if it is determinate that one and only one drawing is now on this piece of paper, there may be nothing which is determinately a drawing now on this piece of paper. Similarly, even if it is determinate that one and only one language is now current in a certain place, there may be nothing which is determinately a language now current in that place. The indeterminacy does not matter for most practical purposes, but it is there.

It would be incautious to conclude that the general terms 'drawing' and 'language' are themselves indeterminate in reference. For they might pick out determinate classes of objects, even if the constitution relation in which their materials stand to them is undetermined. This view may or may not be stable under metaphysical reflection. If not, intended reference to drawings or languages in general is as indeterminate as intended reference to particular drawings or languages.

Could the context in which 'that drawing' or 'that language' is uttered resolve the indeterminacy in 'drawing' or 'language'? Perhaps the terms have an indexical component of the same kind as was proposed for 'ear-ring'. Interpretation would require a maximal M-relation with an equivalence class centred on its salient member. For the same reasons as before, that would reduce but not wholly resolve the indeterminacy. Moreover, the paradoxes in this section were told from the standpoint of a time outside the sorites series; such a context of utterance for 'drawing' or 'language' does not single out a salient member of an equivalence class. When we consider a time in the sorites series, however, we might well focus on the content that the word would have had as used at that time, and so on the maximal M-relations with respect to which the corresponding sorites step judgement is correct. Thus the idea of context-dependence again suggests a psychological mechanism by which each step of the sorites becomes plausible in turn.

8.3   Comparisons

The temporal analogies support several conclusions about the modal paradoxes.

(1)   The modal paradoxes are not illusions produced by literal-minded talk of possible objects and worlds, just as the temporal paradoxes are not illusions produced by literal-minded talk of past objects and times. The analogy is not undermined by the claim that possibilities, unlike times, are to be analysed as sets of propositions, some of which specify the individuals at issue and so prejudge questions of identity. For one can specify a possibility by a counterfactual without listing all the propositions which compose it, just as one can specify a time by a date, and that is how the paradoxes were set up.

(2)   The modal paradoxes give little support to a denial of the S4 principle that if it is possibly the case that it is possibly the case that A then it is possibly the case that A. They may in fact be counter-examples to the principle, for all that has been said here, but we have no good reason to believe that they are. For the temporal paradoxes are not counter-examples to the analogous principle that if it is at some time the case that it is at some time the case that A then it is at some time the case that A. They involve the failure of some other assumption; it will have a modal analogue; why should we suppose that the latter does not fail, and blame the S4 principle instead? Salmon can point to the intuitive plausibility of the other modal assumptions, but he has not shown it to be any greater than the intuitive plausibility of their temporal analogues, at least one of which is false. For what it is worth, the present author's intuitions are equally strong in the two cases. Furthermore, the S4 principle is not behind the modal paradox of section 8.1

(3)   The modal paradoxes give little support to a denial of identity across possible worlds to ordinary objects. For it would be wild to deny them identity over time in attacking the temporal paradoxes. They involve the failure of some other assumption; it will have a modal analogue; why should we suppose that the latter does not fail, and blame identity across possible worlds instead?

Point 3 concerns an *eliminative* attitude to identity across possible worlds. On David Lewis's view, an ordinary person or artifact exists in only one possible world, common sense beliefs apparently to the contrary being made true by relations of counterparthood between similar but distinct objects in different worlds. Lewis does not hold the analogous view that an ordinary person or artifact exists at only one time (1986 pp. 217–20). He is *reductive* rather than eliminative about identity over time; an ordinary person or artifact exists at many times because it is composed of similar but distinct time slices, each of which exists at only one time. Graeme Forbes's use of counterpart theory seems to be intended as reductive rather than eliminative in the modal as well as the temporal case. If the paradoxes are to be given a uniform counterpart-theoretic treatment, it should be at least consistent with a reductive, non-eliminative construal of identity across both worlds and times. Call such a version of counterpart theory *potentially reductive*.

Potentially reductive counterpart theory does not rule out the interpretation of '=' in the modal paradox of section 8.1 as identity. It therefore cannot resolve the paradox by claiming that '=' stands for a non-transitive relation; that move is open only to the eliminative theorist. Nor does it claim that the sorites step identities hold only to a certain degree; as Forbes says, 'the notion of degrees of identity is incoherent' (1985, p. 177). If it supposed the reference of the singular terms to be determinate, it would seem to have only three options: to say that all the identities in the paradox are wholly true, to say that they are all wholly false, or to make invidious distinctions between them. None of these options is attractive. So it looks as though the potentially reductive counterpart theorist should argue that the reference of the singular terms in the modal paradox is indeterminate. Now counterpart theory is not equipped to serve as a general apparatus for applying logic to singular terms of indeterminate reference, for example the results of confused dubbing ceremonies. Yet such an apparatus is desirable; why should it not suffice to resolve the paradox without reference to counterpart theory? The latter's characteristic deviations from classical semantics drop out as irrelevant. Perhaps metaphysical details from the reduction of cross-world identity could be re-used in an explanation of the referential indeterminacy: but such an account is not obviously inconsistent with the use of maximal *M*-relations in this chapter.

9

Criteria of Identity

The phrase 'criterion of identity' has no clear meaning. But has this book not investigated criteria of identity for phenomenal characters, species, people, artifacts? The principles at issue certainly share a distinctive form. What needs to be understood is its significance; why should one prize such principles, and expect to find them? Moreover, not all instances of the form would be counted as proper criteria of identity; what further constraints must be met, and why? Section 9.1 upholds the distinctiveness of the form, on which a criterion of identity for Fs is a relation between non-Fs. Section 9.2 begins to unpick metaphysical and epistemic strands in the use of the phrase 'criterion of identity'. In the relevant sense, a criterion of identity is a metaphysical principle apt to explain epistemic facts.[1]

9.1 Forms

A criterion of identity for Fs is supposed to be at least a necessary and sufficient condition for a pair of Fs to be identical; but it must also be more than that, if the notion is to be of interest. Any demand for a necessary and sufficient condition for such-and-such faces the problem that such-and-such is a necessary and sufficient condition for itself; if the demand is not to be trivially satisfiable, it must be for a necessary and sufficient condition meeting a certain constraint, where such-and-such does not itself meet that constraint. Moreover, it would not do to say just that the constraint is that the condition should be interestingly different from such-and-such, for then the demand would look merely capricious. Why suppose such a condition to exist, or hope to find one?

Sometimes one might require the necessary and sufficient condition to be a definition or analysis of such-and-such. That would

Identity and Discrimination: Reissued and Updated Edition. Timothy Williamson.
© 2013 Timothy Williamson. Published 2013 by Blackwell Publishing Ltd.

be unwise in the case of identity. It is the relation each thing has to itself, and only to itself – which is not a definition but a reminder. There is nothing clearer or more basic than identity in terms of which it could be defined. To require a definition or analysis of identity specifically for Fs would be to compound the mistake; '=' is not ambiguous in its application to different kinds of object. It would be equally wrong to treat a necessary and sufficient condition for the identity of Fs as saying what it is to be an F, for it does not even determine Fhood uniquely, as Frege explained in the case of directions and of numbers. Criteria of identity are not definitions or analyses of anything.

We may say that a necessary and sufficient condition for identity is a criterion of identity just in case it meets the *non-circularity constraint*. However, that is just to label the problem; we still know neither the content of the constraint nor its rationale. The term 'non-circularity' has been chosen not because it has a clear meaning when not used of definitions, but because it lacks one. The constraint will be left hanging in this unsatisfactory state while a more urgent question is addressed, for it has not yet been fully specified what kind of proposition a criterion of identity is to be necessary and sufficient for, and this will in turn affect the non-circularity constraint.

When examples are used to explain what a criterion of identity is, they fall into two kinds (Dummett 1973 pp. 580–1). One is exemplified by the set-theoretic Axiom of Extensionality; sets are the same if they have the same members:

(9.1) $\forall x \forall y (x = y \leftrightarrow \forall z(z \in x \leftrightarrow z \in y))$

(The variables 'x' and 'y' are restricted to sets.) The other kind includes Frege's criterion of identity for directions; lines have the same direction if they are parallel:

(9.2) $\forall x \forall y (ox = oy \leftrightarrow \text{Parallel}(x, y))$

(The variables are restricted to straight lines; ox is the direction of x.) (9.1) and (9.2) differ in form. In (9.2), the identity sign is flanked by terms for directions, whereas the right-hand side states a relation not equivalent to identity between lines which have those directions (distinct lines may be parallel); it is a *two level* criterion of identity. In (9.1), the identity sign is flanked by terms for sets, and the right-hand side states a relation equivalent to identity between those sets; it is a *one level* criterion of identity. It is not easy to understand the phrase 'criterion of identity' on the basis of formally incongruous examples.

A two level criterion of identity for objects of some kind involves a function to such objects from what may not be objects of that kind. The arguments of the function need not be objects at all in Frege's sense; they may be concepts. An example is Frege's criterion of identity for cardinal numbers; the number of things falling under the concept F is the number of things falling under the concept G if the latter can be put in one-one correspondence with the former:

$$(9.3) \quad \forall F \forall G(Nx{:}Fx = Nx{:}Gx \leftrightarrow \exists R(Fx1 - 1_R Gx))$$

('F' and 'G' are restricted to concepts under which objects fall.) Similarly, a two level criterion of identity for sets might say that the set of Fs is the set of Gs if all and only Fs are Gs:

$$(9.4) \quad \forall F \forall G(\{x{:}Fx\} = \{x{:}Gx\} \leftrightarrow \forall x(Fx \leftrightarrow Gx))$$

Of course, some restriction on the variables is needed to avoid Russell's Paradox, which struck down Frege's corresponding Axiom V for value-ranges.[2] In none of the two level criteria (9.2)–(9.4) does the function symbol on the left-hand side appear on the right; perhaps that should be required by the non-circularity constraint for such criteria.

Can either class of criteria be subsumed under the other? One level criteria might be treated as limiting cases of two level criteria in which the function takes everything to itself, but the move looks trivial, and the non-appearance of the function symbol on the right-hand side would no longer be an effective non-circularity constraint. There is certainly a significant difference between (9.1) and (9.4) as criteria of identity for sets; even a restricted (9.4) can act as a set existence axiom, unlike (9.1). No useful purpose is served by treating one level criteria as though they were two level.

Jonathan Lowe has recently suggested that two level criteria can be recast as one level. He proposes to reformulate (9.2) as:

(9.5) $\forall x \forall y ((\text{Direction}(x) \;\&\; \text{Direction}(y)) \rightarrow (x = y \leftrightarrow$
$\exists w \exists z \,(\text{Line}(w) \;\&\; \text{Line}(z) \;\&\; \text{Of}(x, w) \;\&\; \text{Of}(y, z) \;\&\;$
$\text{Parallel}(w, z))))$

(Lowe 1989 p. 6; Ofness is the relation of a direction to the lines which have it.[3]) The claim is suspect, however, and not simply because we lack a criterion of identity for criteria of identity. It can easily be shown that if (9.5) is true, so is:

(9.6) $\forall x \forall y ((\text{Direction}(x) \;\&\; \text{Direction}(y)) \rightarrow (x = y \leftrightarrow$
$\exists w \,(\text{Line}(w) \;\&\; \text{Of}(x, w) \;\&\; \text{Of}(y, w))))$

Directions are the same if some line has both. (9.6) would satisfy any non-circularity constraint satisfied by (9.5), for all the symbols on the right-hand side of the biconditional in (9.6) appear likewise in (9.5). Yet (9.6) does not mention parallelism; it would remain true if 'Direction' were changed to 'Length'. If a criterion of identity for directions is supposed to distinguish them from lengths, (9.6) is not a criterion of identity for directions; by the argument just given, neither is (9.5). Furthermore, (9.5) uses conceptual resources beyond those of (9.2), for if 'Of(x,w)' were defined in terms drawn from (9.2), it would come out as something like '$x = ow$', presumably in violation of the non-circularity constraint on (9.5); the defender of (9.5) must therefore regard 'Of(x,w)', rightly or wrongly, as not definable in such terms. The attempt to reformulate two level criteria as one level is misguided.

Informal criteria are often too inarticulate to fall clearly into either form. Nevertheless, one may display the underlying philosophical concerns more perspicuously than the other. In effect chapter 7 argued this for the case of personal identity, where the two level form made explicit the attempt to trace personal paths through space and time.

The idea of a two level criterion of identity has one obvious advantage. No formula could be more basic (in any relevant sense) than '$x = y$', but some might be more basic than '$ox = oy$', by removing the function symbol 'o' and inserting something more basic than it – as might be claimed for (9.2). Non-circularity constraints make better sense for two level than for one level criteria.[4] Indeed, the clearest example of the latter is the Axiom of

Extensionality, but as an axiom of set theory it is not required to meet any non-circularity constraint at all.

If this book has been concerned with criteria of identity for phenomenal characters, species, people and artifacts, they have been two level; the theory of maximal M-relations is inapplicable to one level criteria. The theory takes as input an incoherent (because non-transitive) two level criterion, and delivers as output a class of coherent two level criteria which are in a precise sense best approximations to the original. What has not been investigated is the source of the input. Why should we have two level criteria of identity in the first place? An answer to the question should not be held responsible to every current use of the phrase 'criterion of identity'; ambiguity and confusion are too rife for that. The answer can give its own sense to the phrase; what present purposes require is that its sense should include the examples discussed in earlier chapters. When but only when the point of the criteria is understood, it should be possible to infer the appropriate non-circularity constraint.

9.2   Functions

The word 'criterion' in philosophy has justly fallen under a cloud. For it was used with the effect of conflating two quite different questions, the metaphysical 'What is it for this to be so-and-so?', and the epistemic 'How can we know that this is so-and-so?'. Both are indifferently rendered as 'What is the criterion for its being a so-and-so?'.[5] The equivocation has been observed still active in the phrase 'criterion of identity'. Writers on personal identity, for instance, have not always been clear about the difference between explaining what it is for the person here now to be the person there then and explaining how we can know that the person here now is the person there then. Appeals to 'what would settle a question of identity' further the confusion. The ambiguity can be traced back to Frege's introduction, via his translator, of the phrase 'criterion of identity' for a means of recognizing an object as the same again. In the passage 'If we are to use the symbol a to signify an object, we must have a criterion for deciding in all cases whether b is the same as a, even if it is not always in our power to apply this criterion' (Frege 1884, section 62), the final clause points to a metaphysical reading without quite closing off an epistemic one: an algorithm may decide all arithmetical questions of some kind, even if it is not always in our power to apply the algorithm when the numbers are too large, and yet the algorithm is a way of knowing the answer to the question, not that in virtue of which the answer is correct. The metaphysical reading no doubt harmonizes better with both the use to which Frege puts the criterion and his overall realism, but the epistemic reading is in places more literal.

The metaphysical and the epistemic questions are not, of course, unrelated. What counts as knowledge of so-and-so depends on what counts as so-and-so. Nevertheless, the questions are distinct in meaning, and any relation between their answers needs to be argued for, not prejudged in the choice of terminology. The relation will not be equivalence in the present case, for some identity propositions are unknowable truths.[6]

Should the ambiguity in 'criterion of identity' be resolved in favour of the metaphysical or the epistemic reading? This book concerns necessary and sufficient conditions for identity propositions. Where the two readings diverge, the metaphysical one follows those conditions, and the epistemic one therefore does not. Where the two readings converge, it matters less which is chosen. The metaphysical reading looks more appropriate.

Unfortunately, the metaphysical reading is itself unclear. What is it to say what it is to be so-and-so? A criterion of identity may be a necessary and sufficient condition for an identity proposition in metaphysically more basic terms, but what does 'metaphysically more basic' mean, and why suppose that such conditions exist? Is some kind of reduction in demand?

As section 9.1 noted, the criteria of identity at issue are two level. They concern identity propositions with complex singular terms; it is not evidently hopeless to seek more basic necessary and sufficient conditions for such propositions. However, that does not answer the questions in the previous paragraph. Indeed, two level criteria raise further questions. For they involve a function from items other than those whose identity is at stake to the latter; what is the metaphysical significance of the function and its arguments? One of the functions discussed took tokens of phenomenal characters to types; another took spatio-temporal locations to people. The relations between argument and value are very different; no point of space-time is a token of a person. Other cases are different again: the relation of concepts to numbers, for instance. Can a uniform account really be given from a metaphysical point of view?

There is a radically reductionist view on which two level criteria are metaphysically uniform. For given the equivalence of $ox = oy$ with Exy, it is formally possible to identify ox with the equivalence class of x under the relation E, just as Frege identified the direction of a line with its equivalence class under the relation of parallelism. On that view, the argument of the function in any two level criterion of identity would stand to its value as member to class. Technical difficulties arise if the equivalence classes are too large to form sets, but the point need not be pressed, for the identification with equivalence classes is anyway quite implausible in many of the cases above. A person is not a class of spatio-temporal locations.[7]

Can two level criteria of identity be conceived in a less radical but equally non-epistemic way, as different principles for 'slicing up reality'? What is missing is a metaphysically uniform relation between the arguments and values of the functions on which the criteria depend. Without one, 'slicing' lacks a uniform sense, and the metaphor does no more than collect some vaguely similar cases; the prospect of theoretical understanding has been cut off. The conception is too nebulous even to rule out the possibility that one kind of thing might have many different criteria of identity: they would not be incompatible, of course, but one would be equivalent to $f(x) = f(y)$ and another to $g(x) = g(y)$, where f and g are distinct functions onto the kind in question (either from the same domain or from different ones). Furthermore, a non-circularity constraint is needed to avoid the trivialization problem, but none has emerged, nor any reason to believe that one can be satisfied. 'Every kind of thing has a criterion of identity': as a metaphysical generalization, the claim is contentless.[8]

A common thread becomes visible from an epistemological standpoint. The arguments of the function can be seen as indexing potential presentations of objects of the relevant kind to knowing subjects; the value of the function is the presented object. A phenomenal character is presented as the character of that token, a species as the species of those animals, a person as the person there then, an artifact as the one made of those materials, a direction as the direction of that line, a set as the extension of that concept. Perhaps the relation of argument to value should be compared with that of sense to reference, not (for example) with that of part to whole. Criteria of identity may address the problem of recognizing an object as the same again more literally than was allowed above.

The epistemological turn immediately raises a host of problems. If criteria of identity are infallible recipes for working out whether one is presented with the same object as before, there are none. If they are fallible rules of thumb, they do not provide necessary and sufficient conditions for identity propositions. If they are not means of recognition but necessary and sufficient conditions for the truth of a claim to recognize, why suppose that they can be given in terms more basic (and in what sense?) than those of the claim itself (the non-circularity problem)? What counts as a presentation in the relevant sense? Can a phenomenal character be presented as the one that would be intermediate in quality between these two, a species as the one with such-and-such a genetic profile, a person as my maternal great-great-grandmother, an artifact as the most valuable in the room, a direction as north, a set as the intersection of all sets containing a given set and closed under a given operation? What of objects which are not or even cannot be presented to a subject: very sub-atomic particles and very inaccessible cardinals, objects in the remote past or at the centre of the sun?

The trick may be to combine metaphysical and epistemological elements, without confusing them, in a judicious mixture. If we can recognize objects of a given kind, those objects are such that we can recognize them.[9] It should be possible to explain our recognitional capacity, and one may hope to extract from that explanation an account of what it is about those objects that enables us to recognize them in the way we do. Sometimes the feature will be a contingent one; if faces varied intra-personally more or inter-personally less, we could not recognize people by their faces. But we can also have knowledge of personal identity by following a person around; the spatio-temporal continuity on which that depends is not obviously contingent. The word 'recognize' may not be the happiest here, suggesting as it does knowledge of identity after separation rather than a process of keeping track. What matters is that the upshot should be *knowledge* of identity (or non-identity, discriminatory capacities being as much at issue as recognitional ones). The subject is therefore at least moderately reliable in appropriate ways. The idea is that an explanation of this reliability will trace it to rough or smooth correlations between the cues to which the subject responds and the conditions which are in fact necessary and sufficient for the presented objects to be identical. In order to establish the correlations, one needs a statement of those conditions addressed to the question: when is the object presented in situation x the same as the object presented in situation y? Without such a statement, no effective comparison could be made with the features of the situation to which the subject is consciously or unconsciously sensitive. The statement would be of two level form, adverting to both the objects and the situations in which they are presented; it might as well be called a two level criterion of identity. A merely pleonastic criterion of identity would provide no basis for an explanation of the reliability of a specific kind of recognitional process; that is the origin of the non-circulatory constraint.

The emerging concept of a criterion of identity is quite a vague one, a gesture towards certain kinds of inquiry: but that does not matter if, as here, it is not used in attempts to make precise theoretical claims. Nor does the argument promise criteria of identity for unrecognizable objects, if such exist. The point is not that they would lack necessary and sufficient conditions for persistence (in the case of objects in time), but that such conditions might be incapable of non-trivial restatement. Even for recognizable objects, the argument is too tenuous to offer any guarantee that a criterion will be found: but it does give the search for one a rationale, by sketching an explanatory role for the criterion to play.

The strategy exploits the fusion of mind-directed and world-directed elements in the concept of knowledge: most obviously, belief and truth. Given a capacity to know about the identity and non-identity of objects of some kind, the need to explain the mind-directed elements drives the criterion of identity towards non-triviality, the need to explain the world-directed elements drives it towards necessity and sufficiency, and the fusion of both kinds of element as knowledge prevents it from splitting under the strain.

The strategy does not in any way imply that subjects who recognize objects must themselves know (however implicitly) a necessary and sufficient criterion of identity for those objects; the explanations of reliability from which it might emerge are to be given by the theorist, who may not be one of the subjects. Our ability to recognize a person does not depend on our possession of a complete criterion of identity for persons; the length and difficulty of the philosophical debate on the matter makes it likely that we have no such criterion. By the same token, we do not associate personal names and our general term 'person' with a complete criterion of identity.

A primitive man might be able to recognize the star Sirius in the sky (by ordinary standards) while believing it to be a hole in a slowly moving heavenly mantle through which light shines: it would be destroyed if a god replaced the mantle by a different one with holes in the same places, but the gods can be relied on to do nothing so foolish. He may have a name for Sirius, and define a general term for stars by pointing to examples. He does not know a correct criterion of identity for stars. Might it therefore be indeterminate what object he is recognizing? The argument of this book does not force an answer. The view that his thought is indeterminate between Sirius and various gruesome mereological sums is consistent with what has been said, but so is the view that the star is singled out as the object of his thought by its causal salience. In either case, recognition by ordinary standards has occurred while the subject lacks what the philosopher seeks.

Even if extreme examples are ignored, an ordinary subject who recognizes an object by ordinary standards will usually be unable to state a non-trivial, complete and correct criterion of identity for objects of that kind, and will be unsure how to describe problem cases. It seems pointless to insist that the subject nevertheless knows such a criterion. If genuine recognition involves such a criterion, ordinary standards being too lax, then it almost never occurs.

What recognition may require is that an *approximate* criterion of identity should be implicit in the subject's practice, even if the subject cannot make it explicit. For the cues on which the recognition depends should be at least locally reliable conditions for identity. The theorist is then faced with the task of working the approximate criterion into an exact one. It has been the theme of this book.

Appendix
Maximal *M*-Relations and the Axiom of Choice

The Axiom of Choice says that for any set X of non-empty sets, there is a function f such that for all $x \in X$, $f(x) \in x$. The Axiom, at one time controversial, is now for most working mathematicians an item of standard equipment (Jech 1973 pp. 1, 11–14, Moore 1982, Hallett 1984 pp. 155–64, Maddy 1988 pp. 487–9 and 737); the need for its use is naturally greater in some branches of mathematics (topology) than in others (number theory). This attitude seems to be a sensible one. The purpose of this appendix is not to discuss the plausibility of the Axiom but to establish its connection with the use of maximal *M*-relations in the text. However, one's view of the Axiom may itself be sensitive to these proofs. Perhaps the Axiom gains some confirmation from the need to invoke it in proving the existence of sets independently predicted on philosophical grounds, as in the case of maximal *M*-relations.

The maximal *M*-relations in the text are relations between individuals – token experiences, animal populations or the like – rather than pure sets – sets which can be built up out of the null set by application of the power set operation, perhaps transfinitely many times. Such relations, as sets of ordered pairs, are themselves impure. An appropriate set theory for the following proofs will therefore allow such individuals. An example is ZFU, Zermelo-Fraenkel set theory with 'ur-elements'. The independence of the Axiom of Choice was in fact proved for such a theory long before it was proved for pure set theory (Fraenkel 1922).

For the application of the Axiom of Choice, relations must be treated as sets of ordered pairs or the like. This raises a metaphysical problem: a criterion of identity is usually expected to work for all possible worlds, not just this one; now the existence of a set

Identity and Discrimination: Reissued and Updated Edition. Timothy Williamson.
© 2013 Timothy Williamson. Published 2013 by Blackwell Publishing Ltd.

surely requires the existence of its members, but then the set of ordered pairs that serves as a criterion of identity in one world will not serve in another, since it will not relate objects that exist in the latter world but not in the former. To overcome this problem, one could think of a relation as being *realized* by different sets of ordered pairs in different worlds and apply the Axiom of Choice to pick a maximal *M*-relation for each world separately rather than for all collectively. However, that would leave two further problems unsolved. First, it would not help with transworld identities. Second, since there are distinct maximal *M*-relations in a given world, some kind of transworld Axiom of Choice would be needed to prove the existence of a complete criterion by picking one maximal *M*-relation for each world. For this reason, incidentally, one cannot avoid appeal to the Axiom in those cases where the relevant set of individuals is always finite, or countable, for it does not follow that the class of choices which need to be made is finite or countable. A bolder approach would be to apply the Axiom directly to a class of ordered pairs of possible individuals and worlds (Williamson 1989 suggests a metaphysical picture that would justify this approach).

Once individuals or sets in distinct possible worlds are considered simultaneously, it becomes a live possibility that there are 'too many' of them to form a set. For David Kaplan has given an argument which could be interpreted as a *reductio ad absurdum* of the assumption that there is a set of possible worlds (Davies 1981 p. 262, Lewis 1986 pp. 104–8). In that case, one should regard the worlds as forming a proper class, a class 'too large' to be a set. The appropriate background would then be a theory with quantification over classes too: set theory in the style of von Neumann, Bernays and Gödel rather than Zermelo and Fraenkel. Moreover, the existence of maximal *M*-relations would then be equivalent to a global form of the Axiom of Choice, the assumption that there is a function f such that for each non-empty set x, $f(x) \in x$. The domain of such a function is a proper class rather than a set, as in the local form. Local Choice does not entail Global Choice, but the latter is still provably consistent with standard class theory (for a comparison, although not in the context of a theory with individuals, see Felgner 1976). Variants of the results below can be proved for maximal *M*-relations over a proper class (equivalents M 7S and M 8S of Global Choice at p. 122 of Rubin and Rubin

1963 are useful). The existence of maximal *M*-relations in this case thereby becomes slightly more controversial.

This equivalence between the Axiom of Choice and a form of philosophical analysis is not an isolated phenomenon; Carnap's notion of a quality class behaves in the same way (Williamson 1986 pp. 390–94).

THEOREM

The following propositions are equivalent:

(a)   The Local Axiom of Choice.
(b)   Let M be a reflexive symmetric relation on a set Y and F an equivalence relation on Y such that $F \subseteq M$; then there is an equivalence relation E on Y such that $F \subseteq E \subseteq M$ and for any equivalence relation E' on Y, if $E \subseteq E' \subseteq M$ then $E = E'$.
(c)   Let M be a reflexive symmetric relation on a set Y; then there is an equivalence relation E on Y such that $E \subseteq M$ and for any equivalence relation E' on Y, if $E \subseteq E' \subseteq M$ then $E = E'$.

PROOF

(a)$\Rightarrow$(b). The Axiom of Choice is equivalent to Zorn's Lemma, that a non-empty partially ordered set in which every chain has an upper bound has a maximal element (Jech 1973 pp. 9–11). The set R of equivalence relations G on Y such that $F \subseteq G \subseteq M$ is non-empty (it includes F), partially ordered by inclusion, and the union of any chain in R is an upper bound in R for that chain. Let E be a maximal element of R.

(b)$\Rightarrow$(c). Let F in (b) be identity.

(c)$\Rightarrow$(a). Let X be a set of non-empty sets. Define Y as

$$\{\langle x, 0, 0 \rangle : x \in X\} \cup \{\langle x, 1, y \rangle : x \in X, y \in x\}.$$

Define a relation M on Y by: $<x, i, y>$ has M to $<x', i', y'>$ if $x = x'$ and either $y = y'$ or $i = 0$ or $i' = 0$. M is reflexive and symmetric. Let E be as in (c) and $x \in X$. $<x, 0, 0>$ has E to at most one triple of the form $<x, 1, y>$, where $y \in x$, for no two such triples have M to each other. Suppose $<x, 0, 0>$ has E to no such triple. Thus its equivalence class under E is $\{<x, 0, 0>\}$. Let $y \in x$; then the equivalence class of $<x, 1, y>$ under E is $\{<x, 1, y>\}$, for the only other element it has M to is $<x, 0, 0>$. Let E' be like E except that it has the equivalence class $\{<x, 0, 0>, <x, 1, y>\}$. But then $E \subseteq E' \subseteq M$, contradicting the maximality of E. So if $x \in X$, $<x, 0, 0>$ has E to exactly one triple $<x, 1, y>$, where $y \in x$. The function which takes x to y is the required choice function for X. QED

It can easily be checked that the above arguments go through when the word 'symmetric' is deleted.

Notes (to the First Edition)

Chapter 1 Concepts of Indiscriminability

1 The vast psychological literature on discrimination will not be discussed in this book (see e.g. Luce and Galanter 1963). The omission may be rationalized by the hope of a theory applicable to all possible discrimination, not just to human and allied kinds. The relevance of psychology to the study of discrimination is comparable with its relevance to the study of knowledge.

2 A mathematical analogy: direct discriminability might be thought of as a recursive relation, indirect discriminability as a recursively enumerable but not recursive one. If cases of discriminability and indiscriminability by direct means are always recognizable as such, then the same goes for discriminability but not necessarily indiscriminability by indirect means. A possible disanalogy: the extension of a recursively enumerable relation can be listed in such a way that each pair it contains will sooner or later appear; if the domain of objects of discrimination is not enumerable, there may be no method for listing the extension of direct or indirect discriminability.

3 The concepts of reflexivity, symmetry, transitivity and non-transitivity can be extended to cover intentional constructions, by use of substitutional rather than objectual quantifiers in their definitions.

Chapter 2 Logics of Indiscriminability

1 Lenzen 1978 is a general introduction to epistemic logic; Hintikka 1962 is a seminal work.

2 The principle that identity entails sharing of properties and relations may not validate (LL) or its equivalent for all languages (Richard 1987). However, variables will not be used here in the fine-grained way necessary to produce this slippage. In particular, a difference of variable in a characterization of knowledge is not to be understood as signalling a difference of presentation in the knowledge so characterized; $a = b, \boxed{K}\, a = a \vdash \boxed{K}\, a = b$ is a correct sequent.

3 Chellas 1980 provides the technical background for the ensuing discussion of principles of propositional modal logic.

4 The easiest way to see this is to note that both of the rules mentioned

Identity and Discrimination: Reissued and Updated Edition. Timothy Williamson.
© 2013 Timothy Williamson. Published 2013 by Blackwell Publishing Ltd.

in the text are valid when $\langle\!\langle k \rangle\!\rangle$ is interpreted as some sort of non-epistemic *necessity*, whereas this is not so of $A \vdash \langle\!\langle k \rangle\!\rangle A$ or $\langle\!\langle k \rangle\!\rangle (A \lor B) \vdash \langle\!\langle k \rangle\!\rangle A \lor \langle\!\langle k \rangle\!\rangle B$.

5   Humberstone 1988 also discusses links between epistemically interpreted iteration principles and concepts of discrimination.

6   Background material is to be found in Hughes and Cresswell 1968 at pp. 189–95.

7   See n. 2.

8   The model also validates the schema $\boxed{\text{K}} \sim \boxed{\text{K}}$ ($\langle\!\langle k \rangle\!\rangle A$ & $\langle\!\langle k \rangle\!\rangle \sim A$), which yields the system sometimes known as S4.1 (it is given an epistemic interpretation in Kripke 1963 at p. 71). Thus (2.3) is not derivable in S4.1. Note that S4.1 is not a subsystem of KT5.

Chapter 3   Paradoxes of Indiscriminability

1   Some of the many relevant discussions are Dummett 1975 and 1979, Wright 1975, 1976 and 1987, Platts 1979, Peacocke 1981, Linsky 1984, Travis 1985 and Burns 1986.

2   (3.2) entails the converse sequent $\langle\!\langle k \rangle\!\rangle a = b$, $Fb \vdash Fa$ by substitution and the symmetry of indiscriminability.

3   The role of classical logic in these arguments will not have been overlooked.

4   Compare Dummett 1975 p. 265 and Peacocke 1981 p. 121. There are certainly many vague adjectives whose comparatives are not vague, at least not to anything like the same extent: 'tall' for example (if being taller than something does not require being tall). However, when such cases are unproblematic the vagueness is not rooted in observationality; if the adjective were purely observational, its comparative would be too. Dummett argues at pp. 9–12 of 1979 that (in his terminology) the supposed incoherence of simple observational qualities does not extend to simple observational relations, because there is no appropriate concept of indiscriminability for n-tuples of the relevant items and in particular that term by term indiscriminability (as in the antecedent of (3.2+)) is inappropriate because a simple observational relation is not determined by the simple observational qualities of its terms. For instance, if a is indiscriminable from b it does not follow that a has the relation of indiscriminability to c if and only if b has. Dummett's inference from his own definitions is not being challenged, but there is a non-trivial class of n-adic predicates which seem to be threatened with incoherence in just the way that monadic observational predicates are; (3.1a+,b+) are as plausible for 'redder than' as (3.1a,b) for 'red'.

Chapter 4   Concepts of Phenomenal Character

1   Might identity in character be indeterminate? The possibility will be discussed in the next chapter. It would not upset the argument in the text, for (4.2) and (4.3) would have it *determinately* the case that examples of the kind appealed to do not occur, which is absurd.

2   If the domain includes merely possible experiences, discriminability will also need to be cross-world, presumably requiring the existence of a world in which the objects of discrimination co-exist and are discriminated; it may be required that the relevant cognitive capacities are the same in this world as in the actual one. Experiences might then be individuated in such a way that an experience cannot have different phenomenal characters in different worlds (compare the problem discussed at pp. 134 and 140 n.9 of Peacocke 1981; see also Wright 1987 p. 254).

Chapter 5   Logics of Phenomenal Character

1   If M is not reflexive there are no M-relations. If M is not symmetric, an M-relation is simply an N-relation, where N is the conjunction of M and its converse (for purposes of this book it is convenient to take relations as classes of ordered pairs, rather than in the sense of Williamson 1985); N is symmetric. Thus even when M is not interpreted as matching, it might as well be assumed to be reflexive and symmetric.

2   Another related issue in the philosophy of mind is the supervenience of the mental on the physical. Some maximal M-relations may assign the same phenomenal character to experiences with physically indistinguishable bases, and this may be regarded as ruling them out as criteria of identity for characters.

3   Proof: Consider any linear sequence of 2n experiences, each of which matches only itself and its immediate predecessor and successor (if any). Since no three experiences match each other, any M-relation has at least n equivalence classes. Just one M-relation E has exactly n equivalence classes: start at one end of the sequence and divide it into pairs; thus E is a maximal M-relation, the only one to obey the Minimality Constraint, and experiences are uncontroversially the same (different) in character if and only if E holds (does not hold) between them. Thus if two experiences match, their uncontroversial sameness or difference in character depends on whether the number of experiences before them in the sequence is even or odd. This is a global rather than a local feature, and it can be shown not to be equivalent in the circumstances to any first-order condition on matching as n varies.

4   However, a sequent may preserve truth on the supervaluation without preserving it on every valuation.

5   The argument is given in Evans 1978 and Salmon 1981, clarified in

Lewis 1988 and Stalnaker 1988 and amplified in the appendix to Salmon 1986 and Wiggins 1986.

6   The objection is made in Parsons 1987; I choose it because I know of no better in the proliferating literature on the subject.

7   For related difficulties in the interpretation of many-valued semantics see Dummett 1958/9.

8   See also Clark 1985, Dummett 1955 pp. 34–6 and 1957 pp. 52–7, Hausman 1967 pp. 79–90, Linsky 1984, Peacocke 1981 p. 126, Putnam 1956, Wright 1975 pp. 354–7 and 1987 pp. 253–4. If M were not symmetric, the appropriate right-hand side would be $\forall z((Mxz \leftrightarrow Myz)\ \&\ (Mzx \leftrightarrow Mzy))$. This condition ensures that no formula in the first-order predicate calculus whose only predicate letter is M even weakly discriminates between x and y, in the terminology of Quine 1976b. The effect of (5.7) is thus an 'identification of indiscernibles', a refusal to make a distinction without a (certain kind of) difference; see Quine 1960 p. 230 and Wiggins 1980 pp. 199–201.

9   Proof: By the Axiom of Choice, there is a choice function for the equivalence classes of the relation of matching the same experiences; for any experience x, let x^* be the chosen element from the equivalence class of x. For any equivalence relation E on experiences, let $E\#$ be such that $E\#xy$ just in case Ex^*y^*. $E\#$ is clearly an equivalence relation. Since x^* matches the same experiences as x and y^* as y, Mx^*y^* entails Mxy, so $E\#$ is an M-relation if E is. Moreover $E\#$ includes matching the same experiences, for if x and y match the same experiences then x^* is y^*, giving Ex^*y^* and therefore $E\#xy$. Let g be the function which maps the equivalence class of x under $E\#$ to the equivalence class of x^* under E; g is well-defined and 1–1 by definition of $E\#$. Thus $E\#$ has no more equivalence classes than E has. Now let E be a maximal M-relation which obeys the Minimality Constraint. Since $E\#$ is an M-relation, some maximal M-relation F includes $E\#$. F has no more equivalence classes than $E\#$ has, so no more than E, so it too obeys the Minimality Constraint. F includes matching the same experiences because $E\#$ does; thus it satisfies the constraint in (5.9). QED

Chapter 6   Paradoxes of Phenomenal Character

1   For references see n. 1 to ch. 3.

2   Compare Dummett 1975 p. 264, Wright 1975 pp. 338ff. and 1976 pp. 233ff.

3   Peacocke 1981 and Sainsbury 1988/9; compare Wright 1975 pp. 348–51, 1976 pp. 237–40 and 1987 pp. 250–61.

4   There is a different sense in which a phenomenal relation between two experiences might depend on the phenomenal character of their mereological sum, or something of the kind, as well as on their

individual phenomenal characters; see n. 4 to ch. 3.

5 Predicates true of all experiences or of none are phenomenal predicates which do not vary in extension. Are there any others? That depends on the topology of experience. If two experiences are unrelated by the ancestral of matching, an invariant phenomenal predicate can distinguish between them and the answer to the question is 'Yes'. If every two experiences are related by the ancestral of matching, the answer is 'No'.

6 The arguments considered in this section are suggested by work of Crispin Wright, especially 1975 pp. 335–37 and 1976 pp. 230–2, but do not follow it in detail. His position is modified in Wright 1987.

7 See Hart 1979 and Sorensen 1988 ch. 4. Intuitionists may object (Williamson 1988a), but I assume that most readers are not intuitionists. For the inadequacy of intuitionist logic as a solution to sorites paradoxes see Cargile 1969 and Wright and Read 1985.

8 The denial of this principle at p. 228 of Nozick 1981 has some claim to be a *reductio ad absurdum* of the analysis of knowledge there expounded. The principle is endorsed at Dretske 1970 p. 1009 and Barwise and Perry 1983 p. 195.

9 A sorites paradox for 'known to be F' could be constructed on the assumptions that (a) the knowledge operator has a KT4 logic and (b) every instance of (6.6) is known. If the steps of the sorites are short enough (b) is plausible, and it will do no harm to assume a KT logic for very rational subjects, but the S4 axiom itself may fail for such objects: they can know that x_i is F without knowing that they know. The epistemic theory predicts this from the vagueness of the concept of knowledge (Sorensen 1988 pp. 242–3).

10 Might different omniscient speakers answer in different ways, meaning what we mean by 'red' and with no change in the relevant facts? The difference would matter only if one but not both answered 'Yes' to some question. Then one omniscient speaker would refrain from answering 'Yes' to a question to which it is a correct answer (because the other omniscient – and truthful – speaker gives it): but then the former speaker is holding something back from us, whereas it may be assumed that both intend to be fully informative.

Chapter 7   Generalizations

1 It is assumed that only one object can be at a given location. The effect of relaxing this constraint is discussed at pp. 390–2 of Williamson 1986.

2 Diachronic species identity presents a new set of problems. A recent discussion of species identity is Splitter 1988.

3 Parfit 1971, Perry 1972 and D. K. Lewis 1976 provide particularly relevant background. One option they discuss is that persons may

overlap; compare n. 1. Parfit and Lewis also mention the problem of longevity in a single body, where gradual change accumulates to utter transformation; it displays a different way in which transitivity could break down.

4   Locations not occupied by any person are excluded.

5   The remark in the text invites Butler's charge of circularity, and excludes a reply to him in terms of the concept of apparent memory (Perry 1975 pp. 135–55, Wiggins 1980 pp. 152–4, Parfit 1984 pp. 219–22). The point is more pressing because the memory condition must fail in cases of fission if it is to be sufficient for personal identity. However (a) the argument in the text is schematic and could apply to a condition revised in the light of this diffi-culty; (b) circularity is not a decisive objection to an account that aspires only to say something true, informative and illuminating about personal identity; (c) the claim is that the non-transitivity problem is appropriately dealt with in a certain way, not that the result faces no other problems. Note that the third disjunct in the definition of M ('x is y') introduces no circularity, since it concerns the identity of locations, not persons.

6   If M is not reflexive and symmetric, the smallest reflexive symmetric relation to include it is given by the formula $Mxy \lor Myx \lor x = y$. The argument then proceeds as in the text.

Chapter 8   Modal and Temporal Paradoxes

1   One could distinguish between a cut from P_r to P_{r+180} and one from P_{r+180} to P_r, depending on the orientation of the workman to the disc. The argument can be adapted accordingly.

2   To be precise, the difference between x and y is the least positive real number z such that either $x = y + z$ or $y = x + z$ (modulo 360).

3   A square bracket means that the endpoint is included in the interval, a round one that it is not.

4   Proof: any equivalence class of an M-relation is included in a half-open quad-rant. Four of these quadrants would not cover the whole circle if two of them overlapped.

5   It might be necessary to choose anti-clockwise rather than clockwise counting; $\{[0, 90), [90, 180), [180, 270), [270, 360)\}$ and $\{(0, 90], (90, 180], (180, 270], (270, 360]\}$ are distinct partitions, although there may be no corresponding physical difference.

6   What follows is loosely based on an ingenious suggestion made by Eli Hirsch.

7   For more on the comparison between modal and temporal paradoxes see Quine 1976a, Over 1984 and 1986, Salmon 1984, Forbes 1985 pp. 188–9, Lowe 1986, Lewis 1986 pp. 217–20. The Methuselah case mentioned in n. 3 to the previous chapter is also relevant.

Chapter 9   Criteria of Identity

1   The concept of a criterion of identity is discussed in Quine 1950, Dummett 1973, Strawson 1976, Gottlieb 1979, Wiggins 1980, Pollard 1986, Lowe 1988 and 1989, Noonan 1988.

2   For more on these examples see Wright 1983 and Boolos 1986/7.

3   Lowe says that (9.5), presumably unlike (9.2), makes the sortal-relativity of the criterion quite explicit (ibid.). However, this reflects not the one level/two level contrast but the unrestrictedness of the variables in (9.5), which requires the explicit relativizations to directions and lines, whereas (9.2) uses sortally restricted variables. Either formula could be recast in the style of the other. That (9.2) concerns identity only for directions is in any case quite explicit in the intended reading of 'o'.

4   Lowe's charge of circularity against Davidson's one level criterion of identity for events appeals to a cloudy notion of presupposition (Lowe 1989 pp. 7–8).

5   The form of the question also insinuates that there must be one and only one criterion for so-and-so, or at least that something is wrong with so-and-so if there is not.

6   Example: let P be an undecidable proposition of mathematics and for any proposition Q let $f(Q)$ be Plato if Q is true and Aristotle otherwise; either '$f(P) =$ Plato' or '$f(P) =$ Aristotle' expresses an unknowable truth.

7   How can we be so sure? Were I the class of my space-time co-ordinates, each of them would be essential to me, as a class's members are to it; but I might not have been here now. That argument could be met by a retreat only as far as the view that a person is a class of space-time-world co-ordinates (worlds will not contain people – since people contain worlds – but only things on which people supervene). However, if a person is a class of quintuples $<x, y, z, t, w>$, what is the class of corresponding quintuples $<w, x, y, z, t>$? It is something isomorphic to a person which is not a person: but there are no such things. Both views also need fancy footwork to accommodate the fact that I am *wholly* inside my room. A more radical objection is that we are not classes of any kind. Classes are abstract; we are not. We are unities; classes are not. We smile; classes do not (or only in an irrelevant sense, when most members of them do). Such arguments are probably sound, but may gain more persuasive force than they deserve from the sheer unfamiliarity of what they attack.

8   It is not denied that the claim has metaphysical content when some restriction is understood: for instance, to cases in which the arguments of the function are spatio-temporal locations and the values are things of some specified kind at those locations. Such content lacks the generality requisite for present purposes.

9   Recognition is individual rather than collective here: as that F, not just as an F (compare the distinction between criteria of identity and criteria of application).

Additional Notes (to the Revised Edition)

Chapter 1   Concepts of Indiscriminability

p. 14:   Graff 2001 announces itself as arguing for the transitivity of phenomenal indiscriminability, but turns out to argue for the transitivity of looking the same as instead (p. 905). They are not the same relation, even when phenomenal indiscriminability is restricted to visual respects.

   To understand looking the same, it is vital not to confuse *sameness of appearance* and *appearance of sameness*, where sameness is exact sameness in a given respect or respects, and appearances of sameness are analogous to appearances of any other relation, such as kicking. Here is a case of sameness of appearance without appearance of sameness. John and Mary are unaware of each other but have similar visual systems. John looks at a sphere. Meanwhile, elsewhere, Mary looks at another sphere of the same colour and size from the same distance in the same lighting conditions. The way John's sphere looks to him is the same as the way Mary's sphere looks to her. What occurs is sameness of appearance between the two spheres but neither appearance of sameness nor appearance of difference, because nobody is aware of both spheres. Conversely, here is a case of appearance of sameness without sameness of appearance. I have two complicated figures in plain view. I notice no difference between them. They look to me to be the same. On a purely visual basis, I judge that they are the same. That is an appearance to me of sameness in shape between the two figures. However, you point out to me some clear differences that I had missed. One of them has a line to which no line in the other corresponds. I could see the line all along in the first figure and did not

Identity and Discrimination: Reissued and Updated Edition. Timothy Williamson.
© 2013 Timothy Williamson. Published 2013 by Blackwell Publishing Ltd.

hallucinate a corresponding line in the second, but I failed to make the comparison in enough detail to notice the difference. All along the two figures slightly differed in their appearance to me. Thus there is not the relevant sameness of appearance with respect to shape.

Sameness of appearance is of course a transitive relation, just as sameness of anything else is (recall that 'sameness' here means exact sameness, not an approximation). To that extent I agree with the conclusion of Graff (2001). But having an appearance of sameness is not a transitive relation, even when the objects in question appear together. For example, imagine a sorites series of colour samples C_0, C_1, ..., C_n from red to yellow laid out like the spokes of a wheel, so that C_n is next to C_0. When $0 \leq m < n$, C_m looks the same colour as C_{m+1} (appearance of sameness in colour), but C_0 does not look the same colour as C_n.

Neither sameness of appearance nor appearance of sameness is equivalent to indiscriminability. Indiscriminability does not entail sameness of appearance. For example, in that sorites series each C_m may be too close to C_{m+1} for one to discriminate them in colour under the given conditions: for all one is in a position to know, they are exactly the same shade. But since C_0 obviously differs in appearance from C_n with respect to colour, so does C_m from C_{m+1} for some m. Thus C_m and C_{m+1} are indiscriminable but differ in appearance. Hence the transitivity of sameness of appearance does not imply the transitivity of indiscriminability. Nor does indiscriminability entail the appearance of sameness. For example, in the Müller-Lyer illusion, the two lines are indiscriminable in length, because they are the same length (indiscriminability is reflexive), but they lack the appearance of sameness in length, because one of them appears to be longer than the other.

The foregoing points about looking the same are closely related to points about feeling the same made at p. 93. For more on looking the same, non-transitivity, and related issues see Williamson 1994, pp. 172–9, Raffman 2000, De Clercq and Horsten 2004, Deutsch 2005, Hellie 2005, Farkas 2006, Pelling 2007, Chuard 2010, Keefe 2011 and Breckenridge forthcoming.

Chapter 4   Concepts of Phenomenal Character

p. 49:   For an earlier occurrence of the non-transitivity problem see Russell 1914, p. 148: 'it is important to realize that two sense-data may be, and *must* sometimes be, really different when we cannot perceive any difference between them. [...] In all cases of sense-data capable of gradual change, we may find one sense-datum indistinguishable from another, and that other indistinguishable from a third, while yet the first and third are quite easily distinguishable'. He refers to it as an old point emphasized by Poincaré (1893 p. 29), from whom he took the example of weights. Poincaré regarded such cases of non-transitivity as characteristic of physical (as opposed to mathematical) continuity.

Chapter 6   Paradoxes of Phenomenal Character

p. 93: The points made in the additional note to p. 14 about looking the same have analogues for feeling the same.

Chapter 7   Generalizations

p. 124: For most of the applications considered in this book, the relation M is arguably either necessary, and therefore not sufficient, for identity in the relevant respect, or sufficient, and therefore not necessary (usually the former). However (7.4) and its quantitative analogues also apply to equivalence relations that M overlaps but is neither necessary nor sufficient for. They may sometimes constitute the best approximations to M. A more general treatment will consider such cases in detail. See De Clercq and Horsten 2005 for significant progress in that direction, using both qualitative and quantitative standards of comparative closeness. Also relevant are Delvaux and Horsten 2004 and Carrara and Gaio 2009.

Chapter 8   Modal and Temporal Paradoxes

p. 128: The work cited as Williamson 1989 appeared as Williamson 1990. It is an early sketch of the necessitist metaphysics of quantified modal logic later developed in Williamson 1998 and now, more thoroughly, in Williamson 2013.

p. 138: My views on the relation between vagueness and identity are developed in: Williamson 1994 pp. 252–6, 1996 (to which Wiggins 1996 replies), 2002 (to which Edgington 2002 replies) and 2003 pp. 707–12.

p. 142: For a reply to the objection to Salmon's use of modal paradoxes against the S4 principle see Salmon 1993. In broad terms, the dispute between Salmon and me concerns which paradoxes are sufficiently similar in their assumptions to be likely to have similar diagnoses. For the time being, I leave it to the reader to judge. In the long run, the issue will be decided (so far as it ever is) by which overall theories of vagueness and of modal and temporal metaphysics do best.

Chapter 9   Criteria of Identity

p. 145: It is worth noting that Frege's criterion of identity for directions is not obviously correct. As Miroslava Andjelković once remarked to me, it identifies what are usually regarded as opposite directions, since the line from A to B *is* (and so is parallel to) the line from B to A. Perhaps we should treat it as a criterion of identity for *slopes* instead. In that case a different criterion is needed for (oriented) directions, perhaps using an equivalence relation on ordered pairs of two points rather than on lines.

p. 147: The question 'What is the criterion of identity for directions?' may be construed as asking either 'When do lines have the same direction?' or 'When are directions identical?' Frege's answer 'When they are parallel' fits the former question, not the latter, for it specifies a relation other than identity between lines, not directions. Lowe thinks the latter question more fundamental, and claims that Frege's criterion can be reformulated to answer it: 'When some line with one is parallel to some line with the other'. In the text, I make three points against this view: (a) Lowe's construal does not permit a principled rejection of a clearly inappropriate answer to the question. (b) On pain of circularity, Lowe's answer uses expressive resources ('Of' as primitive) beyond those of Frege's, and thus is not a mere reformulation. (c) Lowe's question seems to make the hopeless demand for something more basic (in some sense) than '$x = y$'. Lowe's reply (1991) does not address (b) or (c). In this note I follow him in discussing only (a).

Presumably, an appropriate answer to the question 'What is the criterion of identity for directions?' will mention parallelism. Given Frege's construal, one can explain why: the point is to say when lines have the same direction without mentioning directions. Given Lowe's construal, no such explanation is possible. Why is it wrong to answer his question 'When some line has both'? Lowe agrees that directions are identical if and only if some line has both. Indeed, his preferred equivalence entails the new one (the only point here is that someone who uses his equivalence should not reject the new one as false; Lowe seems to misread the book as claiming more for the entailment). Nor can Lowe accuse the new answer of circularity or total uninformativeness. Yet it is clearly inappropriate, for it does not mention parallelism. It does not even distinguish directions from lengths, and Lowe rejects it for this reason. However, he leaves it as an unexplained datum that what the identity of directions consists in must differ from what the identity of lengths consists in, whereas what the identity of cats consists in is the same as what the identity of dogs consists in, according to Lowe (1998 p. 45). He gives no basis of principle on which to reject the claim that each separately consists in the existence of something having both. In contrast, the Fregean approach makes the obvious explanation available. Directions and lengths have different criteria of identity because two lines (line segments) can have the same direction and different lengths, or *vice versa*. This contrast in explanatory power provides a good reason for preferring Frege's approach to Lowe's.

Lowe later returned to the issue, arguing that the Fregean explanation of the difference 'is no explanation at all, for if it were correct parity of reasoning would require us to say that *heights* and *widths* must have different criteria of identity because two plane figures can have the same height and different widths, or *vice versa*—yet heights and widths are both kinds of lengths, being vertical and horizontal lengths respectively, and so must in fact share the *same* criterion of identity, namely, that of lengths in general' (1998 p. 47). Since Lowe's attempted reductio takes for granted that the criterion of identity for lengths is one-level, contrary to the Fregean two-level view, it fails to refute the Fregean explanation. Even if we assume that heights and widths are the very same things, as Lowe (ibid.) explicitly refrains from doing, what follows is only that one should not, strictly speaking, ascribe a two-level criterion of identity to heights or widths themselves, but rather speak of answers to the non-equivalent questions 'When do plane figures have the same height?' and 'When do plane figures have the same width?'. A two-level theorist might have expected that anyway. Of course, if one identifies heights with equivalence classes of plane figures under the same-height relation, and widths with equivalence classes of plane figures under the same-width relation, then one cannot also maintain that heights and widths are the very same things; but the interest of two-level criteria of identity is not restricted to logical constructionist views. Lowe goes on to deny that one can explain why lengths and directions have different criteria of identity, on the grounds that the different criteria are simply built into the meanings of the sortal terms (ibid.). But this is to mistake the challenge. He is not even entitled to assume that lengths and directions *do* have different one-level criteria of identity, since the coinstantiation criterion above works for both lengths and directions. Of course, there are many obvious differences between lengths and directions, just as there are many obvious differences between cats and dogs, but it does not follow that they differ in their one-level criteria of identity. By contrast, the Fregean, who focuses on the questions 'When are things identical in length?' and 'When are things identical in direction?', can easily explain why they have different answers. For more on one-level identity criteria see Noonan 2009.

p. 153: Historically, discussions of criteria of identity have mixed together considerations of logic and semantics, metaphysics and epistemology, with insufficient sense of the distinctions. Although chapter 9 protests against the confusion, it still employs the terminology and tries to find useful work for it to do. I now think that the term 'criterion of identity' and its associated ideology do far more harm than good in philosophy; we should abandon both. The only theory of identity itself we need is a completely general, purely logical one. Nevertheless, we must speak of identity ubiquitously in metaphysics (and elsewhere), just as we must use quantifiers, negation and conjunction. What remain of two-level criteria of identity are abstraction principles, which have an independently established role in mathematics and logic. For example, the theory of rational numbers requires the principle that $p/q = r/s$ if and only if $ps = qr$, where p and r are integers and q and s are non-zero integers, which we can think of as in some sense abstracting the rationals from ordered pairs of integers. Again, the structure of an order relation R on a set X is identical with the structure of an order relation S on a set Y if and only if there is an order-isomorphism from $<X, R>$ onto $<Y, S>$.

For some more general discussion of identity criteria see Carrara and Giaretta 2003, 2004, Horsten 2010, and Leitgeb forthcoming.

References (to the First Edition)

Armstrong, D. M. (1961): *Perception and the Physical World*, Routledge and Kegan Paul.

Austin, D. F., ed. (1988): *Philosophical Analysis: A Defense by Example*, Kluwer.

Barwise, J. and Perry, J. (1983): *Situations and Attitudes*, MIT Press.

Bolzano, B. (1851): *Paradoxien des Unendlichen*, tr. by D. A. Steele as *Paradoxes of the Infinite*, Routledge and Kegan Paul, 1959.

Boolos, G. (1986/7): 'Saving Frege from contradiction', *Proceedings of the Aristotelian Society*, 87.

Burns, L. (1986): 'Vagueness and coherence', *Synthese*, 68.

Cargile, J. (1969): 'The sorites paradox', *British Journal for the Philosophy of Science*, 20.

_____ (1979): *Paradoxes: A Study in Form and Predication*, Cambridge University Press.

Chellas, B. F. (1980): *Modal Logic: An Introduction*, Cambridge University Press.

Chisholm, R. M. (1967): 'Identity through possible worlds: some questions', *Nous*, 1; in Loux 1979.

_____ (1970): 'Identity through time' and 'Reply to Strawson's comments', in Kiefer and Munitz 1970.

Church, A. (1982): 'A remark concerning Quine's paradox about modality', Spanish version in *Analisis Filosofico*, 2, English version in Salmon and Soames 1988.

Clark, A. (1985): 'A physicalist theory of qualia', *Monist*, 68.

Davies, M. K. (1981): *Meaning, Quantification, Necessity: Themes in Philosophical Logic*, Routledge and Kegan Paul.

Dretske, F. (1970): 'Epistemic operators', *Journal of Philosophy*, 67.

Dummett, M. A. E. (1955): 'The structure of appearance', *Mind*, 64, page refs. to reprinting in Dummett 1978.

_____ (1957): 'Constructionalism', *Philosophical Review*, 66, page refs. to reprinting in Dummett 1978.

_____ (1958/9): 'Truth', *Proceedings of the Aristotelian Society*, 59; in Dummett 1978.

_____ (1973): *Frege: Philosophy of Language*, Duckworth.

_____ (1975): 'Wang's paradox', *Synthese*, 30, page refs. to reprinting in Dummett 1978.

_____ (1978): *Truth and Other Enigmas*, Duckworth.

Identity and Discrimination: Reissued and Updated Edition. Timothy Williamson.
© 2013 Timothy Williamson. Published 2013 by Blackwell Publishing Ltd.

—— (1979): 'Common sense and physics', in Macdonald 1979.

Evans, M. G. J. (1978): 'Can there be vague objects?', *Analysis*, 38; in Evans 1985.

—— (1982): *The Varieties of Reference*, Oxford University Press.

—— (1985): *Collected Papers*, Oxford University Press.

Evans, M. G. J. and McDowell, J. H., eds. (1976) *Truth and Meaning*, Oxford University Press.

Felgner, U. (1976): 'Choice functions on sets and classes', in Muller 1976.

Fine, K. (1975): 'Vagueness, truth and logic', *Synthese*, 30.

Forbes, G. (1983): 'Thisness and vagueness', *Synthese*, 54.

—— (1984): 'Two solutions to Chisholm's Paradox', *Philosophical Studies*, 46.

—— (1985): *The Metaphysics of Modality*, Oxford University Press.

Fraenkel, A. A. (1922): 'Der Begriff "definit" und die Unabhangigkeit des Auswahlsaxioms', tr. as 'The notion "definite" and the independence of the axiom of choice' in van Heijenoort 1967.

Frege, G. (1884): *Die Grundlagen der Arithmetik*, tr. by J. L. Austin as *The Foundations of Arithmetic*, Blackwell, 2nd ed., 1974.

French, P. A., Uehling, T. E. and Wettstein, H. K., eds. (1981): *Midwest Studies in Philosophy VI: The Foundations of Analytic Philosophy*, University of Minnesota Press.

—— (1986): *Midwest Studies in Philosophy XI: Studies in Essentialism*, University of Minnesota Press.

Goodman, N. (1951): *The Structure of Appearance*, Harvard University Press.

Gottlieb, D. (1979): 'No entity without identity', in Shahan and Swoyer 1979.

Grice, H. P. (1941): 'Personal identity', *Mind*, 50; in Perry 1975.

Gupta, A. (1980): *The Logic of Common Nouns*, Yale University Press.

Hallett, M. (1984): *Cantorian Set Theory and Limitation of Size*, Oxford University Press.

Hardin, C. L. (1988): 'Phenomenal colours and sorites', *Nous*, 22.

Hart, W. D. (1979): 'The epistemology of abstract objects', *Aristotelian Society*, sup. vol. 53.

Hausman, A. (1967): 'Goodman's ontology', in Hausman and Wilson 1967.

Hausman, A. and Wilson F. (1967): *Carnap and Goodman: Two Formalists*, Nijhoff.

Hintikka, J. (1962): *Knowledge and Belief*, Cornell University Press.

—— (1972): 'Knowledge by acquaintance – individuation by acquaintance', in Pears 1972.

Hughes, G. E. and Cresswell, M. J. (1968): *An Introduction to Modal Logic*, Methuen.

Humberstone, I. L. (1988): 'Some epistemic capacities', *Dialectica*, 42.

Jackson, F. C. (1977): *Perception: A Representative Theory*, Cambridge University Press.

Jackson, F. C. and Pinkerton, R. J. (1973): 'On an argument against sensory items', *Mind*, 82.

Jech, T. J. (1973): *The Axiom of Choice*, North Holland.

Kiefer, H. E. and Munitz, M. K., eds. (1970): *Language, Belief and Metaphysics*, SUNY Press.

Kripke, S. A. (1963): 'Semantical considerations on modal logic', *Acta Philosophica Fennica*, 16, page refs. to reprinting in Linsky 1971.

Lenzen, W. (1978): 'Recent work in epistemic logic', *Acta Philosophica Fennica*, 30.

Lewis, D. K. (1976): 'Survival and identity' in Rorty 1976; with postscripts in Lewis 1983.

——— (1983): *Philosophical Papers*, vol. I, Oxford University Press.

——— (1986): *On the Plurality of Worlds*, Blackwell.

——— (1988): 'Vague identity: Evans misunderstood', *Analysis*, 48.

Lewis, H. D., ed. (1976): *Contemporary British Philosophy: Fourth Series*, Allen and Unwin.

Linsky, B. (1984): 'Phenomenal qualities and the identity of indistinguishables', *Synthese*, 59.

Linsky, L., ed. (1971): *Reference and Modality*, Oxford University Press.

Loux, M., ed. (1979): *The Possible and the Actual*, Cornell University Press.

Lowe, E. J. (1986): 'On a supposed temporal/modal parallel' and 'Reply to Over', *Analysis*, 46.

——— (1988): 'Substance, identity and time', *Aristotelian Society*, sup. vol. 62.

——— (1989): 'What is a criterion of identity?', *Philosophical Quarterly*, 39.

Luce, R. D., Bush, R. R. and Galanter, E., eds. (1963): *Handbook of Mathematical Psychology*, vol. 1, Wiley.

Luce, R. D. and Galanter, E. (1963): 'Discrimination', in Luce, Bush and Galanter (1963).

Macdonald, G. F., ed. (1979): *Perception and Identity*, Macmillan.

Mackie, J. L. (1976): *Problems from Locke*, Oxford University Press.

Maddy, P. (1988): 'Believing the axioms', I and II, *Journal of Symbolic Logic*, 53.

Marsh, R. C., ed. (1956): *Logic and Knowledge*, Allen and Unwin.

Minkoff, E. C. (1983): *Evolutionary Biology*, Addison-Wesley.

Moore, G. H. (1982): *Zermelo's Axiom of Choice: its Origins, Development and Influence*, Springer.

Muller, G. H., ed. (1976): *Sets and Classes*, North Holland.

Nagel, T. (1974): 'What is it like to be a bat?', *Philosophical Review*, 83.

Noonan, H. W. (1988): 'Substance, identity and time', *Aristotelian Society*, sup. vol. 62.

Nozick, R. (1981): *Philosophical Explanations*, Oxford University Press.

Over, D. E. (1984): 'The consequences of direct reference', *Philosophical Books*, 25.

——— (1986): 'On a temporal slippery slope paradox', 'Is there a temporal slippery slope paradox?' and 'Reply to Lowe', *Analysis*, 46.

Parfit, D. A. (1971): 'Personal identity', *Philosophical Review*, 80; in Perry

1975.

—— (1984): *Reasons and Persons*, Oxford University Press.

Parsons, T. (1987): 'Entities without identity', in Tomberlin 1987.

Peacocke, C. A. B. (1981): 'Are vague predicates incoherent?', *Synthese*, 46.

—— (1986): 'Analogue content', *Aristotelian Society*, sup. vol. 60.

Pears, D. F., ed. (1972): *Bertrand Russell: A Collection of Critical Essays*, Doubleday.

Perry, J. (1972): 'Can the self divide?', *Journal of Philosophy*, 69.

Perry, J., ed. (1975): *Personal Identity*, University of California Press.

Pettit, P. and McDowell, J. H., eds. (1986): *Subject, Thought and Context*, Oxford University Press.

Platts, M. B. (1979): *Ways of Meaning*, Routledge and Kegan Paul.

Pollard, S. (1986): 'Identity criteria', *Logique et Analyse*, 29.

Putnam, H. (1956): 'Reds, greens and logical analysis', *Philosophical Review*, 65.

Quine, W. V. (1950): 'Identity, ostension and hypostasis', *Journal of Philosophy*, 47; in Quine 1953.

—— (1953): *From a Logical Point of View*, Harvard University Press.

—— (1960): *Word and Object*, MIT Press.

—— (1976a): 'Worlds away', *Journal of Philosophy*, 73; in Quine 1981.

—— (1976b): 'Grades of discriminability', *Journal of Philosophy*, 73; in Quine 1981.

—— (1981): *Theories and Things*, Harvard University Press.

Quinton, A. (1962): 'The soul', *Journal of Philosophy*, 59; in Perry 1975.

Richard, M. (1987): 'Quantification and Leibniz's Law', *Philosophical Review*, 96.

Rorty, A. O., ed. (1976): *The Identities of Persons*, University of California Press.

Rubin, H. and Rubin, J. E. (1963): *Equivalents of the Axiom and Choice*, North Holland.

Russell, B. A. W. (1918): 'The Philosophy of Logical Atomism', *Monist*, 28; page refs. to reprinting in Marsh 1956.

—— (1950): *An Inquiry into Meaning and Truth*, Allen and Unwin.

Sainsbury, R. M. (1988/9): 'Tolerating vagueness', *Proceedings of the Aristotelian Society*, 89.

Salmon, N. U. (1979): 'How *not* to derive essentialism from the theory of reference', *Journal of Philosophy*, 76.

—— (1981): *Reference and Essence*, Blackwell.

—— (1984): 'Fregean theory and the Four Worlds Paradox: a reply to David Over', *Philosophical Books*, 25.

—— (1986): 'Modal paradox: parts and counterparts, points and counterpoints', in French et al. 1986.

—— (1989): 'The logic of what might have been', *Philosophical Review*, 98.

Salmon, N. U. and Soames, S., eds. (1988): *Propositions and Attitudes*, Oxford University Press.

Sanford, D. H. (1981): 'Illusions and sense-data', in French et al. 1981.

Shahan, R. W. and Swoyer, S. C, eds. (1979): *Essays on the Philosophy of W. V. Quine*, University of Oklahoma Press.

Shoemaker, S. (1975): 'Phenomenal similarity', *Critica*, 7; in Shoemaker 1984.

____ (1981): 'The inverted spectrum', *Journal of Philosophy*, 78; in Shoemaker 1984.

____ (1984): *Identity, Cause and Mind*, Cambridge University Press.

Sorensen, R. A. (1988): *Blindspots*, Oxford University Press.

Splitter, L. J. (1988): 'Species and identity', *Philosophy of Science*, 55.

Stalnaker, R. (1988): 'Vague identity', in Austin 1988.

Strawson, P. F. (1976): 'Entity and identity', in H. D. Lewis 1976.

Suppes, P. (1969): *Studies in the Methodological Foundations of Science*, Reidel.

Tomberlin, J. E., ed. (1987): *Philosophical Perspectives, 1: Metaphysics*, Ridgeview.

Travis, C. (1985): 'Vagueness, observation and sorites', *Mind*, 94.

van Fraassen, B. C. (1971): *Formal Semantics and Logic*, Macmillan.

van Heijenoort, J. (1967): *From Frege to Gödel: A Source Book in Mathematical Logic*, Harvard University Press.

Wiggins, D. R. P. (1980): *Sameness and Substance*, Blackwell.

____ (1986): 'On singling out an object determinately', in Pettit and McDowell 1986.

Williamson, T. (1985): 'Converse relations', *Philosophical Review*, 94.

____ (1986): 'Criteria of identity and the Axiom of Choice', *Journal of Philosophy*, 83.

____ (1987/8): 'Equivocation and existence', *Proceedings of the Aristotelian Society*, 88.

____ (1988a): 'Knowability and constructivism', *Philosophical Quarterly*, 38.

____ (1988b): 'First-order logics for comparative similarity', *Notre Dame Journal of Formal Logic*, 29.

____ (1989): 'Necessary identity and necessary existence', *Proceedings of the Fourteenth Wittgenstein Symposium*, forthcoming.

Wright, C. J. G. (1975): 'On the coherence of vague predicates', *Synthese*, 30.

____ (1976): 'Language-mastery and the sorites paradox', in Evans and McDowell 1976.

____ (1983): *Frege's Conception of Numbers as Objects*, Aberdeen University Press.

____ (1987): 'Further reflections on the sorites paradox', *Philosophical Topics*, 15.

Wright, C. J. G. and Read, S. L. (1985): 'Hairier than Putnam thought', *Analysis*, 45.

Additional References (to the Revised Edition)

Bottani, A., Carrara, M. and Giaretta, P., eds. (2002): *Individuals, Essence and Identity: Themes of Analytic Metaphysics*, Kluwer.

Breckenridge, W. (forthcoming): *'Look' Sentences and Visual Experience*, Oxford University Press.

Carrara, M. and Gaio, S. (2009): 'Approximating identity criteria', in Munz, Puhl and Wang 2009.

Carrara, M. and Gaio, S. (2012): 'Towards a formal account of identity criteria', in Trobok, Miščević and Žarnić 2012.

Carrara, M. and Giaretta, P. (2003): 'Quattro tesi sui criteri d'identità', *Rivista di estetica*, 21.

Carrara, M. and Giaretta, P. (2004): 'The many facets of identity criteria', *Dialectica*, 58.

Chuard, P. (2010): 'Non-transitive looks & fallibilism', *Philosophical Studies*, 149.

De Clercq, R. and Horsten, L. (2004): 'Perceptual indiscriminability: in defence of Wright's proof', *The Philosophical Quarterly*, 54.

De Clercq, R. and Horsten, L. (2005): 'Closer', *Synthese*, 146.

Delvaux, S. and Horsten, L. (2004): 'On best transitive approximations to simple graphs', *Acta Informatica*, 40.

Deutsch, M. (2005): 'Inentionalism and intransitivity', *Synthese*, 144.

Edgington, D. (2002): 'Williamson on vagueness, identity, and Leibniz's law', in Bottani, Carrara and Giaretta 2002.

Farkas, K. (2006): 'Indiscriminability and the sameness of appearance', *Proceedings of the Aristotelian Society*, 106.

Identity and Discrimination: Reissued and Updated Edition. Timothy Williamson.
© 2013 Timothy Williamson. Published 2013 by Blackwell Publishing Ltd.

Graff, D. [now D. Graff Fara] (2001): 'Phenomenal continua and the sorites', *Mind*, 110.

Haller, R. and Brandl, J., eds. (1990): *Wittgenstein — Towards a Re-Evaluation*, 3 vols., Hölder–Pichler–Tempsky.

Hellie, B. (2005): 'Noise and perceptual indiscriminability', *Mind*, 114.

Horsten, L. (2010): 'Impredicative identity criteria', *Philosophy and Phenomenological Research*, 80.

Keefe, R. (2011): 'Phenomenal sorites paradoxes and looking the same', *Dialectica*, 65.

Leitgeb, H. forthcoming: 'Criteria of identity: strong and wrong', *British Journal for the Philosophy of Science*.

Loux, M. and Zimmerman, D. (2003): *The Oxford Handbook of Metaphysics*, Oxford University Press.

Lovibond, S. and Williams, S., eds. (1996): *Essays for David Wiggins: Identity, Truth and Value*, Blackwell.

Lowe, J. (1991): 'One-level versus two-level identity criteria', *Analysis*, 51.

Lowe, J. (1998): *The Possibility of Metaphysics: Substance, Identity, and Time*, Clarendon Press.

Munz, V., Puhl, K. and Wang, J., eds. (2009): *Language and World: Papers of the 32nd International Wittgenstein Symposium*, Austrian Ludwig Wittgenstein Society.

Noonan, H. (2009): 'What is a one-level criterion of identity?', *Analysis*, 69.

Pelling, C., (2007): 'Conceptualism and the (supposed) non-transitivity of colour indiscriminability', *Philosophical Studies*, 134.

Poincaré, H. (1893): 'Le continu mathématique', *Revue de Métaphysique et de Morale*, 1.

Raffman, D. (2000): 'Is perceptual indiscriminability nontransitive?', *Philosophical Topics*, 28.

Russell, B. (1914): *Our Knowledge of the External World: As a Field for Scientific Method in Philosophy*, Open Court. Ref. to edition with a new introduction by J. Slater, Routledge, 1993.

Salmon, N. (1993): 'This side of paradox', *Philosophical Topics*, 21. Reprinted in Salmon 2005.

Salmon, N. (2005): *Metaphysics, Mathematics, and Meaning: Philosophical Papers I*, Clarendon Press.

Trobok, M., Miščević, N. and Žarnić, B. (2012): *Between Logic and Reality: Modeling Inference, Action and Understanding*, Springer.

Wiggins, D. (1996): 'Reply to Timothy Williamson', in Lovibond and Williams 1996.

Williamson, T. (1990): 'Necessary identity and necessary existence', in Haller and Brandl 1990, vol. 1.

Williamson, T. (1991): 'Fregean directions', *Analysis*, 51.

Williamson, T. (1994): *Vagueness*, Routledge.

Williamson, T. (1996): 'The necessity and determinacy of distinctness', in Lovibond and Williams 1996.

Williamson, T. (1998): 'Bare possibilia', *Erkenntnis*, 48.

Williamson, T. (2000): *Knowledge and its Limits*, Oxford University Press.

Williamson, T. (2002): 'Vagueness, identity, and Leibniz's law', in Bottani, Carrara and Giaretta 2002.

Williamson, T. (2003): 'Vagueness in reality', in Loux and Zimmerman 2003.

Williamson, T. (2013): *Modal Logic as Metaphysics*, Oxford University Press.

Index

Andjelković, M., 168
appearance of sameness, 165–6
Armstrong, D. M., 49
artifacts, 112, 126–41, 150, 151
Axiom *see* Choice; Extensionality

Barcan principle, 26
Barwise, J., 162
Berkeley, G., 121
Bolzano, B., 116
Boolos, G., 164
Breckenridge, W., 166
Brouwerian principle, 38
Burns, L., 159
Butler, J., 163

Cargile, J., 103, 162
Carnap, R., 156
Carrara, M., 167, 170
Chellas, B., 158
Chisholm, R. M., 120, 126
Choice, Axiom of, 69, 70, 72, 113, 154–7, 161
Chuard, P., 166
Church, A., 19

Clark, A., 161
colours, 114
counterpart theory, 127, 135, 142–3
Cresswell, M. J., 159

Davidson, D., 164
Davies, M. K, 155
De Clercq, R., 166, 167–8
degree, predicates of, 94–5, 133, 143
Delvaux, S., 167
Deutsch, M., 166
directions, 81–2, 83, 145, 146–7, 150, 151, 164, 168–70
discrimination, 5–8 *see also* indiscriminability
drawings, 136–41
Dretske, F., 162
Dummett, M. A. E., 83, 85, 88, 145, 159, 161, 164

Edgington, D., 167
error, margin for, 104–6
Evans, M. G. J., 80, 119, 160
Excluded Middle, Law of, 78

Identity and Discrimination: Reissued and Updated Edition. Timothy Williamson.
© 2013 Timothy Williamson. Published 2013 by Blackwell Publishing Ltd.

experiences, 48–9, 55–62, 73–5,
    82–5, 89–101, 160
Extensionality, Axiom of, 83, 145,
    146, 147–8

Fara, D. G., *see* Graff, D.
Farkas, K., 166
feeling the same, 167
Felgner, U., 155
Fine, K., 77, 78
Forbes, G., 126, 127, 130, 135,
    143, 163
Fraenkel, A. A., 154
Frege, G., 81–2, 83, 145, 146,
    148–9, 150, 168–70

Gaio, S., 167
Galanter, E., 158
Giaretta, P., 170
Goldbach's Conjecture, 15–16
Goodman, N., 82
Gottlieb, D., 164
Graff, D., 165–6
Grice, H. P., 122
Gupta, A., 130

Hallett, M., 154
Hardin, C. L., 12
Hart, W. D., 162
Hausman, A., 83, 161
Hellie, B., 166
Hintikka, J., 38, 158
Hirsch, E., 163
Horsten, L., 166, 167, 170
Hughes, G. E., 159
Humberstone, I. L., 44, 159

identity
    criteria of, 83, 144–53, 164,
        168–70
    determinacy of, 80–1
    necessity of, 34–5

ignorance, 5, 73–5, 79, 87, 92, 97,
    103–8, 115, 120, 133, 140
indeterminacy, 73–5, 79–81, 87,
    97, 107–8, 113, 115, 119–20,
    133–5, 138, 140–1, 143, 153,
    160
indiscriminability
    analysis of, 5, 8
    and appearance of sameness, 166
    direct/indirect, 20–1, 41, 82–7,
        159
    inferential/non-inferential,
        13–14, 29, 40, 41, 42, 47
    by instruments, 114
    intentional/non-intentional,
        9–10, 14–23, 25, 27, 35–41,
        45–6, 47, 52–64, 89–91
    of kinds, 22–3
    non-transitivity of, 4, 11–18,
        20–1, 27, 29–32, 34–42,
        49–62, 88, 89–90, 114,
        166–7
    and observational predicates,
        43–7, 89–92
    perceptual, 11–13, 16–18, 114
    and phenomenal characters,
        49–94
    and phenomenal predicates,
        95–101
    reflexivity of, 10, 27, 28, 31,
        166
    and sameness of appearance, 166
    symmetry of, 10–11, 27, 28–9,
        31
information, 8, 12, 99–100

Jackson, F. C., 13
Jech, T. J., 154, 156

K (modal system), 31, 33, 37, 40,
    44
KT (modal system), 31, 33, 44, 162

KT4 (modal system), 31, 33,
    38–41, 44, 162; *see also* S4
KT5 (modal system), 32, 34–8, 41,
    44–5, 159
Kaplan, D., 155
Keefe, R., 166
knowledge
    de re/de dicto 9, 30, 47, 56
    and discrimination, 5–8
    identifying, 37–8
    inferential/non-inferential,
        13–14, 29, 40
    of knowledge, 31–2, 36, 38, 39,
        40, 41, 162
    non-closure of, 10–11, 29–30,
        40, 47, 56
    and reliability, 12, 104–6,
        151–3
    see also ignorance
Kripke, S. A., 26, 27, 159

languages, 137–41
Leibniz's Law, 7, 9, 14, 21, 27–8,
    80, 90, 94, 122, 158
Leitgeb, H., 170
Lenzen, W., 158
Lewis, D. K., 117, 142–3, 155,
    161, 162–3
Linsky, B., 159, 161
Locke, J., 121
looking the same, 165, 167
Lowe, E. J., 146–7, 163, 164,
    168–70
Luce, R. D., 158

M *see* KT
M-relation, defined,
    68
Mackie, J. L., 122
Maddy, P., 154
matching, defined, 66
maximal *M*-relation, defined, 68

memory
    and knowledge, 6, 163
    limitations of, 17–18, 59, 61–2,
        99–100
    and personal identity, 121–2,
        163
Minimality Constraint, 72–4, 76–7,
    79, 86–7, 113, 115, 132, 133,
    134, 160, 161
Minkoff, E. C., 115
Moore, G. H., 154

Nagel, T., 48
necessity
    epistemic, 25–6, 29–33, 56
    metaphysical, 25
    see also possibility
Noonan, H. W., 164, 170
Nozick, R., 162
numbers, cardinal, 115–16, 146,
    151

observational predicates, 43–7,
    88–92, 94, 95–6, 100, 159
operational definitions, 114
Over, D. E., 163

painfulness, 90–4, 96, 100–1
Parfit, D. A., 119, 162–3
Parsons, T, 161
Peacocke, C. A. B., 85, 159, 160,
    161
Pelling, C., 166
Perry, J., 117, 122, 162, 163
persons, 116–22, 147, 148, 150,
    151, 153, 162–3, 164
phenomenal character, defined, 48
phenomenal predicate, defined, 95
phenomenalization, inner, defined,
    97–8
phenomenalization, outer, defined,
    98

Pinkerton, R. J., 13
Platts, M. B., 159
Poincaré, H., 167
Pollard, S., 164
possibility
    epistemic, 25, 29, 31–3, 38, 40
    metaphysical, 25, 38, 40, 142
    see also necessity
possible objects, 63, 127, 128,
    142–3, 155, 160, 168
presentations, 9, 15–23, 30–1, 33,
    37–8, 51–60, 112, 150, 152
provability, 15, 25, 32
Putnam, H., 161

qualia, 82–3
quantities, operational, 114
Quine, W. V., 161, 163, 164
Quinton, A., 122

Raffman, D., 166
Read, S. L., 162
Reid, T., 121
relations
    as classes of ordered pairs,
        154–5, 160
    closeness of, 123–4, 167–8
    and Leibniz's Law, 9, 14, 19
    observational, 46–7, 159
    phenomenal, 95, 161–2
reliability see knowledge
Richard, M., 158
Rubin, H., 155
Rubin, J. E., 155
Russell, B. A. W., 17, 82, 85, 146,
    166–7

S4 (modal principle), 31, 127, 135,
    142, 167–8; see also KT4
S4.1 (modal system), 159
S5 (modal principle), 32; see also
    KT5

Sainsbury, R. M., 161
Salmon, N. U., 80, 126, 127, 129,
    130, 135, 142, 160, 161, 163,
    167–8
sameness in character, defined, 66
sameness of appearance, 165–66
Sanford, D. H., 13
semantics, possible world, 32–4,
    37–8
sense data, 17–18, 166–7
sets, 83, 145, 146, 150–1, 154–5
Shoemaker, S., 48, 75
similarity, 48–9, 82, 123
Sorensen, R. A., 103–4, 162
sorites paradoxes, 43, 46–7, 88–97,
    99–108, 113, 115, 126–43,
    162, 166, 167–8
species, 114–15, 150, 151, 162
Splitter, L. J., 162
Stalnaker, R., 161
Strawson, P. F., 164
structure of an order relation, 170
subjective kind of quality, defined,
    49
supervaluations, 77–8, 97, 102,
    108
Suppes, P., 114

T (modal principle), 30; see also KT
Travis, C., 159

uncontroversialness, defined, 75, 77

vagueness, 78–81, 104–8, 138,
    159, 167
van Fraassen, B. C., 77

Wiggins, D. R. P., 118, 122, 161,
    163, 164, 167
Wittgenstein, L., 100
Wright, C. J. G., 81, 83, 159, 160,
    161, 162, 164